ANTONIONI

Sam Rohdie

ANTONIONI

BFI Publishing

First published in 1990 by the
British Film Institute
21 Stephen Street
London W1P 1PL

British Library Cataloguing in Publication Data
Rohdie, Sam, *1939*–
    Antonioni.
      1. Italian cinema films. Directing
      I. Title
791.430233092

ISBN 0-85170-273-2

ISBN 0-85170-274-0 pbk

Designed by Bruce Weatherhead and Ann Langusch

Typeset by Discript, London

Printed in England by
Courier International, Tiptree, Essex

To J. Rhodie

'Ahi, tu Guido Aristarco, che scrivi *leggere un film* invece di *vedere un film*, non ti rendi conto che delitto compi?'

'Oh, you, Guido Aristarco, don't you know the crime you commit when you write *to read a film* instead of *to see a film*?'

Italo Calvino

'Non mi piace Antonioni, non mi piace l'arte astratta e nemmeno la musica elettronica.'

'I don't like Antonioni, abstract art, or electronic music.'

Pier Paolo Pasolini

'Il mondo, la realtà in cui viviamo . . . è invisibile, e quindi dobbiamo accontentarci di quello che vediamo.'

'The world, the reality which we live in . . . is invisible, hence we have to be satisfied with what we see.'

Michelangelo Antonioni

Contents

Acknowledgements

I would like to thank Rolando Caputo, William D. Routt and Richard Thompson of the Cinema Studies department at La Trobe University for reading the manuscript of this book at various stages and offering their help, advice and encouragement. I would like to thank as well Meaghan Morris, Geoffrey Nowell-Smith and Paul Willemen. I am especially indebted to Ann Langusch for her always intelligent, very sharp eye and sense. I am grateful to Beverley Purnell for administrative and secretarial help.

The staff at the library of the Centro Sperimentale di Cinematografia in Rome were very helpful as was the staff at the library of the Australian Film Institute in Melbourne. But I am especially grateful for the help, the efficiency, the efforts of the staff of the Borchardt Library of La Trobe University and above all for the help given to me by Julie Marshall.

I am also grateful to my students; much of the material set out in this book I first pursued in my classes and with them. I must thank the School of Humanities at La Trobe University and its Dean, Ray Pinkerton: the generous leave arrangements for study granted by the University permitted me to do my research and writing, always with encouragement and trust, never with undue pressure.

The stills the book are all from the BFI Stills, Poster and Designs Collection, with the exception of those on pp. 179 and 188, which were kindly supplied by Artificial Eye, and those on pp. 126–7, 130, 134–5, 158 and 185, which are from transparencies provided by Michele Mancini and Ernanni Paterra, to whom thanks. Cover stills are of Jack Nicholson and Maria Schneider in *The Passenger* (MGM/1975).

Introduction

Michelangelo Antonioni made his last feature film in 1982, *Identificazione di una donna*. At the moment he is working on a film, not dissimilar from it in theme, called *The Crew*, to be shot off the coast of Florida. Mark Peploe, who collaborated with Antonioni on the script of *The Passenger* (1975), was involved with the script for *The Crew*; these two films also have elements in common: a change of identity, the dissolution of the narrative, an investigation whose thread becomes lost and slowly disintegrates, a play with perspective and the uncertainty of subjectivity. Though this new film, inevitably, relates to past films, just as inevitably it will differ from them, and not simply as story or setting, but fundamentally, in its approach. Antonioni made short documentaries in the 1940s and his first feature in 1950; but he remains, as he always was, an experimental and contemporary film-maker.

The Crew is based on a short fiction, 'Quattro uomini in mare' ('Four Men at Sea') which Antonioni wrote in 1976. It was set off the coast of New South Wales in Australia.[1] The fiction, which Antonioni narrates in the first person, begins with a 'true' mystery concerning a yacht brought into tow into Coff's Harbour with the owner missing and an unlikely crew of three on board telling a hardly credible story of what had happened to them. It is that story that the narrator muses over and retells; fascinated by the mystery and the improbability, he creates another story equally mysterious and perhaps more improbable as if the purpose of the telling is to maintain, not to clarify the mystery. It is hard to know from the fiction whether there is a 'true' story behind the narration or whether this 'truth' too is invented to deepen the mystery.

Antonioni had some difficulty setting the film up. It was abandoned in 1984 for lack of finance; since then he became very seriously ill. He has partially recovered and the project revived, but the film is yet to be made. In the meantime Antonioni has shot a short documentary for Italian television on the city of Rome for the football World Cup in June 1990 being held in Italy.

In 'Quattro uomini in mare' there are two stories: the one the crew relates on their return to Coff's harbour (and which the narrator disbelieves), and the alternative story which the narrator invents. The stories overlay rather than cancel each other, not alternatives, nor exactly versions of the same, but a substitutive series with no clear first or last, no certitude to cancel out one and assert the other. It is rather more like a fading in and out of different forms of narrative figuration, as in *Blow-Up* (1966), when an image, sufficiently enlarged under the impetus of a mystery, is superimposed on another image, but which is equally mysterious, inconclusive, uncertain, until what becomes most interesting, and most mysterious, is this constantly shifting meaning, and the elusiveness of the narrative itself, losing a thread, picking up another, moving, but to nowhere in particular.

In the story, the owner of the yacht, James Tower, has simply disappeared, presumed drowned. This is a familiar element in Antonioni's work: the disappearance of figures, characters, objects, often into a depth like the sea, or into the sands of the desert, or into a fog which envelops and encloses so that all that is left is the non-figuration of surface, sand and sea which close over any tear within them, the nothingness of mist and atmosphere where identities blur, cloud over. In the narrator's/Antonioni's invention, Tower has not drowned, but remains on board, hidden from the crew; the yacht has been disabled in a storm; the crew is incompetent, brutal, stupid, unable to get the yacht going and must, in their laziness, their lack of skill, wait to be rescued. The crew never notices the presence of Tower, who sleeps during the day, well hidden, and cares for his needs during the night. What is interesting in the narrator's/Antonioni's story is the observation by Tower of his lack of presence, taking himself as an object, not there, and like Locke/Robertson of *The Passenger*, shifting not only between different identities, but between person and non-person, almost, as in the penultimate shot of *The Passenger*, observing his own disappearance, his draining away.

One of the interests in 'Quattro uomini in mare', is the movement between the two narratives and their lack of stability; there is no 'truth' nor 'finality' to ground them in. This narrative untenability is doubled by an untenability of the subject, both 'within' the fiction, Tower observing himself as other, and 'outside' the fiction: the narrator observes his fascinations and inventions, his own play with fictions, his pursuits. 'Outside' is not at all a stable place or clear boundary; like Tower, observing his absence at the borders of it, the narrator observes his absence from the story and yet the presence of his desires in the shape and study of it.

Antonioni's universe is not one in which all difference falls into the same, or difference is so blurred between subject and object, narrator and narrated, image and referent as to abolish these as separate realms, and to abolish therefore any clear place to speak, or any place from which meanings might be securely formed. The places are real but unstable. The interest is not with this instability, nor these losses of place, but rather with the productivity of that instability, the new shapes, the new stories, the new, temporary, subjects which they permit. To lose perspective, to lose identity, which are often 'tragedies' for Antonioni's characters, are opportunities for the films.

In the 1950s, when Antonioni first began to make feature films, much of his work was appreciated in terms of current philosophic-aesthetic positions, partly related to neo-realism, partly to a debased, somewhat vulgar Marxism: either Antonioni was praised for decontextualising his characters from their social settings (the depiction of 'alienation'), or he was criticised for witholding any social meaning by the fact of 'losing' the context (mere 'formalism'). Much of what was new and different in Antonioni's films was neglected by being made socially functional or situated as empty avant-gardism . . . and denounced.

With Antonioni's 'great' trilogy of films of the early 1960s, *L'avventura*, *L'eclisse*, *La notte*, to which perhaps should be added *Il deserto rosso*, there was this same search by critics for meaning, or the criticism of its lack. The terms had somewhat shifted to frameworks of existentialism or the 'objective regard' of the French *nouveau roman*, but the overall critical projects, in part sustained by the heritage of neo-realism, remained relatively constant. Critics then, as before, and later, picked up two sides of Antonioni, and made separate claims for them, that side in which meaning was present, though just on the horizon, a kind of lure, and that other side, at which it was being compromised, lost to patterns and surfaces. There was a philosophic desperation to this criticism; it needed to retain a significance, to hold on to something, even to wrest meaning from the dissolution of meaning.

Antonioni's films oscillate between the positions which criticism has taken. The films pose a subject (only to compromise it), constitute objects (only to dissolve them), propose stories (only to lose them), but, equally, they turn those compromises and losses back towards another solidity: the new story Tower finds in his absence, or the narrator finds in the displacement of the story by the crew, or, in the films, a wandering away from narrative to the surface into which it was dissolved, but in such a way that the surface takes on a fascination, becomes a 'subject' all its own. In 'Quattro uomini in mare', the narrative loops back on itself, simultaneously holding to something, displacing it, and letting it go, but never, definitely, arriving anywhere, certainly not at an explanation: 'Any explanation would be less interesting than the mystery itself.'[2]

The productivity of Antonioni's films does not reside in ideas, but in the stories and images the films generate. The 'point', say in *Blow-Up*, or in *The Passenger*, of the displacement of narratives, of images, of the loss and then recreation of figuration, and the attendant wavering of identity (in the photographer, in the spectator) is what such losses and waverings make possible. These possibilities are not something to be concluded as 'the open-ended work', in the sense that Antonioni's films serve as illustrations of a theory, of 'openness' as an idea; the interest is less in the openness than in its concrete consequences: the narrative becoming pictorial, the pictorial becoming a subject, and one that needs to be looked at, watched in its movement, felt in its duration, but not, ever, an idea to be proved.

Towards the close of *Zabriskie Point* (1969), after Daria learns of Mark's flight to freedom which ends in his murder, she stands outside the house in the desert which, as she watches it, explodes, time and again. The explosions are, within the fiction, purely imaginary though they have a subjective motive; on the other hand, it isn't at all clear from what perspective they are being seen or imagined or who it is that looks. They have an interim, unresolved place between the imaginary of Daria and the imaginary, from another location, of the narrator as in the imaginary and crossed over perspectives in 'Quattro uomini in mare'. The explosion is in a series, but the series can't be read as linear; what comes after is the same as what came before. The differences are not defined by duration, but by changed perspectives, altered scale; and the repetition, by the very fact of it, works as a modifier of sameness. The one-too-many is a difference.

The explosion is an explosion of objects: bits of house, a beam, a box of cornflakes, a scrap of clothing, a refrigerator, a sandwich, packaging, a television set. The objects lose their object-ness to become part of a pattern; within the pattern volume disappears into line, line returns to volume, colour becomes line, density becomes surface; the repetitions and the movements are magical, hallucinatory. Movement is constant, glancing, almost like a sketch, just touching the surface rather than making an incision or mark within it, never fixing, or taking possession.

There are a variety of interpretations and significances that can be concluded from the sequence both psychological and metaphysical, including perhaps the one of the dissolution of the different in the same. But what remains is the concreteness of those images, the precision of their movements, the particularity of their patterns as things in themselves and not as illustrations of something else. At the same time it introduces a wholly new subject in narrative film: non-figurative, informal, unfixed, the subject of the subject dissolved, and that dissolution as the context for something utterly new and unforeseen.

There are two permanent themes in Antonioni's films, but they include not simply matters 'in' the films, 'of' the fictions, but are matters of the films overall: they are the journey, and the investigation, taken by the characters, but equally taken by the films. There are no goals to either and by having nothing in particular to find, anything at all becomes possible, even a subject that doesn't at first look like one: the pattern of a wall, the 'emptiness' of the sea.

All of Antonioni's films differ from each other, and not as matters of story or plot, but in their manner of representing; each has sought something new, each has been an experiment. From 1964 onwards, for example, from *Il deserto rosso*, it is possible to mark in his films a new way of conceiving perspective and subjectivity, and hence new ways of forming images and the narrative of images. The problems which Antonioni has faced have remained relatively constant, but the play and experiment with them has changed from film to film. Just as within his films or within an image, a new shape might appear, fading out the old, within each film it seems a new film is suggested and begins to form. There is another aspect to this difference part personal, part historical, as if the film vibrates with what is current, picks up a contemporary echo, an unheard sound, an invisible image, and then makes these appear. *The Crew* is certain to be different.

In 1980 the city of Bologna honoured Antonioni's achievements with its highest cultural award: the Archiginnasio d'oro. On that occasion Roland Barthes wrote an open letter of appreciation to Antonioni, 'Caro Antonioni . . .'.[3] There was always an ambivalence in Barthes' writings towards more 'theoretical' critics who wanted to systematise, to proclaim, to categorise something as delicate as a novel or a film, as say the film semiotics of Christian Metz seemed to do in its 'theoretical' mania to define. Barthes' letter to Antonioni marked out less what was significant in Antonioni's work than what was valuable and pleasurable, or, more precisely, the pleasure and the significance were not divided, and besides, the letter was a pleasure to read.

Barthes discussed Antonioni and what he called his 'modernism' in terms of categories which weren't like categories at all, at least not in the context of what had been and continues to be part of the theories of cinema. They were 'fragility', 'tenuousness', 'wisdom', 'attentiveness'. Not only did these categories describe qualities in Antonioni but they had the qualities they described. They caressed Antonioni, embraced him but without possessing him. They indicated a complexity and productivity but without the reductiveness of naming (the terms are vague); they had all the delicacy they found and wanted to preserve.

Barthes, more than anyone, helped me to 'see' Antonioni by helping me to get outside a then current theoretical possessiveness, providing me with terms for a divergent critical language; by so doing he allowed Antonioni to possess me. This was not the overthrow of anything, certainly not of the theoretical capital of the immediate past, but a way to use its achievements differently and on films such as Antonioni's where the referent was uncertain, subjectivity unclear and where theories of the object (like semiotics), or those of the subject (like psychoanalysis), did not always seem adequate.

This book is offered as an appreciation of Antonioni's films, their particularity, the concreteness of their images, of their stories, and the productivity and generative power of these, for new images, new stories; it is also offered as a critical discourse alongside the 'language' of Antonioni, which the films have provoked, rather than as response to a demand outside the films.

I can assert, with surety, the newness of the films and my excitement for them, for the most current, the yet-to-be, *The Crew*, as well as for the earliest, *Cronaca di un amore* (1950), or *La signora senza camelie* (1953); as for my discussions of the films, they have been directed largely by the films themselves. I wanted to avoid not so much theory, but the practice of turning film into illustrations of theory; I wanted instead, and in a slight re-turning by Antonioni of a Rossellini phrase, for theory to be confronted by film.

Notes

1. Michelangelo Antonioni, 'Quattro uomini in mare', *Cinema Nuovo*, November–December 1976; it has been translated into English as 'Four Men at Sea', in Michelangelo Antonioni, *That Bowling Alley on the Tiber* (tr. William Arrowsmith) (New York: Oxford University Press, 1986), pp. 54–64.

2. *That Bowling Alley*, p. 59.

3. Roland Barthes, 'Caro Antonioni . . .', *Bologna Incontri* no. 2, February 1980.

Chapter One

Antonioni comes from Ferrara, a small provincial capital in north-east Italy on the Emilian plain not far from the Po river. It is an immensely rich agricultural area with Ferrara at its centre. Antonioni was born in 1913. The Ferrara that he grew up in had a population of around 100,000; its streets are narrow, irregular, medieval. The most notable time of the city however was the fourteenth and fifteenth centuries under the House of Este. It has some of the most dignified and elegant architecture of the period in all of Italy. Ferrara, and more generally the Po valley, figures in many of Antonioni's films: in *Cronaca di un amore* (1950) where Ferrara is the place of Guido and Paola's first love and first 'crime', in the Po valley wanderings of Aldo in *Il grido* (1957), and in some of the settings in *Il deserto rosso* (1964), the fogs, the mist, the encroachment of industrialisation on the valley of which there is an early hint in Antonioni's first documentary on the people of the Po valley, *Gente del Po* (1943). Mist, fog, rivers figure in almost all his films, atmospheres which dissolve shapes, which transform objects, which make the most stable things uncertain. But there is perhaps something else of Ferrara in his films: the rigour and dignity of its architecture, a certain nobility, an appreciation of what is, if not aristocratic, high-bourgeois, immensely cultivated, somewhat distant, not at all 'populist', or extravagant, or in the least vulgar.

Antonioni's first involvement with the cinema was as a critic in the 1930s and in the 1940s, that is in the last decade of Italian fascism and in the period immediately after the Liberation. He first wrote for the local Ferrara newspaper, *Corriere Padano*, from 1935 until early in 1940: mostly film reviews, general articles on the cinema, festival reports, occasionally a short fiction.

The short stories he wrote for *Corriere Padano* were about atmosphere and sensation rather than about character or event; and his film criticism was like this, interested less in character and plot than in mood, a feel and touch of things. Late in the 1930s he attempted to make a documentary film on mad people in an asylum, but the film was never finally made; in 1940, he wrote a treatment for a fiction film in colour, *Terra Verde*, which was not only about colour, but about the shift in colour with changes in the landscape, in the climate; on the one hand the projected film was about the uncertainty of existence, on the other hand, it was about the visual yield of that uncertainty in the way shapes changed, objects altered, colour and its perception shifted. His first documentary, *Gente del Po*, in part like *Terra Verde*, is the documentary of an unstable, moving landscape.[1]

In 1940, Antonioni moved to Rome which was then, as it is now, Italy's film capital; he began to contribute regularly to the film journal *Cinema*, and, after July 1943, for other film and cultural journals: *Film d'Oggi, Cosmopolita, Lo Schermo, Bianco e Nero*. *Cinema*, though in part subsidised by the fascist regime was relatively independent of it; by the early 1940s, it argued for a new realism in the Italian cinema and began to show signs of a definite anti-fascism in its views on the cinema. This new cinema that was asked for by the journal was 'realist', 'populist', socially committed; significantly, it was not all that distant from the cinema that had been demanded by militant fascism, it too wanting a 'political' cinema, film as a political instrument, contributing to the transformation of Italy, to a new revolution.

Antonioni's interests as they began to be defined in his criticism, his fictions, his treatments for film were different than those being worked out in the pages of *Cinema*: it was not that the popular or the social held no interest for him, but that his stress was on matters of form, questions of experiment. *Cinema* wanted new statements. Antonioni wanted more its precondition, a new language. This divide between the social and the formal, between meaning and expression did not fully surface as an issue in Italy until the end of fascism.

1943 was a turning point in the war for Italy: early in that year there were significant strikes and working class unrest in Turin and Milan; on 10 July the Allies landed in Sicily, and on 25 July Mussolini was voted out of power by the Fascist Grand Council; on 8 September, Italy, then under the still 'fascist' government of Marshal Badoglio, declared an armistice and German troops overran north and central Italy. It was the beginning of the Nazi occupation and of an organised Italian resistance movement: the Committees of National Liberation were formed on the very next day; they brought together the six main anti-fascist parties, from the far right to the far left, to co-ordinate a national struggle against the Germans and to seek to co-operation with the advancing allies. Later in the month Mussolini fled to the north and re-established the fascist regime at Salò on the banks of Lake Garda (the Italian Social Republic), which he proclaimed first on German radio.

The fall of the fascist State and the beginning of the Resistance struggle profoundly altered the editorial positions of *Cinema*. Its new open commitment to anti-fascism went along with a denunciation of 'empty aestheticism' in favour of a cinema of realism and social substance which were to be so important for what would be called Italian neo-realism. *Cinema* took a decided turn towards socialism and the communist movement, demanded that art have a clear social mandate, and serve the Resistance and the struggle against fascism. These were not positions shared by Antonioni. He became isolated on the journal and eventually left it, at first to write for other journals, and soon after to begin to make films.[2]

Cinema was edited by the fascist leader's second son, Vittorio Mussolini, and was funded by the fascist state. It was one of three state or part state sponsored film journals (*Bianco e Nero* and *Lo Schermo* were the others) and was perhaps the most interesting and most progressive of them: it was open to the American cinema, to French cinema, to narrative experiments, had a critical political edge and was relatively popular in its appeal, unlike, for example, the rather safe, academic and conservative *Bianco e Nero*.[3] Despite the presence of Vittorio Mussolini, many of those who contributed to the journal and actively determined its editorial policy were either members of the clandestine Italian Communist Party or very close to it: Mario Alicata, Gianni Puccini, Giuseppe De Santis and Luchino Visconti.[4]

Cinema was formed in 1935–36 by a group of intellectuals, including Gianni Puccini, who were working at the time on the *Enciclopedia del Cinema* under Luciano De Feo, a bureaucrat-intellectual, described by Puccini as: 'a fascist, very opportunist, a type quite common then, but all the same, a good guy, full of initiatives and ever ready to protect those under his care.'[5] *Cinema* came directly out of the *Enciclopedia*; the original group of Puccini, Francesco Pasinetti, Rudolf Arnheim, Domenico Meccoli and Aldo Pavolini were later joined by Alberto Consiglio and Giacomo De Benedetti, a mixed group of intellectuals and critics with a variety of aesthetic and political positions. It was De Feo's 'brilliant' idea to appoint Mussolini editor: Mussolini was keen on the cinema, but lazy, weak, ingenuous. His presence on the journal, especially in the late 1930s and early 40s gave it considerable protection. Mussolini gave little time to the journal and was genuinely surprised when later some of the editorial board fled or were arrested for their subversive politics. Puccini again: 'Vittorio didn't have the stuff of tyrants: he was apathetic, tolerant, indifferent and sad. None of us, even when our anti-fascism had become a way of life, of hope, of struggle, was ever able to hate him.'[6]

On the other hand, if Cinema contained, politically, an anti-fascist and communist group, in point of fact the politics of the group did not extend to the criticisms it wrote, or at least it was hard to see how those criticisms were 'subversive', despite a subsequent later rereading of them as 'anti-fascist'. Vittorio Mussolini, referring to the late 30s, remarked: 'There weren't yet any political divisions . . . I have to say that I was never aware that the editorial group of the journal wanted anything other than the success of the fascist cinema; in fact, what they often wanted was a cinema that was even more committed [than the 'fascist' cinema]. The only noticeable differences on the board were related to judgements on various directors and various cinemas.'[7]

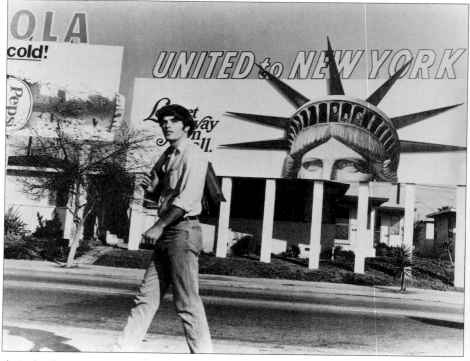

Antonioni's ZABRISKIE POINT *(1969)*
An American landscape

Mussolini, as Puccini noted, and he himself confirmed, was above all a lover of the cinema and especially of the American cinema ('I went to America in 1937 . . . it was a journey of love.'; He met Dorothy Lamour, Betty Grable . . . and President Roosevelt).[8] He wrote an interesting though somewhat excessive and confused piece, more enthusiastic than considered, on the American cinema as *the* model for the cinema of a fascist Italy, like America, young, progressive, adventurous, experimental. His favourite directors were King Vidor, Frank Capra, Ernst Lubitsch, the same as those loved by the 'committed' members of the *Cinema* board who wanted a populist and realist Italian cinema opposed to the artificial conventional genres of Italian films of the 1930s. In fact the tastes, like the 'populisms', of left fascism and a left anti-fascism were remarkably close.

Mussolini was involved in the original idea for Rossellini's 'fascist' war film *Un pilota ritorna* (1942), with a script in part written by Antonioni; in 1938, he worked with Goffredo Alessandrini on *Luciano Serra, pilota*, a film also about heroic fascist aviators, which Antonioni very favourably reviewed for *Corriere Padano*. Mussolini claimed to have been instrumental in devising the last minute rescue at the end of *Luciano*: 'to help the "good guys" in trouble, "our side" always arrived at the nick of time: the XI Cavalry was represented by our bombers with the Ethiopians corresponding to the Indians . . . if instead of Amedeo Nazzari we had used Errol Flynn, it wouldn't have made the least difference.'[9]

Mussolini's enthusiasm for American culture was commonplace, not only among fascist intellectuals, but also, notably, among anti-fascist ones, like Cesare Pavese, Elio Vittorini, Giaime Pintor; it also was shared by the editorial group of *Cinema*, from the most formalist, to the most liberal, or to the most committed and Gramscian.[10] What was interesting about *Cinema* was not only the thin cultural line between 'fascism' and 'anti-fascism' and the fact that different political persuasions could work on the same cultural terrain, but that cultural positions themselves, even when concerned for a renewal of the Italian cinema, were notably vague: something better was wanted, something more serious, but there were no especially clear ideas.

There was considerable unanimity concerning the models for a new, revived cinema; on the other hand, these models were not homogeneous: it included Renoir and René Clair, Carné and Duvivier, Capra and Lubitsch, Giovanni Verga and Faulkner, Hemingway and Zola, Chaplin and Buster Keaton. What they had in common was a search for models outside of the existing practices of the Italian cinema, especially of the 30s, a cinema, which despite its evident merits, was primarily a cinema of genres, of coded stars, characters, narrative conventions, of 'entertainment'.

What characterised *Cinema* was the heterogeneity of its culture and its critical positions, its general openness, its concern for the new; after 1941, however, these positions became more defined, more narrow, more overtly 'political', as the journal increasingly came under the control of the 'left' grouping of Alicata, Puccini and De Santis (especially De Santis); the course of the war, and a few years later the change in the fortunes of the fascist state, only further strengthened this direction. The demand of this group was for a new 'realism' in the Italian cinema; they condemned what they called an empty 'intellectualist-formalist-pictorialism', 'the most frightful and most diffuse of "irrelevances" which divert one from the single and correct road of realism'; 'realism', however, had for them primarily a political, not aesthetic sense, despite the succession of realist writers and film-makers they cited as models and precursors.[11]

It is hard to know precisely what the 'realism' of *Cinema* was, or could be; the journal condemned films which seemed to sacrifice a commitment to the everyday, to the popular classes, to the social reality of Italy, for excursions, not simply into make believe, but into a formalism divorced from political and social ends. If there was a practical example of that realism, it was perhaps

Ossessione (1942), as much a film by Visconti as by the 'left' *Cinema* group who worked on it. What was stressed about *Ossessione* was the subject matter above all other concerns. It was as a result of this move towards the 'left' and to a realism defined by content and morality, that Antonioni, who had worked on the journal during its more liberal, experimental and open phase, and who had, in his criticism, begun to define an aesthetic contrary to that of *Cinema*, found himself isolated and against the tide not only in aesthetics, but because aesthetics and politics were bound to each other, in politics as well.

Italian neo-realism was more mixed and heterogeneous aesthetically than those who constructed the idea of it cared to recognise. Essentially neo-realism was a cultural-political formation defined as absolutely other to fascism, as being the cinema of the Resistance, of Liberation, of a renewed and reborn Italy, of the anti-fascist struggle; hence the 'first' neo-realist films were dated after 1943 and the fall of fascism: *Ladri di biciclette* (1948) rather than *I bambini ci guardano* (1942), *Roma, città aperta* (1945) rather than *Un pilota ritorna* (1942) – though there is little difference in fact in the 'style' of these films, however much there may be a change in sentiment, say in the Rossellini, from fascism to anti-fascism.

Politics was confounded by culture in the definitions of neo-realism; its aesthetic practices were defined as anti-fascist by which was meant everything opposed to the cinema of the fascist period, everything pre-1943. In fact the cinema post-1943, and those who made it, like Rossellini, Visconti, Lattuada, Antonioni, De Sica, Zavattini, Blasetti, were involved in the cinema during the fascist period. The post-fascist cinema had clear continuous links with the fascist past. Neo-realism, identified with the Resistance, with a new Italy, hence with anti-fascism, was mythically defined in terms of an opposition to the cinema of the 1930s, an opposition which on examination did not hold, at least not formally, not with regard to the style and practices of film, and not even always in subject mmatter.

By constructing neo-realism as absolutely 'other' to the cinema of the 1930s, the presence of what was 'neo-realist' in the fascist past was explained as the early presence of an 'other' cinema at the heart of fascism, already contesting it, forming a new culture and a new politics; this 'other', 'anti-fascist' cinema during fascism included the most odd, most various collection of films, film-makers and tendencies, not only Italian, Blasetti and Camerini, but foreign, radically 'other' films, like those of Vidor and Renoir and Clair, and other literatures, like the works of Zola and Cain and Verga, as the models and inspiration of the 'new' cinema within the 'old', of a line of early Resistance to fascism and fascist culture. This 'other' cinema was so vague, so various that on inspection it came to mean nothing other than 'good' films, quality art. This 'quality' was read forward into neo-realism itself; neo-realism too came to mean quality cinema, hence the elasticity of the term, applying well before 1943, at times as far back as the 1910s and 1920s, and as far forward as today.[12]

In 1937, Antonioni wrote a lovely, extremely favourable review of G.W. Pabst's *Mademoiselle Docteur* (1936), which, though commercial, was, for Antonioni, 'still poetry', 'absolutely cinematic', with 'a lightness of narrative touch, like that of an impressionist novelist': 'He has been called intellectualist. He has been accused of hermeticism, and even of romanticism. He seems to me to be an artist. And nothing else need be said.'

Antonioni compared Pabst to René Clair whom he seemed to resemble, but while Clair, to Antonioni, was literary, Pabst was 'visual'. The difference, literary/visual, was the basis for a more telling comparison, especially in view of the way things turned out for Antonioni at *Cinema*:

> More *political*, or perhaps it should be said, more *social* than Pabst, Clair doesn't know how to free himself from literary ideas. And, it is true to say that while for the Frenchman it is the subject that is important, for the Viennese, it is the narration; which is what makes the former less cinematographic than the latter. The latter, let me say again, is a purist. One of the very few purists of the cinema.

The review doesn't speak about meaning or psychology or even of the events of the film, still less of social significance or social relevance. Its interests are in narrative structure, in the function of silences, in the rhythm of events; it is with a lyricism which, however deep and varied, never gets too close, too self-absorbed, manages a 'sense of balanced objectivity'; and it is with the creation of atmosphere: menacing, electric, dark, suspended, 'hiding something perverse, about to strike', 'an oppressive blackness, overtaking every sight, every shot'; the least rustle becomes a cause of fright.[13]

This kind of language, this kind of thought and stress, would by 1943 no longer appear in the pages of *Cinema*; on the contrary it would be condemned as aestheticism: bourgeois, affected, insignificant, frivolous. With the 'left' group firmly in control of *Cinema*, it was as if the cinema itself dropped out of sight. And, fittingly, as in Antonioni's comparison of Clair with Pabst, it is not films which appeared as the models for a new radical, anti-fascist cinema but life, politics, and realistic, melodramatic literature, like the novels of Giovanni Verga . . . from the last century.

Neo-realism as it began to be constructed in the early years of 1941–44 in the pages of *Cinema*, was defined more and more in terms of political substance and morality. *Cinema* became most hostile to a cinema without evident commitment, or only it seemed with a commitment to form without a clear social content. The critical work of Antonioni in those last years on *Cinema* come to be deprecated, and also the work of an entire group of films and film-makers, both genre film-makers of the 1930s, and some of the most interesting, and experimental film-makers of the early 1940s, like Castellani, Soldati, Poggioli, who were condemned in *Cinema* for a formalism without content, for 'irrelevance', for mere intellectualism, decorativeness, emptiness.[14]

Antonioni did not belong with this 'formalist' group, and certainly not with the apologists for the more ordinary films of the 1930s, which he despised, but he no longer belonged with the group of *Cinema* either and its ideology of social realism in which matters of form were deemed subordinate.

Antonioni's views from the mid-1930s to the early 40s, and beyond that, into the post-war period, remained remarkably consistent; those positions, somewhat more nuanced, are largely still held by him today, at least the core of them are, and they had then, as they do now, the same flexibility and productivity, a refusal of certitudes, a sensitivity to change; as things have turned out it was the social 'radical' ideas of *Cinema* that were regressive and tied to a past, whereas Antonioni proved himself more in touch with the present and more open to the future.

In 1940, Antonioni was sent by *Cinema* to cover the Venice film festival. It was a dramatic and frightening time. The festival took place in September. In April of the previous year fascist Italy had invaded Albania and in May reaffirmed its alliance with Nazi Germany. In June of 1940, only a few months before the Venice film festival, Italy officially joined the war on the side of Germany. The Venice film festival had been established by the Italian fascist State in 1934 as part of a broad programme for reviving the Italian film industry and restoring the image of Italian culture abroad. The festival was to serve as a sign that fascist Italy was culturally dynamic (on the evidence of Italian films presented) and culturally open (by the range of foreign films screened and honoured – e.g. Renoir's *La Grande Illusion*). By September 1940 this internationalism was no longer possible; the festival became a fascist film festival; the main films were from Italy, Germany and conquered countries like Albania.[15]

This context for the 1940 festival was only indirectly marked in Antonioni's articles. He sent back three pieces, 'Inaugurazione' and a two part article called 'La sorpresa veneziana'.[16] The festival opened with a German entry, *Opernball* by Von Bolvary. Antonioni was less interested in the film than he was in the spectacle of the opening, in the setting of Venice and in the artistic implications of the war:

> There were no white jackets at the San Marco cinema on opening night, nor low cut gowns. The official opening took place after dark; it was evident in the main hall that the atmosphere was utterly different than it

had been in years past (things were otherwise in the days at the Lido, under bright lights; it is only a memory now; a time that seems to be from a past before we were even born). Now, in war-time, the war was present at the very heart of the festival; with the absence of the Venetian wealthy everything seemed more subdued, austere. The entire event lacked all luxury though there were elegant people (but never before so serious or so silent): actresses, directors, celebrities. There were roses everywhere; it was possible to make use of them to form a lovely picture of life and colour; in that respect the hall seemed set for a gay ball, the only things missing were the Chinese lanterns.

The article concluded:

By midnight everything was over. Officials, film-makers, the public silently left (the darkness made everything still where before, in artificial light, all had been excitement and volubility). The film continued outside though with an altered tone and script. Venice seemed completely unreal and so very dark; lights shimmered along invisible canals as if coming from nearby falling stars; here and there street lamps created strange perspectives. If suddenly the old Venetian masks had appeared from an angle of one of the alleyways none of us would have been surprised.
San Marco square was like a soft field surrounded by tall hedges. At the far end of the square was the bell tower, an enormous black cypress.[17]

Already present in this scenographic, visual *mise-en-scène* of festival-in-wartime themes were sensibilities and interests later evident in Antonioni's films: the dissolution of shapes, the disappearance of objects and their reappearance as other things, still figurative, yet threatened with a loss of identity, a blur of outlines, like the Piazza San Marco become a field skirted by hedges, the bell tower a black cypress, lights on the canals becoming falling stars. The war is present, but as an atmosphere, a quality of light, matters of gesture, comportment ('never before so serious or so silent').

Two years earlier, in 1938, Antonioni had reported on the Venice film festival for *Corriere Padano*; the social attitudes he expressed then were not dissimilar from those he expressed in the 1940 article, but, if anything, his social preferences were more pronounced, at least more outspoken.[18] If, in 1940, he regretted the relative absence of the *bel mondo*, in 1938, he regretted the presence of a very ordinary bourgeoisie and the vulgarisation of the festival: applause at the wrong places, laughter at the gross and the silly; he lamented 'the crowd of ingenuous new spectators', 'the lowering of the tone of things', 'the growth in incomprehension'.
Antonioni, at the time, made a distinction, in a number of his writings,

between the commercial and the artistic, between what was artistically of little value, but nevertheless of considerable appeal, and what was of little appeal, but of considerable value. His assessment of the 1938 festival was that things had gone very well commercially, but very badly artistically; the change in the audience at Venice was already the sign of a social change, a shift in taste. He returned to that idea in an article in 1939 condemning the degradation of the cinema by producers in search of profits who even exceeded the general public in their vulgarity and bad taste.[19] As far as he was concerned the most subtle aspects of culture, cinema or literature were for the very few, and to try to please the very many would be to limit the possibilities of the cinema, to limit experimentation, to fail to go beyond the common and the conventional.

In an article arguing for the introduction of 16mm for feature films to allow for cheaper production and therefore the pursuit of artistic ends free, or at least freer from, commercial demands, Antonioni compared 16mm to the cultural page of the daily newspaper, of reviews, short fictions, cultural notices, specifically reserved for a cultural elite: 'very many among these articles contain, in embryo, little touches which could give life to a new and most special cinema which the general public would only find tiresome, because in a certain sense it would be hermetic, requiring an acute, studied attention that would be, at the same time, of an uncommon delicacy and intelligence.'[20]

Italian film production had virtually disappeared by the beginning of the 1920s, in part due to American competition, in part due to disorganisation within the industry itself. The cinema in Italy for the whole of the 1920s, the first decade of fascism, was essentially American cinema; American preponderance remained until late in the 1930s, but around 1929, Italian production slowly revived with the help of the fascist State.

Film production in the 1930s has roughly been divided into three periods: a period of experimentation (1929–32); a conservative period of fixed genres, State control, an ordered commercialism (1932–38); a period once again of experimentation, less state control, and an enormous increase in production, from a past average of around 20 films per year to well over 100 films per year in the early 1940s (1938–43). For the whole of this time there were intense debates about quality, popularity, art, industry, political commitment, entertainment, the kind of cinema Italy required.

Antonioni's articles were part of that debate as was Vittorio Mussolini's praise of the American cinema, De Santis' condemnation of 'formalism', Alicata's search for models in the novels of Verga. But the debate was also carried on practically in the actual organisation of production, in reactions to changed economic circumstances, and to shifts in political power and cultural emphases. By 1938, for example, there was considerable pressure from producers for an increase in their share of the market which coincided with more general economic needs for greater State control over imports. Restrictions on the American studios, and their response, the withdrawal of films, immediately led to a nearly five fold increase in production which by its very enormity and the fragmentary nature of production spread between scores of small producers, no longer allowed for the control and direction characteristic of 1932–38. The State, which had before helped to contain the Italian cinema within the bounds of a highly coded, conventionalised production of genres, after 1938 argued for a 'free' commercialism, for variety; its policies, necessarily, encouraged considerable experiment: the documentary fictions of Rossellini and De Robertis outside the bounds of existing genres, and the 'formalism' of Castellani and Poggioli, for example, occur in this late period.

Antonioni's writings on film began in 1935–36; his overwhelming concern was to direct the cinema towards what was modern and new, in areas of narrative and of visual style, away from a commercialism and populism in which what tended to be valued, he believed, was what was most obvious and most ordinary: plots, stories, characters, stars. It was precisely when the possibilities of the cinema seemed to open up, after 1938, that his criticisms became more insistent and more confident, and more willing to risk the unpopularity of seeming to be socially exclusive for the sake of a less conventional and more subtle cinema.

The fascist cultural slogan, 'andare verso il popolo' ('go to the people'), which became equally serviceable later to a 'left' populism, and which in the 30s had the practical consequence of the organisation and control of leisure and mass culture by the State, was for Antonioni an idea and a practice which was artistically destructive, to be strongly resisted. The 'people', he wrote, were only competent to appreciate the mediocre and the tasteless: pleasant music, engaging actors, romanticism, cheap sentimentalism, to see only stars, a good story, but utterly oblivious to everything that might be called the 'language' of film, its technical details, those aspects that constituted the cinema for him and where its productivity, its possibility for change, and its 'art' lay: the movement of the camera, lighting, editing, a dissolve, a superimposition, direction, the script. 'There is no understanding, not even the least spiritual accord between artist and spectator over a film; there is only a deep gulf that no one is able to fill.'[21]

With little conviction, and less hope, he proposed, against the force of the slogan 'andare verso il popolo', another slogan, or at least another interpretation: 'portare il popolo verso di noi' ('bring the people to us'), raise them to our level, educate them, don't pander to them. Yet there was always the risk they might respond: 'It's very beautiful . . . but what does it mean?'

His apparent social elitism was above all an elitism for a particular kind of artistic practice and culture, rather more than for the virtues of a particular class, though inevitably, and unfortunately, the two often went together; in any case, it had interesting and by no means self-evident political implications, not least for the cinema itself.

Antonioni's politics at the time were informed by a vague liberalism, opposed to fascism and the war, but also distanced from them. The practices of art and criticism were for him functions separate from politics. Though indirection in writing on political-cultural matters was an established style during the fascist period, Antonioni's interest was in the indirect itself, less in the war, for example, than in its reflection in things, as in his description of opening night at Venice in 1940. Such writing may have been necessary at the time, but when the necessity was no longer there Antonioni continued to see things in a similar manner, and was condemned for it: formalism, lack of commitment, apoliticism, empty aestheticism.

For the most part all reference to political and social matters were absent from Antonioni's writings, or were only present obliquely, by implication. But two articles, one written in 1935, the other in August/September 1943, after the dismissal of Mussolini, directly concern the relation of politics to film: the 1935 article, for *Corriere Padano*, refers to the cultural positions of left fascism on *Critica Fascista*; the 1943 article, for *Lo Schermo*, refers to the left, largely communist group of writers, on *Cinema*.[22]

The 1935 article is one of Antonioni's first critical writings; it concerns the relation of director to scriptwriter. *Critica Fascista* had maintained that because Italy needed a cinema of political commitment, national propaganda, and fascist revolution, the writer, rather than the director, was of paramount importance for a film. A film of this kind, for these purposes, needed to be able to state unequivocally, without adornment, its social messages and political meanings; a concern with form, an attention to style, the fantasies of film directors, the desire for fantasy itself, for the transfiguration of reality, the ability to pursue impulses freely, personally, without direction, wherever these led, these were not desirable in a 'fascist' cinema.

Antonioni did not disagree: if it was propaganda and politics that was wanted, then indeed, writers ought to prevail; if on the other hand you wanted art:

> it is the director, who, in the end, determines the real art of the cinema . . . but we perfectly agree with *Critica Fascista* which affirms 'the need for a programmed production with a precise direction: a cinema of revolutionary inspiration'. This programmed cinema will be a very powerful propaganda arm that will deeply affect the people and will be a most effective means by which fascism can affirm throughout the world what is essential and irreplaceable about it. In that case the personality

of the writer should take precedence over the wishes of the director.

The script, in the 1930s, as it was in the 1950s, when Antonioni, and others, like Rossellini and Fellini, fought against the tyranny of the script ('la sceneggiatura di ferro', the 'iron-clad script'), was an instrument of control; in 1935, to enable the state to exercise political control; in the 1950s, to enable the producer to ensure a certain kind of cinema. Antonioni was not arguing for a general liberty, but for the specific liberty of the film director, not only the liberty for fantasy so much as the right to work at a particular level: of shots, of editing, of lighting, of sound, and to experiment with these possibilities, not in a set direction determined by a script and a story, but rather where things might lead, into areas not yet established, for an imagination not yet fully formed and realised, in short, as it was argued in the 1950s, for experiment, for change.[23]

The social snobbism of some of Antonioni's writings of the period are of a piece with this resistance to a political, committed, pre-set cinema; in both cases it was an argument for an openness and unconventionality which Antonioni found threatened both by commercialism and by political populism, which together seemed to limit those activities which Antonioni regarded as important: playing with the specific means of the cinema and playing with them to no particular predetermined end.

Much of this position philosophically derived from Benedetto Croce, but in this particular instance, in this specific context, Antonioni's defence of the values of an uncommitted cinema was in direct contrast to the most radical, most articulate positions of fascist populism, and even if they came from a revulsion which was more aesthetic than political, more a matter of taste than of social conscience, it was precisely that taste and that aesthetic that was at issue, that was being threatened or being denied by a social-political nationalist ideology; the defence of those individual, personal and aesthetic values implied a political and even, perhaps, an anti-fascist position.

The more outspoken anti-fascism of the 'left' group at *Cinema* opposed its national populism to the populism of fascism; if its aesthetic positions were somewhat broader than those of *Critica Fascista*, or at least more clearly defined and more open to European culture, it nevertheless had an ideological programme which it believed the cinema ought to serve and a social function which it ought to execute. It was interesting, and telling, that the place on which Antonioni took his stand was not ideological, still less social or political, but practical, technical.

When Antonioni wrote, not long after – it would be the dominant note of all his criticism – an appreciation of *Night* by Gustav Machaty, it was not for its social themes, nor even for its narrative, or at least not for a narrative conceived simply in terms of story and events, but for its qualities of light, its contrast of tones, its evocation of an atmosphere, of feelings difficult to grasp and for that reason, all the more effective:

> *Night* in fact is a film made of light and shade. The most beautiful effects are achieved by the contrast of the one with the other . . . Everything is presented behind a veil of sensations. Nothing is very clear, no protagonist is ever looked at directly, the photography itself is always in dim light, but one has the exact sense of the life lived by the characters.[24]

It might have been a description of *Il grido* (1957) made twenty years later; all of his criticism has a quality that recalls his films, like this one on American crime/detective films which evokes the desolation of *Cronaca di un amore* (1950): '. . . this bleak, heavy world, where hurt reigns and death lies in wait at every corner, unseen, simply sensed . . . The dark alleyways, the dirty, black houses that exude squalor, the figures that hurry by . . .'[25]

In the midst of the upheavals of 1943, in the very months of the fall of the fascist regime and the organisation of the Resistance, Antonioni wrote, in the August/September 1943 issue of *Lo Schermo*, an impassioned plea for the artist not so much to be free from those events, clearly impossible, but to be free from attending to them and to their social import and political demands, and instead to be free to carry on the demands of art: its forms, its techniques, its languages. It was a position far removed from a 'neo-realism' of social commitment and the impetus to portray the immediate historical realities as in Visconti's *Ossessione*, or, most dramatically, a couple of years later, in Rossellini's *Roma, città aperta*. As his 1935 article in defence of the film director was directed against left fascist intellectuals on *Critica Fascista*, the target for this article was the anti-fascist, largely communist intellectuals on *Cinema*, including Visconti, and for reasons which were remarkably similar.

The article is the most theoretical and in a sense most 'political' statement Antonioni ever made; it is clearly indebted to Crocean idealism and liberalism. It is difficult adequately to imagine the way things were and how they felt in the autumn of 1943 in Italy, but Antonioni's statement seems by any measure quite extraordinary. Certainly, there is nothing like it in any of the film journals at the time; Antonioni, was, at least in print, moving well against the tide.

Antonioni's central point is quite simple: the cinema has its own specific values and these need to be thought of independently of the war, of social distress, of political necessities; and that effort, not to get caught up, to attend to your art, that was what was difficult: the first responsibility of the film-maker was to the cinema.

The example Antonioni quoted was the Soviet cinema of the 20s: Pudovkin, Eisenstein, Room. These film-makers for him were first of all 'men of the cinema.' 'For none of them social problems, however violent and complex, overcame aesthetic problems, even if the former were a stimulus to their art.' The 'politics', the 'morality', the very worth of that cinema rested with its language and its style; the morality of the film-maker was in the loyalty given to fantasy, to the language of art; that loyalty was, for Antonioni, absolute. And it was precisely now, in the midst of political chaos, that such a morality, such fantasy, and such an assertion of individual feelings against social demands and populist ideology was required:

> One can't help hearing the rumblings, the laments, that are so crucial in the history of humanity and behind which there are all those problems that everyone so well knows. But these are problems of a social kind, before which an older right of the artist to isolation needs to be affirmed . . . One needs to respond with one's *own* language . . . and if this language touches on being art, it will have accomplished a valuable social responsibility. Because the pleasure which art gives is not merely an illusory pleasure; today more than ever it appears as the most human of all happinesses.

Antonioni quoted Gide: 'If social questions now preoccupy my thoughts, it is because my creative demon has left me'; he cited James Joyce's negation of political passions; he mentioned Matisse's worst canvas, his only 'political' one, which depicted, symbolically, France's military defeat and national humiliation by Prussia. For Antonioni, these examples had contemporary import; they affected him and they affected the Italian cinema. He was particularly interested in the positions taken by the editorial group of *Cinema*:

> In fact, today, there is a group of young intellectuals whose predominant activity is with the cinema or with literature who are particularly attentive to the most trying daily realities. Many of them (not all) have our esteem and there can be no doubt that their actions are governed by the purity of their feelings, but these are informed by a principle according to which the urgency of social problems diminish the force of artistic problems.
> . . . The artist ought not to seek to avoid speaking his *own* language. If, by dedicating himself to other work, he ends by killing that voice, it would suggest that his artistic needs were not sufficiently compelling. In the contrary instance the work of art will be born, and in it contingent events and set programs will be brought to an abstract level.

The Italian cinema, at that precise historical moment, seemed to Antonioni too subject to a concern with content in its attempts to avoid charges of commercialism, of escapism, of an interest in illusions and illusory happinesses, and above all for fear of not 'participating' in current political and social events; its gritty realism was sometimes programmatic, academic, artificial, parading itself as a sign of truth; in fact, such 'truth', to him, often resulted in the avoidance and repression of fantasy and dream, and even of ideas. He criticised Amleto Palermi's *La peccatrice*, scripted by film 'theoreticians' at the national film school (the Centro Sperimentale di Cinematografia), Umberto Barbaro, Francesco Pasinetti and Luigi Chiarini, for being scholastic, over-rationalised: 'it is like sipping a lemonade without sugar: there is good in it . . . but it is difficult to taste it . . . it is too reasoned . . . the result is a kind of didactic exercise for students at the film school.'[26]

Critics most concerned with social content put forward a notion of style which was essentially formal and decorative, style as an empty 'writing', as calligraphy; they failed to see that style was a way of thinking, of concretely realising ideas by attending to framing, light, angles, movement, acting, gesture. It is interesting, I think, that Antonioni condemned both an academic formalism and a populist social content-ism for the effect both had on experiment, on imagining, in their denial not simply of the unplanned, but of the possibilities inherent in the actual activity of making a film, which could not, which ought not, according to Antonioni, be unduly set in advance. It was not only the contingency of events that needed to be accepted and attended to, but the contingency of one's reactions, the surprises in 'capturing' events before the camera, the new possibilities, not simply of reality, but of images made of it. For Antonioni, style was a concrete, material matter to be worked on, compared to which 'commitment' seemed abstract; for those who argued commitment, style at best was only a means to higher ends.

To privilege the social for Antonioni was a way of avoiding everything specific to the cinema for things external to it. It was not that social matters were to be ignored, so much as a question of the level at which they were to be realised in the cinema. To Antonioni it was not directly, not as an obvious content, but rather in the then devalued areas of style, of technique, of language, of personal feeling; it was, as the title of his article indicated, a *questione individuale*, all the more impelling in 1943 against the force of political events, and, perhaps, the even greater force of national-populist ideology.[27]

Notes

1. See Michelangelo Antonioni, 'Terra Verde (Sunto per un film)', *Bianco e Nero* vol. 4 no. 10, 1940; see also below Chapter Nine, p. 163. At least half of the original footage of *Gente del Po* was lost during the war; Antonioni edited the final version which is nine minutes long in 1947. His treatment-article for the film appeared as 'Per un film sul fiume Po' in *Cinema* no. 63, 25 April 1939. See pp. 25–26 for Antonioni's description of the film he never made on the asylum.

2. See Aldo Tassone, 'Michelangelo Antonioni critico cinematografico (1935–39)', *Bianco e Nero*, July–September 1985.

3. These three leading film journals were founded more or less at the same time during 1935–36, years which marked a major commitment by the fascist government to the Italian cinema: the founding of the film school, increased aid to film production, the building of Cinecittà, the launching of the Venice film festival. *Bianco e Nero* was edited from the film school which was directed by a liberal fascist, Luigi Chiarini, who employed and worked closely with the Marxist Umberto Barbaro who taught at the school; both wrote extensively for the journal and largely determined its policy. The journal was academic, conservative, idealist; if an aesthetic line could be discerned it was largely indebted to Crocean idealism.

4. See in particular the following articles which appeared in *Cinema*: Giuseppe De Santis, 'Per un paesaggio italiano', 25 April 1941; Giuseppe De Santis and Mario Alicata 'Verità e poesia: Verga e il cinema italiano', 10 October 1941; and their 'Ancora di Verga e del cinema italiano', 25 November 1941; Giuseppe De Santis 'Il linguaggio dei rapporti', 25 December 1941; Luchino Visconti 'Cadaveri' 10 June 1941, and 'Il cinema antropomorfico', 25 September and 25 October 1943.

5. Gianni Puccini 'I tempi di "Cinema"', *Filmcritica* vol 2 no. 5, 1951.

6. Ibid.

7. Dario Zanelli (ed.) 'Quel mio grande e ingenuo amore per il cinema' (intervista con V Mussolini) *Cinema Nuovo* nos. 284–285, August-October 1983, p. 14.

8. Ibid., p. 15.

9. Ibid.

10. Mussolini's writings for *Cinema* include: 'L'emancipazione del cinema italiano', 25 September 1936; 'Un momento critico', 25 November 1938, p. 307; 'Alcune cifre', 25 December 1938, p. 379; 'Importazione ed esportazione cinematografica', 25 November 1939; 'Constatazioni', 10 May 1941. The 'L'emancipazione . . .' article has been translated in *Filmviews* no. 135, Autumn 1988, which also includes a very interesting piece by Emilio Cecchi, 'American Literature and the Cinema', which represents a less favourable view of American culture: see my introduction to both these translations, 'Fascist Italy and the American Cinema', in the same issue; my view of these matters now is somewhat different than it was then.

11. Vittorio Caldiron, 'Il gruppo Cinema 1941–43 nella cultura d'avanguardia', *Cinema Nuovo*, 1 May 1957, p. 274.

12. F. Casetti, A. Farassino, A. Grasso, T. Sanguinetti, 'Neorealismo e cinema italiano degli anni '30', *Il neorealismo cinematografico italiano* (Venice: Marsilio editore 1975), pp. 331–385; the article is fascinating on the relation between Italian neo-realism and the fascist period.

13. Michelangelo Antonioni, 'L'ultimo Pabst', *Corriere Padano* 21 September 1937.

14. Mino Argentieri, 'I "formalisti italiani"', *Cinema 60* nos. 147–149, September–October, November–December 1982, January–February 1983.

15. See Luigi Freddi, *Il cinema* (Rome: L'Arnia, 1949), still the best history of the fascist state organisation of the cinema in the 1930s written by the first head of the Direzione generale di cinematografia. See also Michelangelo Antonioni 'Per una storia della mostra', *Cinema*, 10–25 September 1941, pp. 151–152, 187–189; P.V. Cannistraro, *La fabbrica del consenso: fascismo e mass media* (Bari: Laterza 1975).

16. Michelangelo Antonioni, 'Inaugurazione' *Cinema* 10 September 1940; 'La sorpresa veneziana' *Cinema* 10 September 1940; 'La sorpresa veneziana' *Cinema* 25 September 1940.

17. Antonioni, 'Inaugurazione'.

18. Michelangelo Antonioni, 'Taccuino', *Corriere Padano*, 14 September 1938.

19. Michelangelo Antonioni, 'Umori del pubblico', *Cinema*, 25 July 1939, pp. 52–53.

20. Michelangelo Antonioni, 'Elzeviri a passo ridotto', *Corriere Padano*, 23 July 1938, p. 3.

21. Michelangelo Antonioni, 'Dell'educazione artistica', *Corriere Padano*, 2 March 1937.

22. Michelangelo Antonioni, 'Colpi di sonda. Cinematografo: soggetto e regia', *Corriere Padano* 28 March 1935; Antonioni refers in the article to a piece written in *Critica Fascista*, 15 March 1935; and Michelangelo Antonioni, 'La questione individuale', *Lo Schermo*, August–September 1943, pp. 11–12; see also Michelangelo Antonioni, 'La pazienza del cinema', *Cinema* no. 7, 30 January 1949 pp. 198–200, in which Antonioni refers favourably to a piece written for *Bianco e Nero*, December 1948, by Benedetto Croce.

23. See Lorenzo Cuccu, *La visione come problema* (Rome: Bulzoni, 1973), pp. 54–57, for a discussion of the battle of 'authors' in the 1950s in Italy (but also in France) against the producers ('mercanti di spettacolo') and the tyranny of the script to enforce an obedience to certain generic codes against personal and individual experiments, or at least against what was the not-yet-coded.

24. Michelangelo Antonioni, 'Machaty e il suo "notturno"', *Corriere Padano*, 30 June 1936, p. 3.

25. Michelangelo Antonioni, 'Sotto i ponti di New York', *Corriere Padano*, 9 February 1938.

26. Michelangelo Antonioni, 'La settimana cinematografica di Venezia: *La peccatrice* di Palermi', *Corriere Padano*, 4 September 1940.

27. See A. Asor Rosa, *Scrittori e popolo* (Rome: Samonà e Savelli, 1964; reissued in paperback by Einaudi in 1988) for a discussion of the effects of national populist ideology on Italian culture. Asor Rosa was at the time, and is now, a communist party intellectual (he was recently appointed editor of the Italian Communist Party weekly, *Rinascita*); his attack on populist orthodoxy was new and courageous: its provincialism, its romanticism, its narrowness, the damage it had done to Italian culture.
     There is an interesting essay on Antonioni by the Marxist Italian philosopher Galvano Della Volpe also written in 1964 which isn't all that distant from some of the positions Antonioni took in 1943 in the sense that 'correct ideology' without attention to writing, to style, was, for Della Volpe, only half the battle. See Galvano Della Volpe, 'Antonioni e l'ideologia borghese', in Carlo Di Carlo (ed.), *Michelangelo Antonioni* (Bianco e Nero, 1964) pp. 63–64.

Chapter Two

In 1959, Antonioni reflected back on the 1930s documentary he never made on the insane as a first example of neo-realism: documentarism, concern with factual reportage, non-intrusiveness, spontaneity, responsiveness to the real as it presented itself, 'the people' as protagonists, the strange in the everyday, and a certain catching of things as they occurred, 'in fieri', being surprised by them, watching a reality whose end was not known in advance, and observing, at the same time, one's own gaze, catching oneself in the 'other'.

The first time that I was behind a camera – it was a 16mm Bell and Howell – was in an insane asylum. The director of it was a very tall man and had a face, which, with the passage of time, came to resemble that of his patients. I then lived in Ferrara, the city where I was born, a small wonderful city in the Po valley, ancient and silent. We decided, my friends and I, to make a documentary on the insane. The director of the asylum wanted to help me at all costs and rolled around on the floor to show me the reactions of the patients to various external stimuli. But I wanted to make a documentary from reality, that is from among the insane; I was so insistent that in the end the director said: 'Go ahead.'

We set up the camera, got the lights ready, arranged the mad people in the room according to the requirements of the first shot, and I have to say that they obeyed with humility and made every effort not to go wrong. They were very generous in this way and I congratulated myself on how well things had turned out. At last I gave the order to turn on the lights. I was very excited. All at once the room was bathed in light. For a split second the patients remained immobile, as if turned to stone. I have never seen on the face of any actor such profound, such total fear. Let me stress that it was only an instant; then an indescribable scene took place. The mad people began to contort themselves, to scream, to roll around on the floor as the director had done. There was a hellish uproar. The mad desperately tried to protect themselves from the light as from a prehistoric monster who had attacked them; their faces, which at first, in the quiet, were able to contain their madness within human limits, now appeared crazed, devastated. It was we, now, who were paralysed before this spectacle. The cameraman even lacked the strength to stop the motor of the camera or I to give any order whatever. It was the asylum director who cried 'Stop! Shut off the lights!' And in the room, returned now to semi-darkness and silence, we saw a knot of bodies twitching as if in the last shudders of a death agony.

I have never forgotten that scene. But it was with it that we began to speak, without knowing it, of neo-realism.

This happened before the war.[1]

In 1939, Antonioni wrote a treatment in *Cinema* of what was to be his first documentary on the people of the Po called 'Per un film sul fiume Po'.[2] Much more clearly than in the insane asylum film, the Po film had many of those characteristics that would be identified with neo-realism. The treatment was featured in *Cinema*; it seemed to conform to the 'new' cinema the journal wanted: realistic, populist, documentary truth . . . the poetry of reality. Nevertheless, there was a sensibility at work in the article-treatment which somewhat shifted these apparent neo-realist concerns.

First, there is the river itself. Antonioni was brought up in the Po valley, in Ferrara. The river not only had a social-populist interest for him, which he expressed in the article, but a visual and philosophical one. The Po figures in a number of Antonioni films. In *Il deserto rosso* (1964), notably in the sequence of the party in the cabin by the river, Antonioni used the river and its mists and fogs to distort shapes and surfaces, to blur and alter perspectives, and to create an atmosphere of uncertainty and fragility. The film in which the Po is most evident is *Il grido* where it is a permanent presence whose horizons, mist, fogs, changing tones provide not only a landscape for the emotions of Aldo but a play of alterations in shapes, and a tenuousness of mood and in life itself. And though it isn't the Po, it is beside a river in Milan where the two lovers first meet in *Cronaca di un amore* and where Guido seeks to murder Paola's husband; in *L'eclisse* (1962) the river is a place of death for the drunk who stands in for Piero; it is the place for the suicide of Rosetta in *Le amiche* (1955), and of attempted suicide in *Tentato suicidio* (1953). In these later films, as in this earliest one, the Po, the river valley, the mists, the fogs are not simply background, atmosphere in which a drama takes place, but the subject of the drama, or at least as much the centre of the narrative as the events within it, as if in this featuring of the river, in its aesthetic interest as light and pattern, in its effect on objects and figures, Antonioni was beginning to offer a new notion, certainly a new subject for narrative, much more radical, for example than the atmospheric effects suggested (and suggested to him) by American crime films.

In part, the appeal of the Po for Antonioni in his article-treatment is the mutability of the river: full to the point of flood in winter, dry, emptied out, in late summer. His interest is in the visual possibilities offered by change rather than in their philosophic or social implications. In the article, following a paragraph on the traditional pursuits along the river, the gestures of that traditionalism, their softness, their slowness, their gentleness, and the permanence and repetitiveness of these and the things that go with them, the boats, the nets, the woods, the river itself, Antonioni continued: 'But not even for objects do the years pass in vain. Even for the Po comes a time for reawakening. And now there are iron bridges on which long freight trains rumble night and day, buildings, six stories high, stained with enormous windows vomiting dust and noise, docks, warehouses, smokestacks, other canals with banks of cement; in short a modern world, mechanical, indus- trialised, which places the harmony of the old in crisis.'

Antonioni takes no position about that change, certainly not a position of regret. Change simply is, and whatever its human or social consequences – Antonioni is not uninterested in these – what matters to him is the opportunity to record new shapes and formations, even if these are formations which may lead to social dissolution. It is not something to denounce or lament. Quite simply, and independently of social matters, Antonioni is extremely positive about what he sees as he was about the opening night at Venice, not for the fact of the opening, or of the war, but for the sight of it, the coming of new and 'unreal' shapes, the chance to seize upon something as it, at that moment, disappears, changes. This kind of sensibility is not outside history as it is beside it, registering its effects on surfaces, on objects, on movements.

The Po article begins:

It is not at all a sentimental assertion to say that the people of the Po valley are enamoured of the river. In fact a halo of deep feeling, one should say love, surrounds this river which, in a certain sense, is the despot of the valley. The people of the valley *feel* the Po. Precisely how they *feel* it we don't know: but what we do know is that it is something there in the very air which, like a kind of subtle witchcraft, affects one immediately.

The article has two subjects: the people of the Po and Antonioni observing them. Just as the feelings he senses in others are not named, neither are his own feelings made clear. What he sees, where the camera rests, marks a fascination, not an explanation. Antonioni is not being coy; he doesn't know. The purpose of making a film is to discover things, but the film is not the consequence of that discovery, rather the process of it. This gives not only the Po documentary, but all his films, a concreteness and immediacy of image combined with a vagueness of meaning. The image is not the consequence of a thought, but the thought itself taking shape, finding itself. The images may be concrete, but they often represent variable things in uncertain perspectives. This way of observing was the exact contrary to the sureties of meaning his colleagues on *Cinema* thought valuable, or the sureties of form theorised at the film school.

Some of Antonioni's very early critical writings, around 1937, repeat idealist commonplaces on the documentary: the need for 'poetry', art *and* reality, interpretation and truth, a lyrical spiritual truth, not a mechanical document of reality. What gives the writings an extra interest is not the ideas and the programmatic strictures, but the specifics of his criticism, taking Flaherty to task, for example, for allowing 'fiction' to overcome 'document', for losing the sense of the interest of the real in a set of false, superimposed events. Antonioni asked for two things from the documentary: the cinematographic, by which he meant those things that adhere to the specifics of colour, tone, light, movement, gesture; and the lyrical, by which he meant a personal, subjective response, expressed in 'style' to the life and the reality seen.

N.U. – NETTEZZA URBANA *(1948)*
The anonymous street cleaners

These ideas, somewhat vague in statement, were not so in realisation, not only in his own documentaries, but also in his fictions, from the very first to the most recent; the heart and subject of his films are not with the fiction as a narrative of events, nor with the 'realities' screened, but somewhere between the two, in which the fiction becomes an objective set of events which Antonioni 'finds' as they take place, recording them and his feelings towards them, maintaining, simultaneously, a spontaneity and a distance: the fiction becoming a documented reality, the reality becoming transformed into a new reality ('at once lyrical and cinematographic') in the reaction to it. It took great delicacy – hence the need for specific criticisms, specific works – to tread the fragile division along which document and fiction play.[3] It was not a matter of 'theory' for Antonioni, but of practical example.

One of the films Antonioni saw at Venice was Veit Harlan's *Jud Süss* which Harlan made in 1939; it is a notorious anti-semitic film. Antonioni, with certain exceptions, praised the film. The exceptions have to do with representations of Süss which are programmatic, ideological (racist), which reduce what is complicated to something simple hence, for Antonioni, not believable. His criticism is not strictly speaking ethical, still less 'political', but rather aesthetic: Süss as cruel Jew is unconvincing, shallow, unworkable.

Two scenes of particular horror in the film – the offering of young girls to Süss by the Duke of Frankfurt and the violation of one of them by Süss – are criticised by Antonioni: 'they seem to be episodes of such extreme cruelty as to push all artistic elements of the character beyond any credible human aspect.' On the other hand, scenes in which Süss seems genuinely affected by the feelings of younger people, his fear of death, his generosity towards another Jew, when Süss acts out of his humanity and is not presented as an ideological cipher, when he is like anyone else, 'all these instances,' Antonioni notes, 'give the character an artistic consistency which is moving and familiar.'[4] It is not anti-semitism which Antonioni criticised but the consequences of ideology and its reductiveness; it was the intrusion of a political language with its certainties into an artistic discourse, necessarily uncertain, that he took exception to.

Antonioni's judgement on *Jud Süss* was in fact a reconsidered one; whether or not that reconsideration had anything to do with writing for *Cinema* as opposed to *Corriere Padano* is hard to know, but his earlier review of the film two weeks before for *Corriere Padano* is more unequivocally favourable; the matter of its ideology, of the crudity of its anti-semitism never arises and what was questionable, even unfortunate two weeks later, earlier had been wonderful, marvellous:

> We have no hesitation in saying if this is propaganda, then we welcome propaganda. It is a powerful, incisive, extremely effective film . . . There isn't a single moment when the film slows, not one episode in disharmony with another: it is a film of complete unity and balance . . . the episode in which Süss violates the young girl is done with astonishing skill.[5]

I can't comment on the reasons for the contradictoriness. But there were other lapses of a similar kind by Antonioni, not least his sometimes extreme of social snobbery, even with the excuse of aesthetic sensibility; and there is a single instance of a rather excessive review which at times adopts an official rhetoric in praise of one of the few really 'fascist' films of the period.

During the 1938 Venice festival the Coppa Mussolini prize was shared by Goffredo Alessandrini's *Luciano Serra, pilota* and Leni Riefenstahl's *Olympia*. The Alessandrini was based on a script jointly written by Alessandrini and Roberto Rossellini. The film was 'supervised' by Vittorio Mussolini. Mussolini claims he had a significant role in the film, but it is hard to know. I haven't seen the film, but it was praised in all the film journals and I imagine in most of the press reviews.[6]

It is a patriotic film made contemporaneously with the colonial wars of Italy in north and east Africa, and with those wars as its setting. It is the story of a father and son, military, aviator bravery, loyalty to the fatherland, colonial exile, colonial war. I'm quite sure, judging from the reviews, that the film was indeed exceptional, and deserved much of the praise it received not because it was patriotic, but rather because of its new 'realism', its documentarism, its immediacy, which Rossellini may very well have shared responsibility for; as for Vittorio Mussolini, some of his views on the cinema were quite advanced and progressive. There is no reason to believe that he would have hindered the direction of the film and indeed may have helped it.

Antonioni's review of the film (in fact he wrote about it twice in *Corriere Padano*) is fulsome, excessive, without the fineness of distinction and care for language and culture that Antonioni usually expressed and practised:

> *Luciano Serra* is indisputably the first great Italian film . . . it celebrates many things, from paternal love to the passion for flying, from courage to heroism, but it isn't a film simply of heroism: it is that, and it is, also much more . . . For its vivid humanity . . . this first film of Vittorio Mussolini must be classified among the greatest works of the cinema in our time . . . it is a beautiful film which will please aesthetes and populace alike . . . *Luciano Serra* is a film of the renaissance, of the real renaissance of the Italian cinema. And for it we must give our thanks to Vittorio Mussolini.[7]

And six weeks later, writing on the question of what film ought to represent Italy in New York, Antonioni had only one answer, *Luciano Serra*: 'The name of our most able and intelligent film-maker: Vittorio Mussolini. Yes sir . . .' Yes sir, indeed: Alessandrini was the director.[8]

They were not reviews that are perhaps happy to remember; not only do they seem tasteless, politically suspect, but also they are quite contrary to the aesthetic values which Antonioni sought to advance then, and later. It is worth noting another review, written almost exactly two years later, of Augusto Genina's film *L'assedio dell'Alcazar*, which concerned a Republican siege of fascist and Franco troops at Alcazar during the Spanish civil war; the film certainly had, and served, propagandist ends. *Alcazar*, like *Luciano Serra*, *pilota* before it, was screened at Venice (no prizes) in 1940; Antonioni praised it, not for its rhetoric, its heroic sentimentalism, but rather for contrary qualities: its avoidance of rhetoric, its discretion, its skill in allowing events to speak for themselves, for things not underlined, not shouted, not squeezed out. The value of *Alcazar* for Antonioni was its restraint . . . it is the value too of this more characteristic Antonioni review.[9]

Gente del Po is only a fragment of itself. As a result of mishaps caused by the confusion of war much of the original footage shot in 1942–43 was lost; what remained of the film wasn't edited until 1947. The final film nevertheless is close to Antonioni's 1939 treatment and retains the two subjects he stressed in it: the magic of the landscape and the feelings of the people for it. These subjects are realised in a very special way. The feelings of the people for the Po are evident primarily as reflections in movements and gestures; as for the landscape it fascinates the camera which dwells on this or that aspect of it for its light, its patterns, its variations; the river dividing the planes of the screen, the verticals of the trees lining the banks against the horizontal of the river, the light of the evening on the water, the new shapes, dissolutions of shapes, disappearances and appearances effected by smoke, fog, mist, clouds, light.

The film, though realistic, documenting what it sees, and careful in its attentiveness, seems to have no clear subject: the people are there but not in any sociological way as if what is seen has no reason in particular to be noted except that it is there and the camera becomes interested in it. Often that interest seems different than the apparent subject of the film as if, rather than the camera recording a subject, it is in search of a subject whose identity and outline elude it.

Antonioni is fond of recalling that while he was shooting *Gente del Po* on one part of the river, Luchino Visconti was shooting *Ossessione* on another part. The Visconti is better known: it is taken to be the first 'neo-realist' film and the first 'anti-fascist' film, a combination it would seem of an exemplary aesthetic and an exemplary politics.[10] The link between anti-fascism and neo-realism was for long taken as the essential feature of neo-realism itself. (In fact the 'dates' of neo-realism refer to political events, not aesthetic attributes: 1943, the fall of fascism; 1948, or 1950–51, the end of the hopes of the Resistance with the election of the Christian Democrats to form the first post-war Italian government and the confirmation of its political direction. It is these events which were then read as the determining factors in shaping neo-realism, its early optimism and anti-fascism, its subsequent reformism, conformism. Often in the Italian criticisms of neo-realism it was political reality, not film reality that was being argued.) Antonioni, recalling the simultaneity

GENTE DEL PO *(1943-47)*
The river bank

of the shooting of his and Visconti's film, reflected that he too had been practising neo-realism.[11]

Ossessione occurs on a large stage: the Po valley, the small towns along the river, Ferrara, with a great number of characters each with an identifiable social place. The film combines a nineteenth-century melodramatic opera form with a story and realism based on the American adventure street novel, James M. Cain's *The Postman Always Rings Twice*, much admired by the *Cinema* editorial group.[12] It is a story of passion and violence among ordinary people: a vagabond, an innkeeper, his wife, a homosexual Spanish anarchist. Visconti's realism is a social realism; his characters are social signs; the scene, the setting reflects on current, contemporary Italy; the choice of melodrama is an attempt to relate personal, familial experience to nature (of man) and to history (the nature of society) one echoing the other. The Cain novel provided a plot pretext and a stylistic guide, in its attention to everyday, and violent, reality.

The anti-fascism of the film consists less in its stylistic aspects – other films looking like *Ossessione* were being made – than in its social realism depicting an Italy of poverty, adultery, murder, homosexuality, prostitution in which the bonds of society seemed to be disintegrating, its values and institutions slipping away. This is not a document or observation in the sense that *Gente del Po* is, but rather an argument to which a documentary realism is recruited. At the core of *Ossessione*'s neo-realism and anti-fascism is the reflection in it of a social reality in which the personal is raised to the level of History and the historical brought into line with the Familial. Melodrama suits this concern beautifully.

Thus we have two films, shot at almost the same time, a stone's throw from each other on the river Po, both apparently neo-realist, each utterly different from the other in their concerns and realisation. Nothing could be further from Visconti and the group at *Cinema* who helped make *Ossessione* than the intimacy, quiet and indefiniteness of *Gente del Po*, and nothing could be further from Antonioni than Visconti's and *Cinema*'s opera of the people, its militant populism, its realism with a social message, its ideological programme.

By 1949 Antonioni had already made a number of documentaries: *Gente del Po*, *N.U. – Nettezza Urbana* (1948), *L'amorosa menzogna* (1948/1949), *Superstizione – non ci credo!* (1949), and *Sette canne, un vestito* (1949) and was preparing his first feature film, *Cronaca di un amore*. He had collaborated on a number of screenplays, among them *Un pilota ritorna* in 1942 for Rossellini, and *Caccia tragica* for De Santis in 1947. He had also been assistant director for Marcel Carné on *Les visiteurs du soir* in 1942. He continued during this period to write articles on the cinema. He wrote a very interesting review of Visconti's *La terra trema* when it appeared in 1948.[13]

The Visconti film is based on the late nineteenth-century novel of Giovanni Verga, *I Malavoglia*. The film takes place in the present in the small Sicilian fishing village of Acitrezza between Catania and Siracusa. The actors are non-professionals. They are the real villagers of Acitrezza and they speak their local language. The story, however realistic in setting and character, is a nineteenth-century family melodrama in form. It involves the disintegration of a fishing family which attempts, at first successfully, and then disastrously unsuccessfully, to break the hold of the wholesalers over the fishermen. The family experiences one disaster after another and finally breaks apart almost completely. Because the film is in the local language of Acitrezza, and is not sub-titled into Italian, there is an Italian narrator who relates each scene as the film progresses, summarising events and dialogue.

(The use of the local language of Acitrezza in the film, rather than Italian, is a contradictory choice: it could be argued as a concern for authenticity and, because of the stress on the local, the specific, the film could stand as a criticism of the homogenisation of language and culture practised under fascism; at the same time it might serve as evidence of the film's populism, its concern for the people, their integrity, and so on. But the 'localism' and 'populism' appears in the film as often folkloric, while the choice of a completely obscure language, rather than being evidence of a populism, is on the contrary, evidence of an extreme form of hermeticism, an intense aestheticising, the sign of a 'high', even 'decadent' culture; though the results were very different there was a similar admixture in Pier Paolo Pasolini's early poetry in Friulian of the populist and the decadent, the 'realist' and the hermetic.)

What is interesting about the Antonioni review of *La terra trema* is that the most evident attributes of the film are not even mentioned, or barely so: the non-professional actors, the fact of local speech, the melodrama of family disintegration, petty-capitalist exploitation and its consequences, in short the entire thematic, populist, social-political force of the film either in its formal aspects or in its more evident narrative ones are simply ignored.

Antonioni mentioned descriptive passages in the film which seem to be peripheral to the narrative: the fish wholesalers eating spaghetti, a man laughing against a textured wall on which fascist graffiti is scribbled, 'Ntoni speaking on his boat in the silence of the night, the two sisters, one clever and bright, the other dreamy and nervous, both melancholy in their misery. Antonioni wrote of the movements of Visconti's camera, but as movements almost independent of any clarified narrative sense: he admired its wandering, its fascination with things, but a fascination which remains fascinating for not being over-defined, over-narrativised: 'Movements of the camera that always seem to discover something even if it is only an expression, a gesture; shots that say something even if what they describe is a state of mind, an interior feeling; a photography that always gives, powerfully, an atmosphere.'

It is an indefiniteness about the meaning of things seen and hence, for Antonioni, a respect for their complexity, where they are not concluded in an ideology that are the terms for his appreciation of *La terra trema* but also of other films: *Le Jour se lève*, *Stagecoach*, *Ladri di biciclette*. In his *Terra trema* review Antonioni quoted André Gide on the lasting work which 'bears within itself what disorientates and surprises and therefore endures'; Antonioni added:

> Enduring works are always the fruit of a dialectical relation between the author and the world. Authors intend many things: to describe, to narrate, to unveil, to accuse, to move, and if sometimes one aspect infects another and clarity is compromised, that isn't such a bad thing. Art may be clear but that isn't a reason that it must be.

In 1948, Antonioni wrote a lengthy appreciation of Marcel Carné with whom he worked as an assistant director in 1942 on *Les Visiteurs du soir*. The collaboration was not at all happy: partly for the fact of the war and the hostility of Carné, a Frenchman, working in a Nazi occupied France with an Italian from fascist Italy, but also because there were aesthetic differences and personality differences. Antonioni has stated elsewhere that he learned little from Carné and Carné was not an influence on his work. Antonioni's article on Carné, however – 'Marcel Carné, parigino' – is extremely appreciative.[14]

Antonioni's article began with a quote from the brothers Goncourt: 'Historians are the narrators of the past; novelists are the narrators of the present.' It was a contrast between large History and small history, a History of grand events, of politics and economics, and a history of small and often hidden things, feelings, relations. Antonioni then referred to Flaubert, whom he frequently mentioned in the course of years, and to Stendhal who has a special place for Italians for the evident affection he had for Italy.

Flaubert had a quality of particular value to Antonioni: craftsmanship in writing to the point where writing could be appreciated almost independently of what it was writing 'about', or at least the writing and its subject could be seen in their relations to one another with writing not functioning as a simple instrument for the expression of a content. As for Stendhal, Antonioni described him as a writer not concerned to bring art into line with nature and History, but to use art to analyse contemporary feelings, interior things, and to document these, in the manner suggested in the Goncourt quote.

What interested Antonioni in this small history of feelings was that such feelings could not, by their very nature, be fully grasped or explained. He was also interested in the indirect and necessarily oblique relation Stendhal posed between exterior events and interior sentiments: 'Every approach between art and its times, between cinema and politics, presupposes not so much an attempt at a direct correspondence between images and events, as it does an echo of events in the souls of individuals, where, at the most intimate of levels, sometimes necessitously, sometimes casually, life and art meet, and diverge.' Roland Barthes, more than thirty years later, in an open letter to Antonioni sketched out ideas similar to these: the contrast of large and small histories, the autonomy of a writing, and the opposition between languages of power and languages of art.[15]

With the exception of Renoir (and of course Carné), Antonioni had little sympathetic regard for French cinema, and very little for René Clair. It seemed to him that French films of the 30s, involved as they were with the contemporary politics of the Popular Front, were among the worst of films precisely because the relations history and art, politics and art were conceived too directly and as a consequence events and characters had no more 'reality' than as signs of political and social realities; there was nothing thereby left over. What Antonioni appreciated in Carné was an attention to reality and the rendering of it beyond any mere functionalism:

> With Carné it seems clear that it is not so much a moral that is important as the force with which he grounds reality in facts and represents these with a logic or fateful concatenation, or rather it is the force with which he recreates reality. No act is refused, no consequence shunned, everything is illuminated and interpreted with a precise intuition of the particular.

The quality of the particular, here, 'reality' if you like, is that it is resistant to generality and hence interpretation.

Antonioni went on:

> In the course of things what will define itself as the core of his style will be 'technique'. But this isn't a merely mechanical practice, a kind of grammatical play as an end in itself, but rather a technique which, being aware of itself, resolves and clarifies things, neither dominating nor allowing itself to be dominated. From that flows the fluidity of the narrative of his films, but from it also comes the refinement and intelligence of some of his solutions which he will never renounce. It is not for nothing that the predominantly content-oriented methods of Clair seemed to him intolerable. Beauty for Carné was something that he saw behind the lens, and it is necessary to see with what tenacity he pursued what he defined as '*joli*', or rejected as '*mauvais*', or '*moche*'; and with what lucidity and far seeing surety he mentally placed every shot, in the act of taking it, in an ideal montage: '*dans mon montage*'. Not that there was not any interest in humanity in him, but most of the time it was an unproclaimed adherence . . . he was loyal to 'populist' themes . . . But one cannot place Carné, as has been done, among directors who propose a human

L'AVVENTURA *(1959)*
Anna and Claudia

message, counterposed to those who propose a poetics. Themes certainly enthused Carné, but never to the point of 'forcing him' to give expression to them.

Antonioni's article presents an aesthetic which in general outline he would follow and develop and make more subtle. The article, however, seems quite extraordinary for having been written in 1948, at the height of Italian neo-realism, at the extreme point of its celebration of populism, humanism, love of the people, their goodness, their love, and of a realism whose essential character was the social and political reality of Italy immediately post-war, post-fascism, on the eve of the founding of the Republic, on the 'day-after' of the resistance struggle and the Liberation, a time of political commitment, of *impegno*, which films like *La terra trema*, for example, expressed. To write as he did in 1948 would not have been easy. It placed Antonioni somewhat askew, as in 1943, of both the politics of Italy at the time and the neo-realist politics of the Italian cinema. But it was in fact Antonioni who represented what was new and radically different for the cinema while the then triumphant neo-realism was already being surpassed, with the great exception, of course, of Rossellini.

On his way to Paris to meet Carné, Antonioni had to wait for some time at Nice for a visa. One day he observed a scene of a corpse of a man who had just drowned being dragged up to the beach. Like so many of Antonioni's 'fictions' and like his description of the opening night at Venice in 1940, in this one too the centre of things is displaced, an image takes over from an action. The war is present, but indirectly, primarily as a feeling; and, there is the fascination with death, emptiness, nothingness, the preconditions in Antonioni's works for so much.

> The sky is white; the sea-front deserted; the sea cold and empty; the hotels white and half-shuttered. On one of the white seats of the Promenade des Anglais the bathing attendant is seated, a negro in a white singlet. It is early. The sun labours to emerge from a fine layer of mist, the same as every day. There is nobody on the beach except a single bather floating inert a few yards from the shore. There is nothing to be heard except the sound of the sea, nothing to observe except the rocking of that body. The attendant goes down to the beach and into the bathing station. A girl comes out and walks towards the sea. She is wearing a flesh-coloured costume.
>
> The cry is short, sharp, and piercing. A glance is enough to tell that the bather is dead. The pallor of his face, the mouth full of saliva, the jaws stiff as in the act of biting, the few hairs glued to the forehead, the eyes staring, not with the fixity of death but with a troubled memory of life. The body is stretched out on the sand with the stomach in the air, the feet apart and pointing outwards. In a few moments, while the attendant attempts artificial respiration, the beach fills up with people.
>
> A boy of ten, pushing forward a little girl of about eight, shoves his way through to watch. 'Look,' he says to the girl, 'can you see?' 'Yes,' she says, very quietly. 'Can you see the spit on his mouth?' 'Yes.' 'And the swollen stomach? Do you see it? It's full of water.' The little girl watches

as though fascinated, in silence. The boy goes on, with a kind of sadistic joy. 'Now he's still white; but in a few moments he'll go blue. Look under his eyes; look, its starting.' The girl nods in assent, but remains silent; her face shows clearly that she is beginning to feel sick. The boy notices this and looks gloating. 'You scared?' 'No,' the little girl replies in a thin voice. 'Yes you are,' he insists, and goes on almost chanting, 'You're scared . . . you're scared . . .' After ten minutes or so the police arrive, and the beach is cleared. The attendant is the only one who remains with the policeman. Then he goes off, summoned by a lady with violet hair for her usual lesson of gymnastics.

It was wartime. I was at Nice, waiting for a visa to go to Paris to join Marcel Carné, with whom I was going to work as an assistant. They were days full of impatience and boredom, and of news about a war which stood still on an absurd thing called the Maginot Line. Suppose one had to construct a bit of film, based on this event and on this state of mind. I would try first to remove the actual event from the scene, and leave only the image described in the first four lines. In that white sea-front, that lonely figure, that silence, there seems to me to be an extraordinary strength of impact. The event here adds nothing: it is superfluous. I remember very well that I was interested, when it happened. The dead man acted as a distraction to a state of tension.

But the true emptiness, the *malaise*, the anxiety, the nausea, the atrophy of all normal feelings and desires, the fear, the anger – all these I felt then, coming out of the Negresco, I found myself in that whiteness, in that nothingness, which took shape around a black point.[16]

Many of the images in this brief 'document-fiction-diary' would appear, and obsessively, in other works: the fascination with water, with a surface, which, though pierced, swallows things up, without a trace, into a nothingness; the loss of figuration, of objects losing shape, and the shimmering between that loss and the figure itself, like a corpse, or an image; a subjectivism, but distanced, 'objective'; and a story, as if appearing from nowhere and just as easily disappearing into a void.

In Antonioni's works of the 1930s and early 40s there are traces of future fictions, but also an insistence on the need to find new narrative forms for the cinema, and not from 'life', not in declarations of political or social faiths, but rather from within a new, 'modern' tradition of narrative: Flaubert, Proust, Joyce. It was his modernism that set him apart most from other Italian film-makers of the period and set him outside prevailing social and political ideologies, particularly those being formed by left intellectuals in Italy at a moment of drastic change and upheaval.

Antonioni published three 'fictions' on the cultural page of *Corriere Padano* in 1938 and 1939. The subject of one was a street in Ferrara, peripheral, neglected, forgotten, a street you tended to miss. The story exhibits a fascination with things, with landscape, with the inanimate as holding within it, not only a story in its own right, but one already veering towards abstraction. The look of things becomes the centre of the drama; the subject of the fiction is not an event, but the feel of a wall, the sense of the air, a movement.

The Ferrara street was like the empty Via Alighieri in Ravenna where Giuliana had her shop in *Il deserto rosso* and the only event was a page of newspaper floating down the side of a building and the single presence the shadowy figure of the fruit-seller; or, like the deserted, early morning streets of Rome in *N.U.*, where the only thing present is the dark outline of a sweeper; or, as in *Cronaca di un amore*, the silent streets of Ferrara held by the camera after the figures of the narrative have left; or, as in *La notte* (1960), the streets on the edge of Milan in Lidia's silent walk.

Ritratto is the portrait of a woman drawn by the narrator who longs for her, seeks her attention, describes her every gesture, but whose reality and even image escapes him, in part because her look is elsewhere, not attentive to him, but principally as a function of his place outside and external to the portrait he forms; the reality and the image become confused, contaminate each other, more than the portrait of a woman, it becomes the portrait of a look. The subject shifts as it is being formed and the look which forms it turns back upon itself, meeting its own obsession. It recalls the exteriority, the narrative distance, the objectivity, the confusions of the principal character in Antonioni's most recent fiction, *Identificazione di una donna*.

The third piece, *Uomini di notte*, is about a group of young 'vitelloni' from Ferrara, lost in the fog in their car in the Po valley as are so many of Antonioni's characters: in *Il grido*, in *Il deserto rosso*, in *Identificazione di una donna*. 'It overtook us, suddenly . . . like an enormous wad of cotton stuffing . . . We felt lost, eerily lost in the dark and in the fog, without the comfort of things or the consolation of lights.'

The subject of the story is the fog, losing the outline of things, the disappearance of the figure and the appearance in its place of an image with no subject at all, or at least with a wholly new subject, not of figures, not of a drama, not even of a landscape, but rather more a subject to be formed, taking shape and losing shape:

> Little by little my eyes became accustomed to the dark: I could see the edge of the road, a tree, a road marker, finally, with great relief, a shadow, the dark shadow of a man who came forward, like a spectre on the side of the road . . . soon I saw another and another . . . Then came a group of four or five, close to one another, because of the cold, but separate,

each intent on his own segret. They slowly filed past in a kind of tottering parade, all wrapped up; it was sad to see those coats flapping in a line in the dark; the sadness was a funereal deep sadness which filled me with immense pain . . .

I suddenly had the sense that we were all shadows: the dead and the living, the happy and the unhappy . . . fantasms in the mist . . . [17]

Notes

1. From Michelangelo Antonioni, 'Fare un film e per me vivere', in *Cinema Nuovo*, March–April 1959.

2. Michelangelo Antonioni, 'Per un film sul fiume Po', *Cinema*, 25 April 1939.

3. See Michelangelo Antonioni, 'Documentari', *Corriere Padano*, 21 January 1937; 'La danza degli elefanti', *Corriere Padano*, 8 December 1937; 'Poesia di un documentario: "Los novios de la muerte"', *Corriere Padano*, 25 January 1939; the phrase is from the review of *Elephant Boy*.

4. Michelangelo Antonioni, 'La sorpresa veneziana', *Cinema*, 25 September 1940 p. 221.

5. Michelangelo Antonioni, 'La settimana cinematografica di Venezia: L'ebreo Süss e Il cavaliere di Kruja', *Corriere Padano*, 6 September 1940.

6. Mostra internazionale del nuovo cinema, *'Luciano Serra, pilota'*, *Nuovi materiali sul cinema italiano 1929–43* vol. 2, quaderno informativo 72 (Ancona, 1976), pp. 45–49, which contains full credits for the film, a summary of the narrative, and a selection of reviews in the most important journals.

7. Michelangelo Antonioni, 'Una favola eroica sullo schermo: Luciano Serra italianissimo pilota', *Corriere Padano*, 26 October 1938.

8. Michelangelo Antonioni, 'Per Nuova York', *Corriere Padano*, 10 December 1938.

9. Michelangelo Antonioni, 'La settimana cinematografica di Venezia: L'epopea dell'Alcazar trionfa in un film di Genina', *Corriere Padano*, 5 September 1940. See also Mostra internazionale del nuovo cinema *'L'assedio dell'Alcazar'*, *Nuovi materiali sul cinema italiano 1929–43* vol. 2, quaderno informativo 72 (Ancona, 1976), pp. 12–15.

10. See in particular Casetti, Farassino et al; also the following unsigned editorials in *Cinema* written just at the moment of the overthrow of fascism: 'Vie del cinema nostro', 10 July 1943; 'Questo pubblico, queste masse', 25 July–10 August 1943; 'Editoriale', 25 July–10 August 1943; see as well, Antonio Pietrangeli, 'Analisi spettrale del film realistico', *Cinema*, 25 July 1942, and his 'Verso un cinema italiano', *Bianco e Nero*, August 1942, and Mestolo, 'A proposito di *Ossessione*', *Cinema*, 10 July 1943.

11. Michelangelo Antonioni, 'Fare un film è per me vivere', *Cinema Nuovo*, March–April 1959.

12. See François Cuel 'Il postino suona sempre due volte', *Cinématographe* no. 70, September 1981 for a discussion of the Cain novel in relation to *Ossessione*.

13. Michelangelo Antonioni, '*La terra trema*' *Bianco e Nero*, July 1949, pp. 90–92.

14. Michelangelo Antonioni, 'Marcel Carné, parigino', *Bianco e Nero*, December 1948, pp. 17–47.

15. Roland Barthes, 'Caro Antonioni . . .', *Bologna Incontri* no. 2, February 1980.

16. The translation is by Geoffrey Nowell-Smith and published as 'The Event and the Image' in *Sight and Sound*, Winter 1963/64, p. 14; it originally appeared as 'Il fatto e l'immagine' in *Cinema Nuovo*, July–August 1963.

17. Michelangelo Antonioni, 'Strada a Ferrara', *Corriere Padano*, 8 October 1938; 'Ritratto', *Corriere Padano*, 18 December 1938; 'Uomini di notte', *Corriere Padano*, 18 February 1939.

Chapter Three

Cronaca di un amore was Antonioni's first feature film; it was made in 1950, the same year as De Sica's *Miracolo a Milano* and Rossellini's *Francesco, giullare di dio*. Unlike these, and certainly unlike the Italian neo-realist films made from 1943 until then, the Antonioni had as its subject, not the poor or the peripheral, but the world of the high bourgeoisie, of wealth, fashion, and, fatally, fast cars.

The film begins with an investigation. A wealthy Milan industrialist, Enrico Fontana, having come across some old photographs of his wife and realising that he knows nothing about her, especially not her past, hires a detective agency to find out who she is by finding out who she was. What provoked him were her photographed images. What Fontana finds is not this knowledge but his own death.

The investigation to identify Paola ends by creating an image of her which escapes any clear identification, as if, rather than coming into focus either by a clarifying image or by a narrative, she becomes more blurred, dissolves, and like the narrative itself, and like the life of her husband, seemingly vanishes, ends in an emptiness.

In the pursuit of Paola to find the reality behind her images, the detective discovers an accidental death: a friend of Paola's who was engaged to Guido whom Paola then loved fell down a lift shaft, witnessed by both Paola and Guido. The death was unintended yet wished for; but, after it occurs, rather than Paola and Guido coming together, they separate. What brings them together again is the investigation set in train by her husband to recover that past; again Paola and Guido fall in love. They arrange to kill Fontana as he rounds a slow turn on the open road. That night Fontana learns of the affair between his wife and Guido; driving fast on his rendezvous with murder, the car skids, plunges down an embankment and he dies: though accidental, a rendezvous with death nevertheless. Once again it is a wish come true, and again, after it, the very desire which had provoked his death dissolves: Paola and Guido separate, two lives and a love lost.

This fate of characters, of narrative, of emotions, of desires, and of objects and images to disappear, to lose form and identity, is a permanent feature of all of Antonioni's films, no less in this first feature film than in his most recent, *Identificazione di una donna* (1982), which is also the search for a woman, in 'reality' and for a narrative of a film being planned by the protagonist; real women and images of a woman multiply and disintegrate, to the point not only of their but of the narrative's extinction.

One of the functions of the doubling – twice an accidental death and twice wished for, a love affair duplicated and doubly dissolved, the real losing itself in an image, and the images, as with all images, multiplying, reproducing – is to make identity uncertain; it is an uncertainty that provokes Fontana's quest, but which remains after his death: it invades everyone; it is not just his condition, but a general condition and since it implicates the narrator, positioned at a distance as an observer, it implicates as well the spectator: the uncertainty of identity spreads beyond the fiction to its documentation and reception.

CRONACA DI UN AMORE *(1950)*
Fontana test drives the Maserati

The most interesting comment on *Cronaca di un amore* remains a review of it at the time in *Bianco e Nero* by Fernaldo Di Giammatteo; it concerns, primarily, Antonioni's choice of a narrative position at some distance from the characters which allows the characters an independence from the 'grip' of the narrative, an autonomy from any encompassing knowledge by the narrator, as if the narrator was describing events and characters not which he knew but which he sought to know, which fascinated him, and which he came upon, like the detective, or the reporter of a chronicle, at the moment they occurred, knowing no more and sometimes less than the characters themselves.

The choice of this path is due to the fact that Antonioni continually wants to maintain a certain distance between himself and his characters, and he acts before them with a kind of cold objectivity, placing himself in a relation to the film that he himself described as one of a 'special correspondent'. If the film is looked at carefully it is conducted like the detective who conducts the enquiry, or rather with the curiosity of someone who informs himself of things dispassionately and at a safe distance. The goal is to obtain 'realistic' characters, that are born by themselves, without external restraints. To accomplish this Antonioni never raises his voice, never seeks to impose his position as narrator. He allows his characters to live, he follows them, pursues them, observes them. Sometimes, to better observe them, he isolates them from the world that surrounds them, brings them into close-up. But without it appearing that it is he who asks for this isolation.[1]

The narrator is indeed in a position similar to that of the detective seeking to identify and to find a woman, a character, and a story, but it perhaps places him as well in the same position as Fontana who employs the detective as his agent. It is also the place of the audience positioned to find, by way of images and a narrative, some understanding, meanings, and like the variety of investigators, from narrator to Fontana, the audience too is left only with a fascination and locations from which to project that fascination, but with all certainty denied, all fullness of discovery and conclusion withheld.

This is not a frustration, but rather an opportunity for new possibilities for which the dissolution of certainty and the dissolution of the desire for certainty are preconditions.

Antonioni has used elements of detective fiction to structure many of his films: in *Le amiche* (1955) in the search for the reasons, hence the story, which may have motivated Rosetta's attempted suicide; in *L'avventura* (1959) in the search for Anna; in *Blow-Up* (1966) in the search for a story and a figure within and behind an enlarged photograph; in *Identificazione di una donna* in the search for a woman, a character, and a story. If this search for identity is extended as a search by the main character, not only for the truth of an 'other', but for the truth and identity of oneself, then this form of detection, both a quest and a journey, informs all of Antonioni's films: for example, *Le amiche* (Clelia finding her own loneliness and disconnection in the disconnections of others); *Il grido* (Aldo looking for himself and finding his own death); *The Passenger* (1975) (Locke seeking himself and his death in Robertson, his double); *Zabriskie Point* (1969) (Mark flies to a death arranged for another whose identity he assumes); and stunningly in *Il mistero di Oberwald* (1980) (a mysterious double of the dead king bringing the dead queen back to life only to destroy them both in a suicide of mistaken identities).

What happens in these films is that Antonioni while using many of the narrative structures of detective fiction changes their intent: nothing is discovered, or the quest itself is diverted, loses itself, all conclusion and finality is denied. Not only is the knowledge sought in Antonioni's films not attained, but all certainty tends to be lost; and in *Blow-Up*, in *L'avventura*, in *The Passenger*, in *Identificazione di una donna*, the mystery itself becomes abandoned, other interests displace it, with nothing being solved, nothing definite being secured.

What Di Giammatteo noticed was the extraordinary narrative reticence of *Cronaca di un amore*, extraordinary for its consequences and extraordinary in the context of the Italian cinema of the period, that is, in the context of Italian neo-realism.

> It truly is the technique of the special correspondent. Can this technique be applied to the cinema (to art)? One shouldn't hesitate to say yes and to recognise in this fact one of the values of the film . . . *Cronaca di un amore*, if considered from this point of view, is one of the richest films of the Italian cinema since the war . . . It breaks with the habitual without at the same time separating itself from ordinary experience. One should say, on the contrary, that this experience is enriched in the attempt to find – by means of a technique applied for the first time with such tenacity (even to the point of excess) – a major human complexity in the characters. Antonioni tries to observe his characters from every conceivable angle, without judging them, without proposing something in order to condemn it. The impossibility of overcoming the evil within us or of starting life over again as if the past had never existed must be suffered 'objectively' by the characters from conclusions that they themselves reach from within themselves. The film-maker only indirectly intervenes to help create those conclusions. This is no longer a chronicle, nor even *verismo* (at least not in the usual sense of that term). On the contrary it is a move towards a direction not yet touched upon by the experience of realism of the Italian cinema, which is no mean achievement.[2]

The post-war Italian cinema, to which the term neo-realism has been doggedly applied, was on inspection a very diverse cinema with multiple and opposed directions. It would be difficult, I think, to characterise a classic neo-realism, one that might contain *Roma, città aperta, Sciuscià, Riso amaro, Ossessione, Gente del Po, I vitelloni*, and, perhaps as well, *Cronaca di un amore*. Nevertheless, it might be instructive to take up Di Giammatteo's notice of Antonioni's narrative reticence and 'objectivity' as something strikingly new in the Italian cinema with reference to 'neo-realism'.

What distinguished Antonioni's 'objectivism' from that of other Italian film-makers in the late 1940s or early 50s, was not so much techniques of observation – long takes, relative lack of fragmentation of space and time, a reluctance to intrude, to judge, to comment, to set down an *a priori* knowledge of events and characters – so much as a different set of assumptions about the things observed and which accounts perhaps for that nomination of his style, and perhaps also his feelings, as cold, inexpressive, without love, the exact contrary of what, despite its apparent objectivism, neo-realism was thought of as possessing: warmth, love, the glow of humanity, a hope for the future. It is not a matter here of pessimism or optimism, still less of love or sentiments, but rather the fact that Antonioni took his reticence one step further than the classical directors of neo-realism. Though these directors recorded a world which they refused to judge or to set in a pre-ordained order, to establish an order for (which is a way of judging), they nevertheless believed that such an order existed and for that reason need not be artificially imposed.

Many critics, especially those still wedded to neo-realism, and regretting its passing or, worse, its 'betrayal', appreciated Antonioni's 'distanced narrative', his delicacy, his choice of the small things, his avoidance of the dramatic, his sense of place and atmosphere; but they were disturbed too that this atmosphere and landscape failed to function as explicative or causal: on the one hand the background was moved to the fore; on the other, it seemed just there, of equal weight with character, objectively described, but without the provision of any connections. The context – social, physical – wasn't in his films a determination, or if it was, the precise nature of that determination could not be known, no more than could the identity or the feelings of his characters. It was as if Antonioni had taken his objectivity too far; not only was he distanced from the narrative, and his characters separated and distanced from each other, but they were disconnected too from their context. It was an objectivity that had seemingly gone beyond 'realism'; in the distance of Antonioni's look, in his reticence, indeed, in his refusal to presume to know or to suggest an order, the very reality and identity of things were made insecure. It was a step which many who had been involved in neo-realism found it immensely difficult to take.[3]

The early experience of many Italian neo-realist directors, like Rossellini, in making documentaries involved, in part, a rejection of conventional fictional modes for ones that would be realistic in the sense of not imposing a sense and yet positive for all that because of the sense of things that would shine forth – the actual reality of the world. It is at this point and from the very beginning of his career as a critic, then as a documentarist, that Antonioni marked out his difference: not only did he not presume to know in his films and in his descriptions, but these descriptions of events and landscapes and people and characters refused to yield up any clear meaning. His reluctance

Lucia Bosè as Paola in
CRONACA DI UN AMORE

to know was founded on a perception about the instability, the tenuousness of knowing, what Barthes would describe as the fragility of knowledge, but equally a fragility that adhered to things, to objects, to lives and therefore to the sense of them.

Antonioni's narrative reticence is evident from the beginning, from *Cronaca di un amore*. And it involved not only what was described and the method of description, but also the activity of describing, of narrating, of the position of the narrator, all of which were put into question, rendered unstable, an uncertain place of uncertain knowledge.

Looked at on the level of theme or meaning, many critics, especially in Italy, enjoying the warm humanism of neo-realism, found Antonioni's work cold, depressing and, hopelessly, gloomily pessimistic. Some of this had to do with distance: an objectivity without sympathy; but mostly it related to the sense of disconnection. Even if the social environment weighed down figures in Visconti, De Sica, Rossellini, there was always hope, either for a change in that environment, or in pockets within it: faith, the family, love, affection. No matter how threatening, how awful things were, there were some eternal certainties or a political chance, love or solidarity, a retreat or a way forward. There is still Bruno and human will in *Ladri di biciclette*, the dog who saves the man in *Umberto D*, an optimistic tomorrow in *Paisà* and *Roma, città aperta*, struggles not in vain, not like in Antonioni where ends dissolve, and struggle ceases to have sense.

On the other hand, and Rossellini apart, the way forward charted by these films was often familiar and conventional. What may have seemed grim in Antonioni's themes, was positive, indeed exhilarating at the level of their realisation; his films opened up new narrative and fictional possibilities in the very activity of dissolving what was certain and clear, in rejecting what neo-realism had made positive. And this is most evident visually: by the very fact of destabilising forms and structures, Antonioni permitted new forms to appear, hence new fascinations and new objects to make themselves felt. Neo-realism, on the contrary, and despite the attentiveness it gave to technique and to film language, was conservative, intent on declaring established, unshakeable things, certainties and orders which by the mid-50s even its greatest apologists had to admit no longer held.

The new in Antonioni appears within what is sure and established as a present yet hidden surface making itself seen and felt within what Barthes would call the 'interstices', the line between alternative realities, something new contained in the ordinary and conventional, and which often threatens it, not to be replaced by another 'thing', but rather not to be replaced at all, as when a figure, or an object dissolve into patterns, a landscape, or fog or rain overwhelm a 'subject'. It is something akin to the progressive enlargement of a photograph as occurs in *Blow-Up*: an event becomes an image; the image loses its figure to become dots and tones; then these in turn coalesce into another image, finally into other 'events', but equally unstable, impossible to fix.

In 1986, first at Venice, then in Rome, Antonioni exhibited a series of images which were called *Le montagne incantate* ('The Magic Mountains'). The images were produced by a serial reworking of images: starting with a small water-colour or a collage, roughly in the shape of mountains, Antonioni photographed these and then enlarged the photographs, stopping the enlargement at a point at which, as in a fade-in, fade-out in the cinema, the one image began to disappear and another took shape as if within it, always there but unseen; the definite loses itself in the abstract, and what had not been there gradually becomes an object. In *Blow-Up*, neatly, what appears out of the abstract is the image of death, but then that death, when come upon, no longer exists.

In a different way that same transition between things, events, persons, the loss of one and the appearance in that same place of an other, but equally unstable, occurs in other films: strikingly in *L'avventura* with the disappearance of Anna and the taking of her place by Claudia in turn tainted by the anxiety of, once again, the dispersal of love, of a repeated betrayal, of a loss of feeling; in *Identificazione di una donna*, one woman for another and one woman for the image of a woman; most movingly and obsessively in *Il grido*, Aldo wandering from one woman to the next in search of what he loses until he returns home, full circle, and meets a vertiginous death.

Antonioni is not only fascinated with this process and its visual consequences, but he is especially interested in the precise moment of alteration, compulsively fascinating and yet impossible to fix or even apprehend as when Locke becomes Robertson in *The Passenger*, or more startling, when Locke, in the famous penultimate shot of the film is strange witness of his own death: even the boundaries of subject and object become blurred. That shot is literally a shot of absence, a movement of death.

What is always present in this process, and which distinguished Antonioni as early as *Cronaca di un amore* from other Italian film-makers of the period, is that, involved in this reality of change and variability, is the fact of its apprehension, not only is the world outside changing, but so too is the perception of it. I doubt that Antonioni is interested in a philosophy about uncertainty or lack of surety – points taken up so frequently by those who praise Antonioni and by those who do not – but rather he is interested in the shapes and sights and objects that such uncertainty makes possible. The philosophy may be familiar, certainly dated, but Antonioni's visual practice of it is not.[4]

At the opening of the sequence in Ferrara, in *Cronaca di un amore*, when the detective initiates his investigation of Paola, there is a relatively lengthy shot of the outside of the school where the detective goes to ask about Paola Molon's schooldays. I have no measure of the shot, but its length is well beyond that required by its function to establish place. Shots of this kind, of a dead time, or which are non-functional narratively, are frequent in Antonioni's films and already present in *Cronaca*: for example the shot of the waterside where the two lovers first meet held long after they have left the scene, when the shot lingers to no narrative purpose, or, similarly, the shot of trams crossing a deserted street.

This anticipation-of-an-action shot, or the lingering-after-an-action shot, is connected to another frequent figuration in Antonioni's films, also present in *Cronaca*, when the attention of the camera is caught by something either peripheral to the narrative or utterly unconnected with it, and the camera simply wanders off, focuses on a pattern, or a shadow, an extraneous event, becomes a camera-errant while the narrative is seemingly left to one side. The motives for these very similar yet different figures in Antonioni's films are never made clear but they are places, similar to those within the narrative of events, which mark out transitions, in this case between the narrative and its disappearance as on another register between Anna and her disappearance in *L'avventura*, or the wiping of the photographer from the screen in the last shot of *Blow-Up*. What is interesting about these figures in the films – and they become more frequent in later films – is that they are places in which the narrative is no longer, and which are often referred to appropriately as *temps*

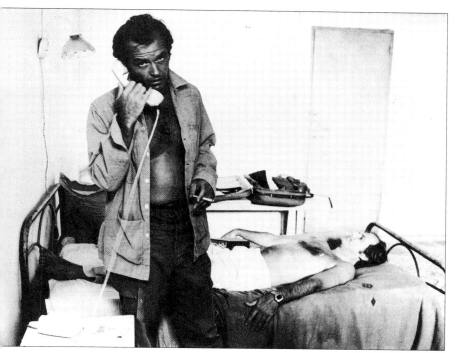

THE PASSENGER *(1975)* *Locke prepares to become Robertson*

morts, this place at which the narrative dies, at which the camera becomes distracted, is often a place in which another non-narrative interest develops: the light and tone of things, compositional frames created by doorways, beams, gates, gratings, the shifting of colour, a shimmering between figure and ground. These are places which are openly non-narrativised, of a pictorial and visual interest which suddenly takes hold, causes the narrative to err, to wander, momentarily to dissolve. They are among the most interesting places of Antonioni's films, at which everything and nothing takes place. The end of

L'eclisse is like this as is the close of *Zabriskie Point*, the house in the desert exploding again and again and producing in that destruction and dissolution, as within the emptiness of the close of *L'eclisse*, something new: new patterns, new forms. And it is there in *La notte* when Lidia drives off in the rain at the party, the camera losing interest in the drama inside the car and the meaning of that escape, for the drama of the form of the car, the rain on the windscreen, the distortions of spaces by light and water and shadow.

There is a lovely description by Michel Butor of a meeting he had with Antonioni at a time just after *La notte* was made, in 1961.[5] One passage of the desciption refers to the fact, often noticed in Antonioni's films and about which Antonioni himself has spoken, of Antonioni's frequent need to continue to shoot an actor or actress after a scene has been played.

> He told us that while shooting, he continues to record the actors on film some few moments after the scene which he set up has been completed; they are in part at least aware of this. Clearly it bothers them since they know about it, but it allows them to be seen in a different way than usual and to rejoin a more anonymous and spontaneous humanity in relation to what they had just done.
>
> Not that Jeanne Moreau was not shot as Jeanne Moreau, but rather, she was taken in a suspended moment where she was no longer Mrs Pontano, but not yet either her own self. Often he preserves these margins, these 'ends' as he would say, because the entire sequence then takes on another sense as a new dimension makes its appearance in the disturbance of the natural.
>
> This seems to me to go beyond what is generally understood as the technique of the cinema, and demonstrates that the thematic of Antonioni's films is illuminated by a sharp original reflection on the very conditions of his own work.

The other remark by Butor which I want to recall also refers to these indefinite moments, in which identity is unclear or at risk, in which things are not one thing nor another, but this time not as between the fiction and some other place, but interior to the fiction and to a character:

> The rare finesse of his psychology, his art of seizing the feelings of his characters in their most sudden reversals, the moments of joy which must become sadnesses, the sadness at the moment after a joyfulness, the sparks of hatred in the eyes of lovers, the coming of despair quickly stifled in the gestures of someone who wants to be thought of as satisfied, the gap, sometimes enormous, between apparent sincere words and actual behaviour . . .

Relative to other, later films by Antonioni, *Cronaca di un amore* is rather eventful, even if some of the most dramatic events are never seen, but are told, mediated in a description; on the other hand, relative to the action and the dramas of the cinema which surrounded Antonioni – Italian, neo-realist, but also that of Hollywood – very little happens in *Cronaca di un amore*: it is, comparatively, almost eventless.

A few years before the Butor interview, Antonioni reflected back on *Cronaca di un amore* – particularly, what hasn't been discussed here, the great length of the shots, the infrequency of cuts, the long duration of sequences. He said the technique came to him instinctively, in the course of shooting, but the motive was in part the one he later expressed to Butor: 'And there was the need to feel the characters beyond the moments that are conventionally important for the spectator, to show them once more, when everything seems already to have been said.'[6]

Much of the drama of Antonioni's films occur here in the dead times, outside of the narrative, when everything is done, when there is silence, or emptiness as if in these spaces not only does the film occur, there precisely where 'things' are eclipsed, but a whole new cinema begins to take shape.

It seems that it is more the image of his wife Paola rather than Paola herself which stimulates and fascinates the industrialist Fontana to the point of wanting to find out the truth, the reality, behind this image – almost as if the reality, in the actual body and presence of his wife is less real than an obscure image of her. Now, rather than the image becoming clarified, even as truths are told and events are provoked, it becomes less clear, the real Paola fades further into obscurity. This happens, among other things, for two reasons: it is not actions we are given but reports of them, that is, just as Fontana begins with what is indirect and a representation, so too the audience (and the characters) find themselves with only images, reports, memories, letters, phone calls, messages, testimonies that refer to events and to character as if it is less things that are important than feelings about them, yet the expression of these feelings remains ambiguous, uncertain; the other reason for that uncertainty is that most actions and some of the characters are doubled.

The death of Fontana – wished for by the lovers to the point of planning his murder – occurs without their intervention and is the symmetrical copy of the wished-for death of Guido's fiancée who plunged to her death down a lift shaft. The result of that death, like the death of Fontana, is that the two lovers, now freed to come together, their wishes come true, inexplicably separate. Fontana's capricious whim to find out about his wife which is provoked in part by a jealousy (a past not known, not possessed by him) is doubled by the jealousy of Paola at seeing Guido dance with the model at the night club and which similarly provokes her whim not only to bid for the dress, but to refuse to play the game of deceit and plot against her husband. The past returns, reinstates itself in the present and causes its own duplication and in a much more complicated fashion than I have indicated: for example, not only can Paola be compared with the dead fiancée of Guido's, but Guido can be compared with her dead husband, with the corpse of Fontana which he stares at in a gaze repeated in other films of the protagonist looking down at a corpse which he or she either resembles or which for an instant they take the place of in their imagination: the corpse in *Blow-Up*, the corpse with whom one changes identity in *The Passenger*, and the similar taking the place of a dead man to die again in *Zabriskie Point*, and, I think it can be argued, in *Il grido*, when Aldo comes full circle, returning to himself, to his past, and to a present emptiness; it also occurs in *L'eclisse* when the drunk is fished out of the river in Piero's car, and in *Le amiche* in the attempted and then final suicide which involves the projections of Clelia.

The double and doubling not only confounds origin with copy, real with image, and multiplies the real along a series of duplicates thus decertifying and skewing any attempt at a final surety and truth; but so often the double is that of death or nothingness, and thus like most images, but particularly photographic images, the trace of something no longer there.

One of the most notable scenes in *Cronaca di un amore* is accurately described by Noel Burch:

> In a later scene during which the lovers take refuge on a staircase, we follow their ascent in a series of long crane shots, and, just as we hear the loud off-screen sound of an elevator door slamming shut, the lovers break off their argument (they are already talking about murdering the husband) and lean over the railing, sharing the same painful memory of Guido's fiancée falling to her death down the elevator shaft. The next shot shows the elevator approaching the camera from a very pronounced downward angle. The shot is invariably experienced by the viewer as a 'subjective' shot, as something the lovers see. Nevertheless, when a tilt, begun as the elevator started upward, brings the camera back to a horizontal position, we realise that it is actually on the other side of the elevator shaft, and that the lovers still looking over the railing are actually facing us and quite a distance away. In both cases, a 'retroactive' match . . . is involved. . . .
>
> We are visually reminded of the lovers' thoughts and words for the few seconds during which the shot appears to be subjective (even though subjective shots are extremely rare in this film). The moment we realise our 'mistake', we are once again 'outside' the characters' minds, and image and word move apart again.[7]

CRONACA DI UN AMORE
The staircase

Not only is the uncertainty of our perceptions involved in this scene and the errors in identifying, in putting ourselves in the place of another which evaporates as no place at all (the 'subjective' gaze of the characters), but it also involves the redoubling of sights, of memories and of wishes, of the compounding of subjects (narrator, spectator, character 'look'), which on the one hand centre on the line between positions, the shifting, variable place at which things are neither clearly one thing nor the other, not past, nor present, not subjective, nor objective, not a fact, nor clearly a desire; and though the scene resolves some of this, as Burch says, 'retroactively', the fascination remains in the in between-ness, and the knowledge that even if a place has been at last arrived at, it will only be temporary, will itself be threatened with erasure, with doubling, with doubt.

The other fascination and compulsion of the scene is the link, obsessive in Antonioni, between desire and death, freedom and obliteration which is perhaps why the desire for both; and the positivity of that desire, suicide, is so familiar a figure in Antonioni's films, from his documentary *Tentato suicidio* to the extraordinary flight to nowhere in the nothingness of fog, towards the possibility of extinction in *Identificazione di una donna*, and even more notably perhaps when Giuliana stops just short of death in the fog in *Il deserto rosso*.

Notes

1. Fernaldo Di Giammatteo, 'Cronaca di un amore', *Bianco e Nero*, April 1951, pp. 73–77.

2. The term *verismo* refers to a literary movement of the late nineteenth and early twentieth century, in which 'truth to nature', even in its most crude and shocking aspects, was an ideal; Zola in France and Verga in Italy were regarded as veristic writers; that ideal was revived by the writers of *Cinema* as worthy of a new Italian cinema which would present the actual reality of Italy on the screen as opposed to the falsity of images presented either by Hollywood or by what was regarded as an imitative-of-Hollywood 'escapist' film industry in fascist Italy. Escapism was identified as having a political, or more precisely, depoliticising function; *verismo*, to the contrary, by exposing reality, without prettifying it, would have a politicising and anti-fascist function, in particular since these writers for *Cinema* felt that the 'reality' of Italy presented on current Italian screens was quite different from the 'real' reality.
    Ossessione, in the terms proposed by the *Cinema* writers, was a perfect veristic film. Certainly the notions of actuality and reality that helped form ideas for this kind of realistic, anti-fascist cinema were very important for the ideology and the practices of Italian neo-realism.

3. See in particular Guido Aristarco, 'Film di questi giorni: *Cronaca di un amore*', *Cinema*, 15 November 1950; and Edoardo Bruno, 'I film . . .', *Filmcritica*, vol. 1 no. 2, January 1951.

4. See Pascal Bonitzer, 'Désir désert' *Cahiers du Cinéma* nos. 262–263, January 1976, and his 'Il concetto di scomparsa' in *Michelangelo Antonioni: identificazione di un autore* (Parma: Pratiche editrice, 1985), pp. 148ff.
    Though the discussion concerns televisual images, painting and Godard, I found some of the ideas in Bonitzer's 'Les images, le cinéma, l'audiovisuel' (*Cahiers du Cinéma* no. 404, February 1988) relevant to Antonioni and especially to Antonioni's *Il mistero di Oberwald*. The relevance lies in Antonioni's concern to present 'strong', certainly askew, unconventional, and at times 'violent' images, violent less for their subject than their form; in *Oberwald* he uses, but then utterly transforms, the television image, to make that image and its formation 'noticeable', hence strong. This need for strong images is noted by Bonitzer and one of its consequences is for some film-makers, like Godard, to seek that strength not in the more familiar and customary images of film, and especially of television, but rather in the less familiar area of painting, of an 'elite', bourgeois tradition; quite often the references are to classical painting. Antonioni is much less direct in this regard than Godard, or say Pasolini, but certainly there is an indirect presence of painting in his films; their 'force' can be felt: Piero della Francesca, Jackson Pollock, Giorgio De Chirico, Giorgio Morandi, Henri Matisse, Georges Braque, and even beyond these particular figures to a tradition of Japanese art which Barthes recognised in his letter to Antonioni.

5. Michel Butor, 'Rencontre avec Antonioni', *Les Lettres Françaises*, no. 880, 15 June 1961.

6. The statement comes from an interview in *Positifsitif* no. 30, 1959; it is requoted in Carlo Di Carlo, 'Vedere in modo nuovo' in Carlo Di Carlo (ed.), *Il primo Antonioni* (Bologna: Cappelli, 1973), p. 17.

7. Noel Burch, *Theory of Film Practice*, (New York: Praeger 1973), pp. 78–79.

Chapter Four

In autumn 1941 Antonioni wrote a short history for *Cinema* of the Venice film festival which began with the festival's own informal beginnings in 1932.[1] Antonioni contrived a history lesson on the deleterious effects on art by politics, not simply that the arts required peace, but that they required autonomy from ideologies and politics:

> The fate of Europe started to grow dark in 1914; from then, in fits and starts, things have worsened, and the disaster of today hardly surprises anyone, least of all the historians. Italy has made a revolution; it has made a war – in Africa – then another war – in Spain – and now it has undertaken a third, all in the space of twenty years. What has been the consequence of this for the cinema? And not only of European cinema but world cinema since world war is the official name for this new war? It is not difficult to imagine. In periods of struggle, stagnation; in periods of peace, great activity. In fact the golden age of the cinema runs from 1925 to 1933, that is directly at the halfway mark of the longest period of truce, while the waters of the world were only stirred by the slightest ripple, the most subtle movement, as when a stone is thrown in the water and the outer circles grow larger and disappear. They were waters which gave only an appearance of tranquillity; only now can one say what currents surged beneath it. There was, however, time to think calmly about the cinema and all could occupy themselves with it: the best men were of that period, and the best works were of that period. Various tendencies, currents, schools emerged: the French avant-garde, German expressionism and so forth; men of culture, reassured, no longer diffident, began to take an interest in the new expressive language of the cinema to which they had no other choice but to concede aesthetic legitimacy . . .

Antonioni refused to place himself or film or culture in the service of any political ends; commitment to a morality was not to be confused, for him, with a commitment to an ideology. What governed this 'politics' of art was not a clear philosophic position (Crocean, idealist), certainly not a political-social one, but rather the need to protect certain artistic practices from much of current practice and theory, both 'fascist' and 'anti-fascist', which demanded that art serve political purposes.

Antonioni's writings in the early 1940s, and immediately after 1945, were marked, particularly in his discussion of neo-realist films, by his distance from the political and social messages these contained, and especially from the then dominant notion of a 'national-popular' culture which emerged from the direct experience of the war, of the Resistance, and of the ideas of the left anti-fascist struggle, put forward in *Cinema*, in the films from the *Cinema* group, by De Santis, Lizzani, Visconti, and then in later films and by later defenders of neo-realism.[2]

In 1945 there was a European music, theatre, cinema festival in Rome. It was the first post-war celebration and exhibition of European works in Italy. Among the films shown were Rossellini's *Roma, città aperta* and Carné–Prévert's *Les Enfants du paradis*. Antonioni's reception of the Rossellini, though favourable, was decidedly cool, much cooler in fact than his reception of *Les Enfants du paradis*, or even Olivier's *Henry V*, whose defects for Antonioni were far outweighed by its experiments with colour and its open admission, indeed celebration, of its own artifice, and by its refusal to be 'realistic'.[3] Antonioni's response to the Rossellini was not so much to any particular details (the kind of details, for example, he noticed in Visconti's *La terra trema*) and it was not at all to the social or political sense of the film, but rather to what he called its morality: honesty, sincerity, objectivity, sobriety as against the prevailing dishonesty and 'boulevard' falseness of most of the immediate 'commercial' post-war Italian cinema: not a word about the Resistance, about heroism, about the nobility of the people, about love, and hardly a word about aesthetics or language. And these few words were measured, relatively unenthusiastic. He was more interested in John Ford's *Stagecoach*.[4]

Lorenzo Cuccu in his book on Antonioni remarked that while Antonioni remained quite outside the political and social commitments of neo-realism, he was attentive to its new film language, to the relations it posed between film and reality for which the work of Rossellini was exemplary and which Cuccu described in terms of 'a look intent to gather the sense of reality, to select and to filter its most significant traits, happily freed of cultural and ideological filters, ready to abandon himself totally to the imperious presence of things.'[5] If this was true of Rossellini's film or of neo-realism generally, it was not a truth either proclaimed or self-evident to Antonioni and possibly, principally, for two reasons: if the external world was a matter of wondrousness for Rossellini, and seizing it a discovery and act of devotion, neither that seizure nor the object possessed presented any further problem for him: if the look was honest, objective, the truth of things, even to the point of their miraculousness, would shine forth. If such a view appeared in its objectivity to renounce what Cuccu called 'cultural and ideological filters', it failed to see that the notion of objectivity it held depended on the fact that the reality of the world already had been filtered; the belief was that the world could be apprehended, and that its meanings were not obscure or in need of artificial dressings. It was the evident sense of the world, its simple clarity that would be yielded up in all its positivity and certainty by the rejection of dramatic models, spectacular plots, emphatic, expressionist acting, melodramatic forms, by the falsities, the dishonesties, the rhetoric that had heretofore obscured and mystified it.

(There was a further reason, perhaps, for Antonioni's specifically luke-warm judgement on *Roma, città aperta*, this most famous of Italian neo-realist films. What was startling about the film at the time was more its subject than its language, more its morality than its narrative structures. Of all of Rossellini's films since then, *Roma, città aperta* is his most melodramatic and conventional. The films after it are more interesting, more experimental, more objective in their gaze, more narratively distant, and, at the same time, more immediate, not for the subject chosen – increasingly, for Rossellini, set further and further back into the past – but for the sense of events being caught as they occurred, for the camera searching for a sense rather than bestowing it, for the felt presence of a narrator and the look of the camera directly implicated in what was being formed, and in the case of the Ingrid Bergman films, the objectivity, almost documentarism, in charting the subjective vision of the Bergman character, showing her pain, but at a distance, the more to make it felt. *Roma, città aperta*, of all of Rossellini, shares most in the ideology of neo-realism defined by subject and morality, but least in the formal, linguistic innovations of neo-realism.)

By the assertion of an objectivity, neo-realism gave back to a post-war world of uncertainty, insecurity and disintegration both hope (things could be known) and truth (the fact of that knowledge itself) which was, for some, immensely reassuring. It was an ideology not of revolution but of reconstruction, a Marshall Plan of the mind.

Antonioni's diffidence towards neo-realism, despite his remark of having practised it unknowingly in 1942 on the banks of the Po, came in part from a different attitude towards commitment and knowledge, but an attitude never-theless shaped, equally to that of Rossellini's, by fascism, the war, and the Resistance, for which perhaps the rubric of Crocean idealism or the idea of a separation between art and politics does not go quite far enough.

Antonioni and Rossellini are in fact worlds apart in their sensibilities; Rossellini belonged to the perspectives of a much older world. He viewed the uncertainties, the malaise of the present not as an opportunity, so much as a misfortune in need of correction . . . and correctable; he spoke of faith, of salvation, of reason. His films moved towards demonstration, didacticism, the unravelling of truths, a faith in rationalism.

Antonioni is too uncertain to be a teacher, and too excited with the possibilities offered by misperceptions, by fragility, by the dissolution of things, to be able to assert otherwise; he too was touched by an interest in objectivity,

I VINTI *(1952) Franco Interlenghi*
in the Italian episode

in the documentation of feelings, but less as a tool or a method than as a stake
in the game.

In Antonioni's 'history' of the Venice film festival, the image in the opening
paragraph of a surface of water rippling outwards to a new calm after a stone
had been thrown while beneath the surface, unknown to anyone, strong
currents were gathering which would utterly destroy all calm, was something
more than a cliché about the inter-war years; it was not only a lesson Antonioni
was reading out, but one that he would over and over again resume: that
things were insecure; that knowledge was, more often than not, partial, false;
that hopes were misplaced; that what was not seen was threatening to overturn
and overrun things held dear and secure. When Pina and Francesco sit on the
stairwell at Via Tasso in *Roma, città aperta*, he comforting her with hopes for
a future through a reflection on a past, despite appearances to the contrary,
and despite even, as things turn out, the killing of Pina which fails to dissuade
either Francesco, or more importantly, Pina's little boy, Marcello, from the
popular struggle against the Nazis, such comfort for Antonioni, in his review,
simply didn't ring true.

 The lesson of the war for him was a lesson about insecurity, disintegration
and the falsity of sureties and of hopes in which the ultimate false surety was
that of politics itself – fascist, or not. This did not imply that one political
position was no better than another, all political faiths be damned, but rather

that it was not the part of an art to compound such surety and certainly not to function as propaganda. At that moment, just after the war, this surety was caught up not simply as theme to neo-realist films, but as a way of looking, and that way was quite different to the way Antonioni then saw things and later would represent them; and, perhaps more to the point, he would examine not simply things, but the regard of them, and find the subject of regard itself – tenuous, hard to grasp, fleeting – at the very centre of his concerns.

Antonioni's second feature, *I vinti*, was made in 1952. The film was in three independent episodes chronicling, as typical of the time, crimes by young people, killings in Italy, in France, in England. What gave these incidents their typicality, hence their social sense, was their senselessness, their apparent lack of motivation, the impossibility of understanding them; Antonioni provides a description only, without that feature usual in films of social and moral import, an explanation. What happens is absurd, illogical, empty of reason: friends go on a picnic to the countryside outside of Paris and one of them is murdered by the others; a young man in England murders an unknown prostitute chosen at random for the satisfaction of it and the satisfaction of a perfect, because motiveless, murder; the murder in the Italian incident is more sensible, has a reason within the plot (though not in the character), but the episode was altered under censorship pressure and is hard to judge; what stands out in this, as in all the episodes, is not only the reticence and distance of the narration, but the presence of the backgrounds and the landscapes as central to the actions, somehow working their way into the souls and psyche of the characters, but in no way that is direct or obvious. The landscapes too are objectively chronicled, but not analysed, nor posited as a cause, a reason, a definite determination which would then allow judgements, responsibilities, actions. If in some social sense these crimes are 'typical', the chronicle of them is specific, and so intensely so that nothing general can be derived from them.

The film has, in its separate incidents, the investigative, detective story pretext of most other Antonioni films and as in these, but more pointed since the absurdity of the crime is so marked, the investigation goes nowhere; what is left is the description of behaviour, the observation of action, the sense of an atmosphere and place, but not the satisfaction of a reason, still less the comfort of a hope.

The film was not well received in Italy, though in France Bazin remarked on the 'compelling beauty' of the French episode, and compared the English one to some of the best sequences of Rossellini – at the time, great praise indeed.[6] Once again, the Italian critics were dissatisfied with what was in fact most valuable about the film: its visual beauty, its narrative reserve. The one was rejected for being merely beautiful, the other for leaving nothing positive, no clear understanding, hence no social sense.

Antonioni complained about the almost complete absence of aesthetic criticism of the film and the contrary insistence on content; he asserted his full right to 'beautiful writing' and its importance for the force of things against a demand, at base moralistic, for the drama of character, or the drama of events, not 'empty' decoration. And, he countered: '. . . one gets to the paradox that I should make beautiful films with ugly images.' His comments on the narration are interesting:

> I am against programmatic injunctions; film isn't an essay and *I vinti* shouldn't be thought that. I wanted to confine myself to the narration of three episodes that seemed to me symptomatic of a particularly painful state of affairs and from which one could possibly draw a moral, but *a posteriori*, not *a priori*. For me the important thing was to narrate the facts, to narrate *tout court* . . . a film has to be judged in these terms; not so much on an ethical plane or a moral one, but on an aesthetic one. Besides, it is well known that you oughtn't to give much weight to the program-matic premises of an author; the work has it own autonomy outside of these, and often opposed to them.[7]

Antonioni wanted to talk of the structures of *I vinti*, his experiments with an objective style, the relation between the camera and external reality, his resistance to editing conventions, to the binding of the viewer into the exchanges of shot/reverse-shot, his need to overcome existing practices and to find new ways of narrating and seeing; his critics, and particularly those still loyal to neo-realism, asked him about matters of content, not realising fully the innovation of narrating a crime without an apparent motive or plausible explanation and the difficulties this set for narration, for psychology, for establishing relations between characters and with an environment, and the consequences of this subject difference for the narrational techniques of the traditional cinema within which entirely different sets of assumptions were assumed about reality and its representation.

I vinti was very far from the film it ought to have been because of changes imposed on the French and Italian incidents by the censors; nevertheless, it remains a major experiment in narration, for Antonioni, and for the cinema, not least in the choice of a subject which tempts social explanation and yet refuses it, renders it fatuous.

Antonioni told an Irish story with regard to *I vinti* and to Italian neo-realism:

> For a good part of the critics I am cold, an intellectual. Why cold? Why intellectual? Because I have tried to find a new way of approaching reality, different from . . . how should I say it? . . . the pietism of Italian realism? When Zavattini says 'let us say everything about man', of course I agree

with him. It all depends on what you mean by man. Do you know the reply of the Irishman who was asked: 'Isn't one man as good as another?' 'Absolutely,' he responded, 'and even more so.' I feel I have something of the irony of the Irishman . . . [8]

La signora senza camelie was made in 1953. It is the story of Clara Manni, Milan shop girl, given a small part in a film, and then, because she is so noticeable in it, so lovely on screen, she is set up for quick stardom as a sex symbol. Without really her consent, possibly against her will, as she was pushed into films, the producer Gianni, an anxious, weak, desperate little man, pushes her into marriage with him, and then just as swiftly out of the cinema of commerce, where her person is her sex and her body, towards the cinema of quality where, presumably, it would be her skills and his respectability that would be at stake . . . in the service of art: *Joan of Arc.*

It doesn't work out. Clara doesn't have the talent. But she, in the midst of a failing marriage and a wrongly set career, is caught within another fantasy, that of the diplomat Nardo who fancies an adventure with an actress, while for Clara he becomes a Prince to save her from everything: at last truth and true love. The real truth turns this fantasy sour while Clara trades it for still another: to really be a serious actress. She rejects Nardo to become what Gianni had tried unsuccessfully to make her. In the end she settles for being a fake desert Princess in abbreviated clothes in a cheap spectacle . . . and she telephones Nardo. In the last shot of her, in close-up, she is being photographed for the press with her new producer to mark their new, nasty cheap film: she is in tears.

Before the narrative of *La signora senza camelie* begins Clara Manni had, in the story, already been snatched from being a shop girl to being made a film actress by the too-much-in-a-hurry film producer, Gianni. When the film opens Clara, wandering outside a Rome cinema at night, finally goes in to watch the close of a film in which she is there on the screen, singing at a night club, entrancing three audiences at once: at the club, at the cinema, and at the 'real' cinema outside of all these other places and from which we look. Comments follow about her and about her performance; the remarks are directed at her or are about her, or are about her and directed at her at the same time; immediately, there is a breach in the subject: is it to Clara Manni that these remarks adhere, or to the image of her, or even to the image of that image? And when Gianni, the producer, there in the rain-wet Rome street, seeks a kiss from her, it is evident that there has been a loss, an unease, a disquiet, created about identity and about person. Thus, from the beginning, when the subject is introduced, it is introduced as uncertain, a shadow between images and projections.

About half-way through the film Gianni makes a movie for Clara, a movie just for her, not the commercial pulp in which she first had a role and made her 'name' (*La donna del destino/The Woman of Destiny*), but a *film d'art*, tasteful, bourgeois. Clara Manni, the ex-shopgirl, ex-torch singer, ex-sex-symbol becomes Clara Manni/Joan of Arc in Gianni's *Giovanna d'Arco*. The film is presented at Venice. Clara Manni is there in the audience as at the opening of *La signora senza camelie* looking at her changed image, measuring her changed self.

The film is a disaster. Clara doesn't have the skill or the stature for the role. She flees from the screening, in tears, to a bus motor-launch to return to her hotel. She is followed out of the theatre and accompanied on the launch by Nardo. Weak, discomfited, she is soothed by all of Nardo's diplomatic and amorous skills: he too has been taken by her image, not the failed one on the screen which she can't now bear, but another one, that simply of the actress, her beauty, her glamour, the adventure; she takes his attention as true love, found at last, in this world of falsity, of deceptive, unflattering reflections. The launch takes them to her stop. The camera positions itself at a distance from an archway of a small Venetian alleyway-street. The camera is there before Nardo and Clara. When they appear and pause under the archway, they are in semi-light making it seem as if it is not they who are there but their shadows, more silhouette than substance. Gradually, the couple move into the light and take shape, then they walk further on, leaving the camera where it had been, but they leave the sense of their absence; visually they seem still to be there in the glow of an after-image.

The scene, if not important to the narrative, is narratively motivated: Nardo in pursuit of his prey; Clara running from an embarrassment, fleeing from herself, fleeing from an image of her which seems not to be her, projected by another, her producer-husband, into the arms of yet another, Nardo, with another image of Clara. A new romance in Venice and yet a romance which has the trappings of the artifice of a film romance, as if Clara, even here outside the cinema, is playing a role, and Nardo along with her, a Prince Charming, but also a Seducer, betraying Clara by means of her own hopes and self-delusions. In this confusion of real and image, subjective desire and the objects it creates, there is a definite narrative sense to the phantasms which appear in the scene under the archway: the phantom impress of Nardo and Clara beneath the archway after they have left it and their shadowy appearance there before they are fully present. And, at a banal level of narrative events, quite independent of any thematic concern with identity, there is, very simply, the motive of a continuous action: Nardo and Clara move from launch, through streets, to hotel, he pursuing her and they forming, imperceptibly, a new couple.

In fact, the narrative of events is not quite continuous: there is the brief moment before their arrival under the archway in which nothing at all happens, as if the camera is there waiting for the action to begin, and then the camera remaining on a narrative emptiness after the couple have departed. This line, very slight, only a tremor, between the fullness of narrative and its absence, is twice doubled in the scene; even when the couple appear they are only shadows waiting to appear again in full light and after they are gone they have not fully disappeared: the narrative is at once present in the feel of their absence and absent by the 'fact' that they have left the scene. It is twice doubled because another relation comes into play: that between the appearance of a character and the appearance of an image.

One of the functions of 'classic' montage is to create a continuity in which time literally disappears; time is caught up in continuity. In this little scene, a scene repeated elsewhere in the film, and repeated in other Antonioni films, time is made to endure by being rescued from continuity in that breath of time between events, or, more precisely, between appearances. And in this 'space' of time, a space in which time both endures and is threatened with dissolution, in which space exists independently of a narrative fullness and which in turn is threatened with dissolution by the return of the narrative, an image of nothing, or at least an image in which nothing 'happens', makes its appearance.

This play is fascinating: it establishes the presence and the regard of an image as independent of narrative and indeed threatened, as is time, by the resumption of narrative. And yet, all this is narratively defined: it is not a pictorialism independent of narrative procedures but rather a notion of image formation, or, more precisely, a practice of image formation in which problems of narrative, of regard, of perspective are crucially involved.

Giorgio Morandi and Jackson Pollock are among Antonioni's favourite painters; there are others: Matisse, Braque, De Chirico. In the scene from *La signora senza camelie* objects and figures take and lose shape, become other while still remaining same, are themselves and not themselves simultaneously, a place between. It has something of the movement of Pollock: line becoming colour, figure becoming ground, shapes appearing and disappearing; and there is the feel, perhaps more obviously, of Morandi: objects losing themselves in a background, in a tone, and backgrounds coming forward into shapes. These are terms for movement which the cinema has tended to repress in favour of the movement of a story. While figures and the narrative in Antonioni's films may lend themselves to be placed in a scene, in a drama, they come to have a life of their own, as images, and to become a source of fascination without the need for a narrative anchor. At the same time, and it is the reason for the fascination, the narrative and the figures are never completely lost, are poised to return and resume shape.

These are delicate, fragile moments when significance is drained, explanation silenced, time and space for an instant rescued from the anxiety of a continuity, as if the entire film has paused, intent on an emptiness against the expectation of the fullness of narrative.

The archway in the Venice *calle* in *La signora senza camelie* is a repeated figuration in Antonioni's films, not only archways, but doorways, entrances, exits, thresholds, often windows. These function to mark boundaries between spaces. Sometimes it is a boundary between an exterior space and an interior one (for example, the very complicated spatial play outside Sandro's apartment in Rome in *L'avventura* of the shifting perspectives between Claudia on the outside and Anna on the inside, and then the reversal of those places and – an autonomous outside gaze by the camera – finding an interest in the rush of the Tiber independently of anything taking place in the narrative and from a perspective which simultaneously overlaps a view from the gallery where Claudia is and the bedroom where Anna is, but is neither of their views. Sometimes it is spatial boundaries within interiors that are marked: the fascinating play of horizontals and interior screens in Thomas's London studio in *Blow-Up*, and sometimes it is the spaces within exteriors that are cut into, isolated: the horizontal and vertical frames provided by the horizon, the water, the cliffs of Lisca Bianca where Anna 'disappears' in *L'avventura*.

These thresholds and dividers between spaces function in the films, as in the small scene in *La signora senza camelie*, within and outside a narrative sense; however 'telling' may be, for example, at Sandro's palazzo, the transfers of perspective and identities between Anna and Claudia in *L'avventura* and which later involve first a transfer of clothes and then of persons (one character disappears and the other takes her place), the scene has a visual interest which compels and fascinates before it 'means' or narratively 'functions'. One of the functions of the reintroduction by Antonioni of space not caught up in events and of time rescued from their continuity is to provide a time and space to look, and hence, since looks constitute things, to establish in that space-time between events a place for the image to make its appearance, or perhaps more exactly, to exist at all. In the 'classical' narrative film the image is seldom disjoined from the drama of events or the action of characters; it has no independence from these, or if it does it is as the merely decorative, at the periphery of narrative. Antonioni has shifted this periphery to the centre of things, has made the image a 'subject' in its own right: its shape, its colour, its movement, its time and the time of regarding it.

A feature of Giorgio De Chirico's 'surrealist' works of the 1920s was the placement of figures in unnatural, unreal perspectives, but formed with a clarity of line which might be termed 'classical'; another quality of these De Chirico paintings is the beauty and sharpness of their light, which, like his lines and perspectives, were unnatural and classical at the same time; objects and figures appeared differently in De Chirico for the distortions effected by his 'unnatural', almost theatrical, lighting and perspective. There are two direct De Chirico 'scenes' I can recall in Antonioni's films: Clara's meeting with Nardo behind the sets in a *papier-mâché* Hollywood–De Chirico 'street' in *La signora senza camelie* and the deserted 'metaphysical' town landscapes in Sicily, towns built by the fascists, which Sandro and Claudia encounter on their disquieting romantic drive towards Noto in search of Anna whom they don't wish to find; and there are reminders of De Chirico landscapes in Lidia's walk through Milan

L'AVVENTURA
'Metaphysical' landscape

in *La notte* and Clelia's walk through her past in Turin in *Le amiche*: unpeopled urban landscapes, objects isolated, in odd perspective, without sense because without context . . . simply there.

There is a striking narrative correspondence in *Blow-Up* (1966) to this displacement of figures and bodies in space: Thomas, the photographer, is forever seizing upon objects he simply 'must have' – the airplane propeller, the broken scrap of a Yardbird electric guitar, a photographic 'shot', a girl, a painting, a dish of food – and then, when he is elsewhere, and they are elsewhere, with that double shift in perspective, he loses interest, throws them away.

In Thomas's studio, in *Blow-Up*, Jane becomes for Thomas, and for the camera, independently of Thomas, an object to be framed among the beams, the disconnected spaces, and the coloured screens; she is there to retrieve, in desperation, the photographs Thomas took of her and her companion in the park, (wilfully because it took his interest) only to become not only not herself (Thomas seeks to remould her, reshape her very rhythms), but a thing for Thomas to photograph again: once again an object to 'take', to compose with.

LA SIGNORA SENZA CAMELIE *(1953)*
'fake desert Princess . . .'

The camera is taken by a similar fascination: framing bodies, placing them in one position and then in another, trying them out from different angles, against different backgrounds. All other purposes, all other ends become lost for this one. These objects and arrangements seem to have a life all their own. The narrative of *Blow-Up* literally loses its way in the pursuit of an image. And though it may be that that loss thematically makes sense, even, if you will, is over-determined by these little stories in which *the* story becomes lost, the independent interest of what displaces it remains and, in that sense, confirms such loss, and celebrates it.

The frames of windows, doorways, beams, uprights, cliffs, horizon lines are means to place objects and bodies in space: in the midst of the break-up of an affair at the beginning of *L'eclisse*, Vittoria becomes fascinated, as does the camera which takes (and leaves) her perspective, with the placement of figures within frames, seen from different angles, within different relations, and hence, by that fact, become different (there is a narrative echo to this in the film: Vittoria seeing herself out of a relation, in a different relation to herself and to Riccardo). It is not that here (or anywhere else in Antonioni) a point is being made about the relativity of things in philosophic or ethical terms, but rather that this relativity offers the possibility of new relations and new identities, narrative ones and visual ones: in *L'avventura* the displacement of Anna and her replacement by Claudia, the refilling of an empty space and the return of story to the fullness of narrative.

In 1953, at the time of its appearance, *La signora senza camelie* was harshly judged by critics who had supported neo-realism for its populism, social representations and political commitment, but had overlooked its experimentalism or had reduced it to fit with older conventions and established assumptions. If, by 1953, it could be argued that neo-realism, however defined, was no longer practised by Italian film-makers, it was still being recommended and used as a measure by Italian critics. Guido Aristarco had been disappointed in *Cronaca di un amore* and even more so with *La signora senza camelie*; what was genuinely new and valuable in Antonioni's work was taken as a shortcoming in so far as it fell short of a hypothetical and seemingly betrayed neo-realism.

> In order genuinely to go forward along the path mapped out by Italian neo-realism and in search of a style, he [Antonioni] must be made aware of the defects of his first film, in order to distance himself from the risk of 'making us admire it, but failing to move us'; giving primary place to technique, forgetting the reasons for which it was sought. If not, his path will fatally become a blind alley. . . .
>
> Antonioni . . . is typical of his generation . . . dissatisfied with the old formulas, he doesn't know how to overcome them; his 'chronicler' credo, his wanting to speak at a distance, his 'objectivity' is nothing other than an incapacity to analyse historically, or else a rather vague fear to say how things are and to assume the responsibility for a precise and exhaustive judgement. . . .
>
> It is precisely the world that the director wants to penetrate that is

absent from the film. Not in a physical sense, but because there are no genuinely typical characters. . . .

Things . . . are schematic, marginal . . . approximate and sometimes even ambiguous.[9]

And from another critic of *La signora senza camelie* equally longing for a neo-realism which he felt had been led astray:

The tired and fragmentary development of the film; its continual wanderings towards gratuitous, secondary, irrelevant motifs; its utter lack of human warmth and its contradictory, episodic structure, preventing characters from assuming a concrete humanity or events taking on their full, painful dramatic significances.[10]

This critical reaction in Italy to Antonioni was in sharp contrast to the appreciation of him in France in part for the different reception and understanding French critics had given to Italian neo-realism, particularly André Bazin and the critics of *Cahiers du Cinéma*. If Antonioni was in any sense one of the heirs or indeed proponents of neo-realism it was of a neo-realism as understood and elaborated by French criticism rather more than by Italian criticism which had tended to identify neo-realism with a social message and consciousness and against whose apparent lack Antonioni felt the need to defend himself:

The meaning of a film always comes later; at first I am only interested in the characters and then, through these characters, I try to paint a picture of their surroundings. I did that in *La signora senza camelie*, where I told the story of some characters, trying to find what influence the world of the cinema had within them. This too is a way of making realism.[11]

The frequent statements by Antonioni in the 1950s that he too was making realism, that he too had made neo-realism, and yet at the same time his opposition to its messages and departure from many of its forms, was motivated in part by the pressure and presence in Italy of that tradition. Antonioni defended himself in two seemingly contradictory directions: by claiming to continue the tradition of neo-realism and equally asserting his right and the need to depart from it; the terms for reconciliation were that he was recording not an external but an internal reality, not a man in search of a bicycle, or a man brought to near suicide by a small pension and straitened circumstances, but rather by the workings of these external aspects within characters.

To make a film today about a man who has robbed a bicycle or rather about a character who is important because he has robbed a bicycle and solely for that reason, above all for that reason – not in order to know if he is shy, if he loves his wife, if he is jealous, and so on, things that are not interesting because the most important thing is this experience, this misadventure with the bicycle which stops him from working so that we must follow him as he searches for his bicycle – a film of this kind, as I was saying, no longer seems to me have any significance. I was led to think: what is it at this moment that is important for us to examine, to take as the theme of stories, of imaginings? And it seemed to me it would be more important not so much to examine the relations between characters as much as to see what of all the things that have happened to them have remained inside them, not so much the transformations in their psychology or their feelings, but the symptoms of these changes that occurred within their psychology and feelings and perhaps also in their morality.[12]

In scenes like the killing of the ants in *Umberto D,* or the lengthy takes in *Roma, città aperta,* where the real time and real space of events was relatively uninterrupted and if not unfocused, or at least unweighted, the actual taking of those scenes, the perception of them, came to the fore as a subject. While the intent may have been to make reality shine forth, another reality, that of the camera and the organisation of things had, if not an equal, certainly a perceptible presence. Much of this was the result of a realistic intention which, by being outside of the conventional (where time and space were highly manipulated yet made invisible by taking the audience along paths of identification with the action), almost inadvertently made its form and technique appear. Hence the excitement with neo-realism by French critics (realism was after all a language, said Bazin) and the homage to film-makers like Rossellini by Godard and Rohmer. By making the world appear as if for the first time on the screen – surprising reality – neo-realism, at the same time, made the language for that realisation palpable and new.

Neo-realism's interest in the exterior, in the world of appearances and the materiality and objectivity of things forced it, contradictorily, to renounce an 'invisible' form of film-making which was tied up, intimately, with forms of narration. For example, to make the scene appear for itself and not as a scene for another, bound in a ceaseless, remorseless line of continuity, in which nothing was present except to be linked to a previous shot and displaced by a successive one (the thin-line of classical narration), neo-realism sought to loosen the narrative hold upon representation, or at least this kind of narrative hold, the consequence of which for neo-realism was the revelation of reality, or in other terms, the reinstatement of the image for the cinema. The visual beauty of much of neo-realist films and particularly those by Rossellini – the sense of seeing things for the first time – had much to do with the breaking of logical rules of narrative continuity.

Antonioni's interest in what was intimate, psychological and essentially invisible – the working of reality within us – resulted in an even greater visibility of form than was characteristic of the best of neo-realist films, primarily because this reality within us included, for Antonioni, the reality at work within him and the feeling that that working inside us of things not only made things uncertain, but ourselves uncertain. By tying perception to the actual shape and status of the external world, he made them both equally subjects of his films, and equally ambiguous and tenuous.

Even though neo-realism may have made the terms of its perceptions visible, they were tied to a notion of the objectivity and comprehensibility of the external world; Antonioni loosened this hold of perception upon reality and calculated its implications. Essentially, neo-realism had a single subject which was the world it sought to represent. Antonioni denied that world any such singularity or objectivity, or rather he conceived of its objects differently. Antonioni's films not only present divided subjects as heros and heroines – the crises of identity for Clara Manni in *La signora senza camelie*, for Locke in *The Passenger*, and the multiplication of doubles in all of Antonioni's films: doubled events and doubled characters, divided and de-centred reality, an ambiguous reality of shifting points, multiple centres.

Lorenzo Cuccu called Antonioni's vision '*la visione estraniata*' (the estranged vision), by which he meant not only a look from outside of events, but – and it is difficult to illustrate in words – a look upon that look.[13] Locke has it in *The Passenger*: he takes on himself the identity of another and looks at himself as that other and regards his own look. At the same time Antonioni gazes, equally estranged, on that multiplication and problematisation of looking which extends itself, uncomfortably, to the audience. As Locke seeks to find himself in the identification with another (dead, gone, like an image), and as he progressively loses himself in seeking to identify himself, with the result that an equally elusive image of him, another image, appears within the old, the audience is similarly placed to identify with Locke and with his image and to interrogate that image and its own regard of it.

Cuccu's idea of the 'estranged vision' is dense and complicated; it involves for him, among other things, the refusal to use the camera for purely diegetic ends, the relative absence of a dramatic motive in the choice of scenes, the non-identification of the structure of the film with the dramatic and narrative material, an attitude of coldness, distance, intellectualism which is part of a refusal to manipulate the drama in an emotional-spectacle direction, and an equal refusal to seek for an audience places of emotional identification, not because of some quirk of personality on the part of Antonioni but rather because of a particular aesthetic position: 'it doesn't represent the form of expression of the world view of the author, but the material on which he chooses to place his gaze in order to decipher the sense of it in its many forms.'

In the 1950s, Antonioni was accused by some critics, particularly on the 'left', of an empty formalism and pictorialism, of being wedded to technique with no apparent social or 'human' purpose, especially in contrast to the humanism and social conscience evident in neo-realism. The kind of possibilities of action and representation such criticism demanded were possibilities 'in reality' like that of finding or not finding the bicycle in *Ladri di biciclette*, or the problem of Clara Manni in *La signora senza camelie* wanting to become a serious actress:

> Really! . . . One doesn't study only by reading Pirandello any more than one forms good taste surrounding oneself with pictures. Does Manni not have other possibilities of studying? Antonioni has nothing to say about this.[14]

Such criticism remained long after the issue of neo-realism ceased to matter: the initial negative reaction to *L'avventura* and the positively vitriolic condemnation of *Zabriskie Point* (one of Antonioni's very best films) all

LA SIGNORA SENZA CAMELIE
Clara and Nardo

involved appeals to a singular, known reality from which Antonioni had unreasonably departed to engage in formal experiments and an aestheticism without apparent purpose.[15]

One of the fascinations of the images Antonioni has constructed, in part by freeing them from functional demands of narration and dramatic story, is their instability to the point of dissolution (not of the image but the subject of the image) and the appearance within one image of another image, or within a single figure, another figure; this too is one of the primary fascinations of his narratives which lose their subject only to find another, Claudia for Anna in *L'avventura*, or a story of science fiction for the story of Ida as her story had displaced the story of Mavi in *Identificazione di una donna*. These images may be beautiful and compelling but this is not a 'mere' pictorialism any more than the disappearance of the narrative results in a film about nothing much more than a technical display.

It would not be difficult on political or ethical-social grounds to justify these strategies along the lines of the world being uncertain, our knowledge of it uncertain, and the depiction therefore of such uncertainty in things and our perceptions of them being not only 'objectively' correct, but the precondition for any knowledge whatsoever. Umberto Eco has written convincingly in defence of Antonioni's 'social commitment' in these terms and has implicitly condemned a 'left' criticism of Antonioni, very virulent in the 1950s and some of whose remarks I have recently quoted, which assumed a definite world and determinate solutions for it. That criticism resulted, not only in a failure to appreciate Antonioni's aesthetics, but a failure to develop a politics more in tune with realities than the politics of his 'left' critics perhaps were, particularly those on *Cinema Nuovo*.[16]

It was the precise absence of conventional political positions in Antonioni's films, as it was the absence of conventional narrative positions in them, that revealed both a new politics and a new aesthetics. And yet all of this writing in defence of Antonioni, Umberto Eco's as well as Barthes' (who spoke of an Antonionian language which resists power and contests it), doesn't always get to the heart of things since it inevitably gives a message to an aesthetic figuration whose very power to move and attract is involved with the dissolution of figuration and hence of the kind of ethical-political messages with which his most impassioned defenders credit him.

On the other hand, once in that system, of defending yourself against the charge of apoliticism and of a mere formalism, it is difficult not to end up at the place you most want to avoid. Certainly, the 'merely' formal is completely inept as a description of Antonioni's films, not because a meaning can be concluded from the forms he creates, nor because the 'nothing' into which figures and narrative dissolve is 'something' after all, but because even when

Antonioni is at his most pictorial and imagistic, his attitude remains essentially a narrative attitude; in any case the division between narrative as a vehicle for meaning and 'the image' as a means for the dissolution of narrative – that way in which the narrative dissolves into an image and 'things' dissolve into no more than images – is never a complete one and seems always to be repaired, reworked, refashioned. Or, in other terms, if the experiments Antonioni accomplishes with narrative are such as to allow the image to appear, to make a space for it by literally creating space and creating time, it always remains in a relation to narrative and to figuration; beckoned by a liberation from all restraints to signify, it nevertheless re-establishes those restraints and the need it gives rise to.

Antonioni's place when filming and constructing a fiction and when filming that actual process of construction is never above the material he is in the process of forming . . . and interrogating. He is, or rather his camera is, at the same level – or, sometimes, at a different level, though not superior, never superior, to his characters. If they go through the world seeking to find things, to identify, and to recognise themselves, so too does Antonioni; and neither he, nor they, emerge as masters. In that sense there is no formalism to his films, or at least no mastery of form since the terms for 'forming' are rigorously interrogative, and the uncertainty Antonioni finds in things, in the world, in images, he finds in himself contemplating them – hence the doubling, hence the returning of the film to its own gaze. But there is something more to this: the fact that a formalism, a pictorialism, especially in the cinema, depends on a view of the world on one side and I, or the film-maker, on the other, mastering it. But Antonioni is not only not in that position, but he is perpetually in a position in which that mastery is at stake, at risk.

There is no camera on one side and characters on the other which it views: it is precisely in the dissolution of that divide and of the inclusion of view and of subjectivity in the figures and objects looked at, but never, because of this way of seeing, fixed, that Antonioni's politics and his formality lie. It is a politics not so much compounded by notions of uncertainty, but of crucially being involved, entering and composing the reality which one is part of, which one interrogates and equally creates. There is no master here, no figures who act like puppets on a string, no independent forms, no dominant presence regarding others from afar.[17]

The Centro Sperimentale di Cinematografia, Italy's national film school, was among a number of institutions set up by the fascist government to help the development of an Italian film industry. The school was there to train not only directors and technicians but also to provide a general cultural education on the cinema: beside courses in acting, camerawork, directing, set design, courses were also offered in theory, film history, aesthetics.

The director of the school was Luigi Chiarini, favoured and favourable to the fascist regime, an intellectual of liberal persuasion, cultivated and with an ideology and aesthetic indebted to the ideas of Croce. One of the leading teachers at the school was the Marxist critic and theoretician Umberto Barbaro. The relations between Chiarini and Barbaro were harmonious and productive and there was no question of Barbaro needing to quit the school because of his Marxist and certainly anti-fascist sympathies (he was forced to quit after the war by the Christian Democrats).

After the war Chiarini worked as a film critic, writer, theorist and film-maker (he collaborated on the script of Antonioni's *Tentato suicidio*). The transition from fascism to democracy did not seem difficult for Chiarini; one of the film journals he wrote for in the 1950s was the 'left', 'Lukacsian' journal *Cinema Nuovo* whose editor, Guido Aristarco, had criticised Antonioni's *La signora senza camelie* for unmotivated and socially unlocated characters, narrative fragmentariness, abstraction. Chiarini was no more favourable to the film than Aristarco was and for similar reasons, but what he concentrated upon was its lack of a good script and a resultant undisciplined and empty formalism – the film exhibited for him a great virtuosity of form, but a narrative and a characterisation lacking in all virtue. Chiarini wrote two articles on the film: an initial review and then an answer to Antonioni's reply to that review. None of the writings, either his or Antonioni's, particularly sparkle, but the issue of the script which they raise is an important one.[18]

Tonino Guerra, who has worked with Antonioni as scriptwriter for almost all his films from *L'avventura* onwards, described, in a preface to *L'eclisse*, nearly ten years after the making of *La signora senza camelie*, the process of script collaboration with Antonioni:

> In Antonioni's films words are only a comment, a background to the images. In the first sketches for the screenplay when we mark out this or that scene everything is entrusted to words.
>
> We rework things, change lengthy dialogue scenes and along the way get ourselves accustomed to the way a particular character speaks. Then, very very slowly, the words fall away and gestures begin to take their place, movements of the characters . . . visual marks on which the story of the film more and more begins to rest. Finally, even the most beautiful lines fall away, those that had so charmed us and seemed so necessary.
>
> For this reason, a screenplay like this, so economical, might give someone who assumes a literary value for the screenplay, a definite impression of bareness, even of poverty. The reason is that Antonioni, obviously, wants to destroy in the word what it retains of literary suggestion in order to give it value as cinematographic suggestion.
>
> But there still remains something to discover even beyond images as

they can be gathered from a written page, some kind of meanings that give a mystery and resonance to what seemed so clear and definite.[19]

Though Antonioni's early films, like *La signora senza camelie*, relative to his later ones, were highly narrativised, in the sense that there were 'events' formed by a story with a not insignificant effect on the outcome of the film, and hence the greater presence in these films of a script and of the script as support and even force behind the images, there was, nevertheless, in these films not only an aesthetic regard for images as such independent of an obvious narrative function, but a strong sense of the constitutive power of the camera and of what it saw, its ability to be able to seize on an 'event' neither planned nor called for: the lingering, the excessive time of the camera's gaze, the *temps morts*, a sudden, spontaneous visual fascination without a definite narrative 'sense'.

To be open to the moment of shooting and the momentary aspects of reality outside of determinations set in advance by the script has been characteristic of Antonioni's films and his way of making them. The apparent 'subjects' of his films – uncertainty, instability, tenuousness – are structured into the way they are made. These are not abstract, philosophical ideas so much as concrete practices in the making of his films, a way of being aware of changes – of gesture, comportment, feelings, in the quality of light – and attentive to these changes and committed to realising them; moreover, and it is difficult to state, that realisation was not so much a matter of 'capturing' the moment and its transitoriness, but of maintaining the hesitancy and fluidity involved in the act of shooting; the image was not a frozen expression of the idea but the idea itself, the actual making of it.

It is a manner as well of being subjective, of including in the activity of shooting all that is working inside you: feelings, impressions, fascinations: 'Perhaps this is a way to be autobiographical, that is to put into a film everything that reality causes to move within you, but immediately, in a completely contingent way.'[20] This attitude, though different from it, was indebted to neo-realism and particularly for the implications it held for the script.

As an aside, it is rather interesting that Antonioni, one of the great landscape artists of the cinema, depicts the landscape as having neither illustrative, nor symbolic, nor even atmospheric weight. If there is a correlation, for example, between the interior landscape of feelings within Aldo in *Il grido* and the exterior landscape of the autumn/winter greys, mist and fogs of the Po valley, it is not that this valley is simple backdrop or setting for Aldo's drama, nor the symbol of it, but rather that it is something that works within him; and the camera looking at the river, or looking at Aldo, or losing itself in the mist, looks at these things with an equal and unweighted intensity. They

LA SIGNORA SENZA CAMELIE
Lucia Bosè in furs

are present together, a contingent yet necessitous reality. It is like the working of things on the inside of Antonioni.

In defending himself against Chiarini's charge that he did not know how 'to see reality' and hence required a strong script to keep this reality in sight, Antonioni remarked on the seeing of reality by neo-realist directors as something outside of and independent of any script and that his work and his sensibilities were part of that non-scripted, spontaneous, instinctive visual stress characteristic of the best of neo-realism.

What Chiarini was asking of Antonioni was a unity between narrative values and images; despite how heavily scripted *La signora senza camelie* is in relation to later Antonioni films, this unity, for Chiarini, was evidently lacking in the film. The falling away of words and of narrative, or at least the division between a narrative, psychological aspect and a visual-imagistic one, that described by Tonino Guerra for the script in *L'eclisse*, and very evident in the equal but separate regards in *Il grido* for the journey of Aldo and for the landscape of the Po, was, in the climate of film-making in the early 1950s in Italy, already something strongly felt by critics who saw *La signora senza camelie*: the narratively useless pauses of the camera and the wandering away from a narrative centre, for example, when Clara speaks on the telephone first to her mother and then to Gianni from the hotel room where she has gone with Nardo, a scene which conventionally is filled with the drama of betrayal, guilt, anguish, misapprehension, anxieties, but which is flattened, de-dramatised, in part by a camera becoming interested in the internal architecture of the room, its framings of the outside and then becoming interested in the spaces in Gianni's home, at the other end of the phone line in Rome. It recalls the scene in front of Sandro's house in *L'avventura* and the wanderings of the camera within Thomas' studio in *Blow-Up*, intent on framings, on objects, on surfaces, on changing perspectives.

Though *La signora senza camelie* depicts scenes of desperation, the effect is of neutrality, of a disengaged objectivity, so that even at the point of the most intense and direct narrative gaze, a division between what is seen and the seeing of it opens up; and this also occurs within the narration by a concentration of equal intensity on occurrences that are central to the narrative, but also peripheral to it, for example (and Chiarini strongly objected to it), the sudden summer shower in Venice which catches out Nardo and his friends and which occurs in the film just before the Venice premiere of the disastrous *Giovanna d'Arco*, and the meeting on the boat launch between Nardo and Clara.

Antonioni wrote:

With regard to the shower on the terrace, Chiarini says: '. . . everything in white and grey tones, with a clarity that makes one marvel at the joyous erupting of the summer storm in the blinding light of the sea and which only serves to say, let's go to the cinema.' If Chiarini had written: it is a beautiful shot but without any significance, only beautiful for certain grey and white tones, decoratively, abstractly beautiful (or something of that sort), I wouldn't have bothered to reply; it is a valid opinion and as such ought to be respected. But he says that the shot gives the sense of a 'sudden summer storm', and gives a sense of the 'sea'. The shot is thus not empty, not abstract. It says simply what it sets out to say: that it is summer, that we are in Venice during the film festival, that one of the main characters is about to go to see a film in which the central female character stars. Thus it is a parenthesis. A shot which functions like the so-called '*flèche*'. And how ought you to say what you mean? '. . . it makes one marvel . . . ,' says Chiarini. Well? I can't understand why, in order to validate the shot, I should have substituted another situation for it. What is so incredible is that a Crocean like Chiarini reduces everything to a matter of content. He is entitled to criticise my film; it is his right to accuse it of poverty, of aridity, but he ought not to take as his example, stressing it, the shower on the terrace, for here, surely, he is mistaken.[21]

Antonioni stressed the purely denotative meaning of the scene in all its literalness; what he emptied from it was its drama and, giving it a parenthetic function in the narrative, he reduced its dramatic importance while adding to its importance as a scene to be looked at. That look neutralised the fictional drama and the anxiety of a narrative continuity; instead it gave to the scene a documentary objectivity: summertime, a shower, summer light, Venice, an action about to occur.

To Chiarini it seemed like a scene of nothing at all. Antonioni's paragraph reverses Chiarini's assumptions; he points out that Chiarini's remarks about an emptiness were in fact a reference to content, that the merely abstract was not abstract at all, and that it was Chiarini, not Antonioni, who had divorced form from content and whose Croceanism had disabled him from perceiving the obvious and perhaps as well something new.

The entire sequence, which is very brief, in fact motivates action and indicates relations: Nardo's decision to go to the cinema to see Clara Manni on the screen and perhaps Clara Manni in the audience; and the look of Simonetta, his current lover, as he goes off from the bar, out onto the terrace on his way to the cinema. The shower of rain bothers Chiarini because it has no sense, says nothing of the relations, states of mind, or if it does the sense is too vague, too fragile to hold. The rain does work somewhere in the characters, but not directly or causatively; in the first instance it is just there, contingent, part of the world. It is not the task of Antonioni to proclaim some meaning for it so much as to regard it, even question it; what Chiarini wanted was an answer.

Antonioni replied to Chiarini's criticisms not only by stressing the relative non-importance of the script and the value of new narrative strategies for the cinema, but the fact that this new conception, in part visual, but primarily a matter of regarding and relating, was the principal virtue of the best of neo-realism.

[Chiarini] advises those directors who don't 'know how to see reality' to place between themselves and reality the mediation of a good script, even if, and especially if, they are neo-realist in sympathy, as if to realise a good script did not necessarily involve 'seeing well'; as if the conquests by neo-realists, by the best of them at least, were not of an improvisational kind (for example, *La terra trema*, *Paisà*, and also *Ladri di biciclette*, if one thinks of the quantity and the richness of the material with which their images are filled thanks to the choice of one exterior rather than another, one angle and not another).

He [Chiarini] ought to know better than anyone else that from the moment the director puts himself behind a camera he opens his eyes to what is the blank page for the writer, the canvas for the painter. . . . At that moment the director is alone, and only he has the chance to create poetry, to translate, let us say it, into poetry, the extremely precious, but nevertheless inert pages of the script . . .

Chiarini had not only been director of the Centro Sperimentale in the 1930s and early 40s, but also the editor of its film journal *Bianco e Nero* : academic, intellectually conservative, idealist, Crocean, intensely serious. Even up to the last months of the fascist regime and as if oblivious to it, *Bianco e Nero* published long articles on the internal harmonious unity necessary for a true work of art, on the distinction between literature and poetry, on the superiority of a European art tradition to the populist spectacles of Hollywood (and presumably of the Italian film industry as well).

Unlike *Cinema*, *Bianco e Nero* was seemingly untouched during the fascist years by the agitation of a liberal anti-fascism for the need to renew Italian culture not by returning to an ideal notion of art, but by upsetting that notion in an almost documentary and spontaneous rendering of the everyday and the ordinary, the actual real experience of 'the people', the spectacle of current reality; just as it was equally untouched by the urging of some fascists for a more committed culture, one that had a definite political function in support of the regime. It maintained its Crocean ideals of the separation between art and politics from the pressures of the liberal left and from the official fascist right (it did, however, from time to time publish 'official' material from state bureaucrats and even ran a lengthy series of articles by Goebbels on the administration of culture, but these had the status more of documents than of a taking of position).

If from the late 1930s through perhaps to the early 50s Crocean idealism touched Antonioni, as it had most of the major figures of Italian culture, especially in his maintenance of the need for an autonomy of culture and art from any political instrumentality, his notions of the art work and the actual practice of his film-making were far from the artistic conservatism and bourgeois art revivalism associated with Croce and to which Chiarini fundamentally belonged. Moreover, and I think this is crucial for Antonioni, his defence of an artistic autonomy had more to do with the demands for commitment from an anti-fascist left than ever it did from the much less demanding and more tolerant official fascism of the 30s and 40s which not only permitted the olympian lack of commitment of *Bianco e Nero*, but permitted the call by the liberal-left *Cinema* for a 'realistic' rendering of the world in opposition to the optimistic and rose-coloured representations preferred by official fascism.

This area of art and politics is difficult to define. It was not that Antonioni was indifferent to social and political events for the sake of the pursuit of formal artistic problems, but rather that he sought their representation in less obvious and sure ways than did his anti-fascist colleagues say on *Cinema*; the issue was not between politics and art but between different forms of representation. To Antonioni, the 'realism' demanded by the critics of *Cinema* was a social realism whose forms of realisation were essentially uncritical towards the problem of viewing reality; his politics were tied up in the need to find new forms as a means for constructing and perceiving new realities. The 'new' realities of left critics were realised by very traditional means: hence the easy accomodation between conservative Crocean idealists and Lukacsian Marxists and the fact that Antonioni disturbed both. For Aristarco, Antonioni's apparent formalism and lack of narrative unity was evidence of a political and ethical failure: not placing man in his enviroment, not typifying social groups, not providing clear social motivations. For Chiarini the same qualities of fragmentariness and formal experimentation, without clear sense or meaning, was evidence of a failure to perceive 'reality': hence the need for a script, for a tighter narrative logic, for a clearer identification of things at precisely those points at which Antonioni was making identification a problem, denying any easy unity and risking the surety of his own perceptions and knowledge.

Chiarini made a double distinction in his criticism of *La signora senza camelie*, one philosophic-aesthetic, the other narrowly technical, both derived from the work of Croce: a distinction between literature and poetry, and a distinction between visual decoration and reality. These distinctions converged on his strictures for the script.

In a Crocean hierarchy of value, poetry stood higher than literature; poetry was not poetry in the accepted sense but rather a set of qualities involving a unified vision, unified by the presence of the author in the work, in effect a personal vision. Literature was altogether a more generic, more convention-alised category. Chiarini transferred the distinction to the cinema: spectacle (*spettacolo*) was the equivalent of literature, *film* the equivalent of poetry. Most of the cinema for Chiarini was spectacle and not film, generic rather than personal, industrial not individual. *Bianco e Nero*, for example, in contrast to *Cinema*, had maintained a more or less permanent hostility to American cinema (*spettacolo*) in favour of the European cinema (*film* – in practice, French and Russian cinema), but really it was a cinema 'in theory', a cinema

The French episode of I VINTI
with Etchika Choureau

desired, whose few examples were in a distant past. (In that sense it was not unlike Croce's liberal politics which mingled a present regret with a hope set in the past; fascism to Croce was an aberration, an unfortunate disruption of a sure to be restored destiny of liberalism). The best of the American cinema for Chiarini – he cited, interestingly, *Death of a Salesman* – partly saved itself from the status of literature, spectacle, generic convention by the strength and individuality of its script, in this case, the Arthur Miller drama.[22] His arguments were not markedly dissimilar from those in *Critica Fascista* on the script which Antonioni had countered in 1935; the politics were the same.

Chiarini praised *La signora senza camelie* only for its camerawork, or more precisely only for the cameraman; that is, the film exhibited a 'merely' technical virtuosity, but that virtue pointed to a directorial lack: it was the cameraman, not the director, the visuals, not the narrative. The film was doubly condemned: it was artistically disunified and it was empty, simply pretty and decorative. The function of a strong script was to militate against this mere formalism and to provide some singularity of vision, hence poetry, and in so doing give the film sense and reality.

> Because of the respect which I have for him [Antonioni], I have advised him to only make films from good scripts because with scripts like the one for *La signora senza camelie* you can't even produce passable literature, that is not even acceptable spectacle, notwithstanding all the formal virtuosity of the film.[23]

Chiarini's general views were not isolated; many of them were shared by critics on the Marxist left. One of the interests of these views is its appreciation of neo-realism in terms of its depiction of social reality, a poetry of reality, but a lack of awareness of the means by which that reality was presented. Antonioni's sensitivity to neo-realism (for its linguistic innovations) was in contrast to the insensitivity of critics who depreciated him (for mere formalism) but praised neo-realism (for its social content). Certainly it reveals how retrograde the cultural politics were, not only of Crocean liberals like Chiarini, but Lukacsian Marxists like Aristarco.

It was, as Antonioni stressed, one of the virtues of neo-realism to loosen the hold and the status of the script and to allow thereby a spontaneity, an instinctiveness and constitutive freedom to the camera. The implications of that new freedom were enormous: the displacement of the centrality of the script was not only an opportunity to experiment with directly 'visual', non-narrativised qualities, but it displaced the dramatic canons of the cinema, the importance of the diegesis around which all else depended.

Chiarini wanted to drag Antonioni back to an art of the past in the name of art and poetry; Aristarco sought to do so, but in the name of radicalism, social commitment, 'reality'. Both were equally reactionary, but the left has more to answer for: its insensitivity to the new and to the radicalism of that new stands as a political failure of major importance. The Gramscian tendency to consider the work of art under a political and pedagogic profile contributed to strengthen the social-populism and sententious moralism of Marxist-democratic critics, like Aristarco, who, in effect, explicitly invited Antonioni to return to nineteenth-century forms, to align a view of a democratic and humanitarian world with a clear rational realism, to be optimistic, and to reject thereby the achievements of modernism and the avant-garde this century, which it explicitly rejected.

Scrittori e popolo by Alberto Asor Rosa is one of the great works of Italian post-war literary and social-political criticism. It was written by someone within the Italian Communist party, but severely critical of the artistic conservatism of Italian neo-realism in literature and painting and of a critical tradition which supported it and confirmed Italian literature in its 'indigenous', conservative and provincial qualities. Asor Rosa, however, made an exception for the neo-realist Italian cinema:

> The cinema, in the absence of a strong national tradition, permitted itself a freer and more unprejudiced invention even from the point of view of style. It didn't by that fact eliminate the weakness of the ideological and cultural complex in which it operated, but in a certain sense it transcended it in the immediacy of its impressions, in the naked 'truth' of its narrative.[24]

If the neo-realist cinema by its language had partly transcended the narrowness of Italian culture, film critics had not. They sought to reimpose that narrowness and especially where the cinema was at its most inventive. The criticisms of Chiarini and Aristarco, moralistic and censorious, and representative of an entire generation, polemicised against every uncommitted and formalist choice as actions which removed from art its social function, its popular content, its political sense. By 1953, when *La signora senza camelie* appeared, Europe was in the midst of the cold war which tended to reaffirm and strengthen all that was worst in this criticism; rather than it being ready to open itself to the broader aspects of European culture, it instead re-emphasised an indigenous populist culture in the name of democracy, the people, progress. At the very time that the social traditions and representations of neo-realism were no longer relevant, these critics implicitly hung on to them and did so in the name of a progressist naturalism. It is, perhaps, what accounts for the sententiousness of that criticism, and its hysteria when faced with the threat to its assumptions by the elegance and formal intelligence of a film like *La signora senza camelie*.

Notes

1. Michelangelo Antonioni, 'Per una storia della mostra', *Cinema*, 10–25 September 1941, pp. 151–152, 187–189.

2. See Lorenzo Cuccu, *La visione come problema* (Rome: Bulzoni, 1973), pp. 160–171; also, for a general introduction to Italian populism, A. Asor Rosa, *Scrittori e popolo* (Rome: Samonà e Savelli, 1969).

3. Michelangelo Antonioni, 'Film di tutto il mondo a Roma', *Film d'oggi* no. 20, 3 November 1945; and also, under the same general title, and reporting on the festival, nos. 16, 19 of 6 and 13 October 1945 respectively; *Roma, città aperta* is discussed principally in no. 19 while *Les Enfants du paradis* is extensively reviewed (and praised) in no. 16.

4. Vice (Michelangelo Antonioni), 'Film di questi giorni', *Cinema*, 25 November 1940, p. 381.

5. Cuccu, p. 169.

6. André Bazin, Michel Mayoux, Jean-José Richer, 'Petit dictionnaire pour Venise' *Cahiers du Cinéma* no. 27, October 1953, p. 19.

7.   Quoted in Lino Del Frà, 'Con una pistola in mano sono subito simpatici', *Cinema Nuovo* no. 30, 1 March 1954, pp. 118–119.

8.   Ibid.

9.   Guido Aristarco '*La signora senza camelie*', *Cinema Nuovo*, 15 March 1953, pp. 185–186.

10. Anon., '*La signora senza camelie*', *Bianco e Nero*, March 1953, p. 81.

11. Requoted in Stelio Martini, '*La signora senza camelie* non offende il cinema italiano', *Cinema Nuovo* no. 6, 1 March 1953.

12. Michelangelo Antonioni (colloquio con), 'La malattia dei sentimenti', *Bianco e Nero*, February-March 1961, pp. 70–71; it has been translated in *Film Culture* no. 24, Spring 1962, pp. 45–46, as 'A Talk with Michelangelo Antonioni on his Work'.

13. Cuccu, p. 34.

14. Guido Aristarco, '*La signora senza camelie*', *Cinema Nuovo*, 15 March 1953.

15. See for example the criticisms levelled at *Zabriskie Point* by Seymour Chatman in his book on Antonioni: *Antonioni or, The Surface of the World* (Berkeley and Los Angeles: University of California Press, 1985) pp. 158–168. Chatman reiterates the kind of criticism Aristarco made of *La signora senza camelie* over 20 years earlier, but with less justification; hence, perhaps, its pompous, lecturing tone: '*Zabriskie Point* is clearly a troubled movie.'

16. Umberto Eco, 'Antonioni "impegnato"', in Carlo Di Carlo, *Michelangelo Antonioni* (Rome: Edizione Bianco e Nero, 1964); see also his '*De interpretatione*, or the difficulty of being Marco Polo', *Film Quarterly* vol. 30 no. 4, Summer 1977 pp. 8–12.

17. See Pascal Bonitzer, 'Désir Désert', *Cahiers du Cinéma* nos. 262–263, January 1976, pp. 96–98.

18. Luigi Chiarini, '*Signora senza camelie*', *Cinema Nuovo*, 1 April 1953; and his 'Ancora sulla *Signora senza camelie*', *Cinema Nuovo*, 1 June 1953; Michelangelo Antonioni, 'Antonioni risponde a Chiarini', *Cinema Nuovo*, 14 May 1953, p. 292.

19. Tonino Guerra, 'Le parole', in Michelangelo Antonioni, *L'eclisse* (ed. John Francis Lane), (Bologna: Cappelli, 1962), p. 27.

20. Requoted in Cuccu, p. 57.

21. 'Antonioni risponde a Chiarini', p. 292.

22. 'Ancora sulla *Signora senza camelie*'.

23. 'Ancora sulla *Signora senza camelie*'.

24. Asor Rosa, pp. 153–164.

Chapter Five

Il grido was Antonioni's fifth feature film; it was made in 1957, just after *Le amiche*. Unlike it, and indeed unlike all of Antonioni's feature films, its setting and central character is the working class: men who work at refineries, road building, trucking, dredging; women who run petrol stations, make dresses, cut reeds; habitations are shacks, cheap hotels, a shed for storing motor oil. In subject *Il grido* is absolutely unlike *Le amiche* which centres on the world of high fashion in Turin, the rich, the bored, and the urban. But both essentially are unspectacular, undramatic films, observations of behaviour, of gesture, unintrusive, at a distance.

Le amiche is the story of Clelia, once poor, from Turin, become a successful couturier in Rome, who returns to Turin to open a branch of the Rome firm; she is competent, secure, kindly, generous. She enters, accidentally, into a fashionable world of rich lonely women and frustrated, mediocre men by chancing on an attempted suicide in the room adjoining her own in the hotel where she is staying when the film opens; she has just arrived in Turin. The attempted suicide – *Le amiche* immediately succeeds Antonioni's short episode film under the title *Tentato suicidio* (1953) – is by Rosetta, in love with Lorenzo, an indifferent, moderately successful artist, married to Nene, a passionate and successful one; the suicide attempt is related to the impossibility of the love, but it is more a gesture, an act, than the real thing. Lorenzo drifts into an affair with Rosetta: it becomes desultory, unhappy, pleading, empty. The second time Rosetta attempts suicide, by drowning in a river, it is not an gesture and she dies.

The film is filled with other couples, other impossible loves between characters seemingly isolated from each other, seeking to find an other in their loneliness, but the acts never connect, seem to touch only other voids; all the relations and all the characters become less and less real not only to others, but to themselves, until they resemble the mannequins at Clelia's boutique opening, absolutely mocked in the applause for the mannequin in the bridal gown. Clelia too finds herself in an impossible love with Carlo, an assistant working on the renovations to the boutique; it isn't quite class, nor even exactly career that separates them (Clelia must return to Rome), so much as a perceived lack of substance. They touch each other, but only momentarily, then, like the others, lose touch. For Clelia the fragility of love isn't the end of things: for Rosetta there was nothing else but this dependence on sentiment and on an other; for Clelia the mutability of the world, of her life, her affections are facts to be faced and opportunities to be seized. Rosetta placed everything on her love for Lorenzo; Clelia knew better than to trust in the unstable, perhaps because her profession was fashion, the world of appearances; it is the world of almost all of Antonioni's main characters: film stars, fashion photographers, directors, architects, journalists, novelists, and, perhaps to be included as well, stockbrokers (*L'eclisse*).

Oddly, Guido Aristarco, who most criticised Antonioni for his lack of social context, his mere decorativeness and an empty formalism, approved of *Le amiche*, the story of the rich, and not *Il grido*, the story of the poor, because for the rich, being out of touch, isolated, seemed to Aristarco to suggest a social motive in the film; whereas for that same condition to prevail amongst the working class, to the point where individual isolation is so strong as to sever even the most basic (working-class) solidarity, was the sign of the return of Antonioni's formalism, social emptiness.

Though the films are vastly different visually, and in setting and social surroundings, they are very similar in the way they look, in their reticence, in the impenetrability of motives, and in that tendency – more marked in *Il grido* than in *Le amiche*, because in *Il grido* the very mists and fogs of the Po valley worked towards that effect – for existences to become unreal, for figures and relations to lose their outlines, their identities, their connections with others.[1]

Aldo, in *Il grido*, works in a sugar refinery. He lives (unmarried) with Irma and their seven-year-old daughter Rosina. When the film opens Irma learns that her husband has died in Australia; for Aldo it is an opportunity to marry; for Irma it is a reason to tell Aldo that she no longer loves him. He is astonished, lost – 'All these years, it has been nothing but lies?' In an instant his world has disintegrated; he leaves Goriano with Rosina. They wander along the Po first together; then later, when she returns to Irma, Aldo is left utterly alone. He goes from woman to woman in search of what he has lost, less Irma perhaps than his securities; in the end, he returns to Goriano, and accidentally, in an image which resumes the very beginning of the film, he falls off the tower in the refinery to his death, accompanied by Irma's anguished scream, the '*grido*' of the title.

Aldo has a number of centres to his life. Each reinforce the other and stabilise him: his work, the town, his loves. When Aldo is first seen in the film he is at the top of a tower at the refinery, balanced and certain. When Irma first tells him that their love is over he tries to resecure her, first by charm then by violence, but there is nothing there. He grabs hold of her but his arms are empty. All of Aldo's securities are lost in an instant; he leaves Irma and Goriano, and though he leaves with Rosina, he has already lost her in having lost Irma, and much of himself.

Aldo moves, for the remainder of the film, through the misty, grey, moist autumnal-wintry landscape of the Po valley, from place to place, woman to

The river bank in IL GRIDO *(1957)*
Aldo and Rosina

woman: with Elvira, the dressmaker, a lover from the past; with Virginia, the petrol station owner, with Andreina, part-time reed cutter along the river, in the season, part-time whore, out of season. But nothing has any substance, neither women, nor feelings, nor place.

All the women have resources Aldo lacks, the main resource being that of flexibility, not believing in certainties, able to contend with change, indeed welcoming it, like Clelia in Le amiche, for the possibilities it might offer, as if the insecurities they identify in the world help clarify their identities.

Aldo seems a shadow wandering through a landscape equally empty, unreal, insubstantial. If Goriano-Irma is thought of as the centre which was Aldo, the loss of it decentres and equalises every other place and relation; each, though different, is the same for Aldo: the women are *not* Irma, the place is *not* Goriano, the work is *not* at the refinery. The film in fact is not that repetitive; very subtly, because of these accumulated emptinesses around and within him, Aldo becomes less and less clear, each contact a further loss of feeling, a further disintegration of person, though nothing is said, no particular drama states it, or underlines it. The camera only watches: Aldo's hand running through his hair, a frown, a blankness in his look, a change in gait, the fact of the wandering itself, of aimlessness and refusal.

The film, which depicts a loss of centre and hence of meaning and hierarchy, at the same time decentres itself by structuring within the narrative alternative places and dramas to focus upon; it multiplies centres, each autonomous, none more important than the other. The gaze of the camera is blank, nothing is

IL GRIDO
Aldo with Elvira

weighted: this equalisation of centres and their pluralisation is not simply a matter of locations within the narrative, or a matter of the theme, but it is a positive aspect of every sequence and often of some shots when an object is of equal weight with person: the drip of water in Andreina's hut, the decoy ducks on the river flats, a bridge across the Po; sometimes this equalisation, this refusal to posit a cause or to construct a symbol, extends to the very atmosphere, to the rain, the mud, the mist as independently present, not the cause of Aldo's distress, not the background to it, but simply there, by the side of it.

Elvira is the first woman Aldo tries to stay with; she lives in a small house in a village beside the Po. He is recruited, virtually on arrival, to repair the engine of a motor boat owned by a friend of Elvira's daughter, Edera. There will be a boat race that afternoon. The incident is peripheral to the narrative; it interrupts Aldo's meeting with Elvira, takes him away to the river, apart from the drama or the emotions of his situation. It has value as fact but not as story and yet it is not de-emphasised, or not relatively to the 'main' action; in fact it displaces it. This 'irrelevance' becomes the centre of the narrative attention.

The event, at most, is an interlude, a kind of pause; it marks a subtle shift away from story to fact, from drama to simple occurrence, and, from story to image. Even if the scene lacks dramatic interest (the race is in itself unimportant and comes to nothing in relation to any plot or character in the film), it is not without visual interest (the movement of the boats; the tonal shifts between sky, bank, water; the unreality of the scene, so distanced, without 'subjects', the boats and their drivers almost disembodied; the seeing of everything, mediated through spray and mist, losing outline), and there is, in the pause, a narrative sense of Aldo's isolation, of these other dramas, so pointless to him, oblivious to him, but important to others – to Edera, for example, who is excited by him, and later, drunk, tries to seduce him. But none of these is exactly the main point. It isn't that a drama is de-emphasised in order to feature a visual design, or even to thematically frame the emptiness around Aldo, but rather that the constituents of drama, or more correctly, the constituents of what is a narrative subject have been markedly altered. It is in its very marginality that the importance of the boat race resides, in bringing forward what for most narratives are background, 'atmosphere'; here atmosphere and background acquire force, and in so doing shift the processes of narrative itself towards gestures, rain, the contingent, the tones of the world; there is a sense to *Il grido* that one is watching not so much a film of fiction, but a documentary narrated in an utterly new manner. There is no crisis here, no drama, no tragic moment, only a duration of objects and persons slipping by, carefully, minutely, precisely observed.[2]

Aristarco, in *Cinema Nuovo*, quoting Lukacs, noticed, and didn't like, the triviality of the boat race. Nor did he like other, apparently peripheral, insignificant events: the episode at the petrol station when the man on the motor scooter takes off without paying, pursued by Virginia, or Rosina's encounter with the mad people on a foggy, damp Po river embankment, the story of the enchantments of Venezuela. They were unimportant and yet they had equal presence with 'significant' scenes. It was evidence to Aristarco of a mere naturalism, a blank documentarism, a failure to indicate meanings, hence to establish a 'reality', by which Aristarco meant an ideology, a social meaning.

The episodic, non-dramatic quality of the film suggested something else to Aristarco, something far worse: a 'fanaticism for the beautiful', 'hedonistic calligraphy', 'meaningless formalism', 'the illusion that technical perfection in and of itself is poetry'. The scenes seemed to be organised for 'photogenic', 'pictorial' effect, rather than obeying 'human necessities', the explanation of character, the revelation of social setting. At worst this was reportage, at best a love of design and an expression of an over-refined, aristocratic taste without social conscience. He doubted whether, as a consequence, 'real and authentic characters actually exist in the film.' Aristarco's writing is moralistic, stuffy.[3]

More than in his earlier films, the sense of hierarchy, of drama, of marked significance was least strong in *Il grido*; the peripheral threatened to spread, to engulf the entire film, as it does, for example, in Antonioni's next film, *L'avventura* (1959), where the peripheral is extended and enlarged, as on Lisca Bianca in the search for Anna, in which the empty landscape displaces the narratively full search, and in which, by the fact of that emptiness new forms can take place, of love (in the narrative), and of sight (in the images). It was indeed difficult to know in *Il grido* what was central. Nothing was that emphatic. Background often stood equal to the characters 'within' it; even the boundaries between inside and out were unclear, hence judgement became less certain, ideology less pronounceable.

Aristarco mentioned, disparagingly, Bresson and Carné as among Antonioni's models, but the chief negative influence for him on Antonioni was Cesare Pavese, the author of the story from which *Le amiche* had been adapted: 'the Pavesian cult of the word was like the cult of the shot for the director.' He quoted a description by Pavese of the process of writing, about which he said, and he may have been right, that it could easily be applied to Antonioni's methods of filming: 'When Pavese begins a narrative, a story, a book, he never has a clear social setting in mind, or a character or characters, or themes. What he has in mind instead is always an indistinct rhythm, a play of events, which more than anything else are sensations, atmospheres.' Aristarco wanted a dramatic cinema; Antonioni was forming a cinema closer to contemporary writing, not action condensed into moments of crisis, but rather more the slow, infinitesimal transformation of things, queried, studied, not immediately enlisting a loyalty, or declaring a sense.

Though *Le amiche*, like *Il grido*, had for Aristarco the same 'poisons of a subtle intellectualism', an over-concern with form, an obsession with visual beauty in *Le amiche*, at least, these aspects were kept within bounds, served moral, ideological, 'human' purposes. *Le amiche* may have been based on a Pavese novel (*Tra donne sole*), but in the film, unlike in the novel, 'style was not all'.[4]

Renzo Renzi also wrote for *Cinema Nuovo*. Later his ideas rigidified and came to resemble those of Aristarco, but in the beginning his view of Antonioni was understanding, flexible and extremely sensitive; being a Lukacsian didn't necessarily entail the crudity of Aristarco, on the contrary.

Because he feels himself an actor in a world which he cannot particularly dominate, Antonioni doesn't propose solutions, doesn't intervene in facts. He limits himself to documenting that world from a psychological perspective. On the one hand, his attitude is cold and distant; on the other, it is that of a responsible participant. In other words, he is within the crisis he describes, but like a knowing accomplice: hence the lack of clear solutions and at the same time the possibility of a moral judgement. In short, it is a process of painful self-consciousness.[5]

If Antonioni seemed to express an uncertainty, if he failed to mark stresses, if he stood back, these positions, to Renzi, were understandable reactions to and expressions of political and social changes. Renzi contrasted the immediate euphoria and desire for change after the war to the conservatism of the decade following, which required different forms of protest, perhaps more individual and subjective in shape, but no less 'social' for that reason; Antonioni, in that sense, according to Renzi, had inherited much from neo-realism and, in his way, was finding a manner not only to represent the present state of things, but also, subtly, to undermine it by representing:

> the mirror of a world where dreams regularly are disappointed, where things stay as they are despite deep, legitimate and very human desires to change things; a world where one is defeated by facts and wins only on the level of consciousness; that is, with inadequate words where one learns to 'swallow' the bitter pill of reality.

There are times when it seems that institutional changes are possible, when they support and stimulate individual desires as they did in the period of the Resistance and the years just after the Liberation, from about 1943 to 1949, the time of great hope which was manifest in the films of Italian neo-realism, until the disappointments of the 1948 elections, the coming to power of Alcide De Gasperi, the conservatism of Italian Christian Democracy. The conservatism in Italy in the 1950s, for Renzi, dictated other, more private, certainly less sure responses, of which Antonioni's was one. Antonioni was not alone; Renzi linked his *Il grido* to recent films by Castellani (*I sogni nel cassetto*), Fellini (*Le notti di Cabiria*), Visconti (*Le notti bianche*), which were also 'intimist' in their approach, but whose intimacy and subjectivity could be taken as positive political signs, at the very least signs of a response to a new, changed present.

It wasn't that Antonioni was being insensitive to what was occuring in Italy, rather it was Aristarco who was, and the rigidity of his ideology. Renzi, though equally Lukacsian, equally troubled by the new conservatism, held to the ideology more lightly than Aristarco, and more intelligently.

Aldo, Elvira, Edera, her boy friend, Rosina watch the boat race from the muddy banks of the river. It is misty, raining. Aldo and Elvira make a bet: if the boat wins Aldo has to take her to the dance that night. The boat comes in third; he takes her anyway. The race, though the centre of attention, has no particular

IL GRIDO
Mists of the Po valley

importance. It is only an event, casual, reported, equal to others, or rather it equalises the 'dramatic' event of Aldo's arrival to the non-dramatic one of the boat race.

During the race the camera wanders both from the race and from the characters; it becomes interested in the line between water and sky which shifts with the movement of the boats, in the long horizontals of the river, land, sky cut by the diagonal of a steel bridge, and the mistiness and dampness of the scene, the mud. These 'things', their photogenic qualities, the greys of the river valley, these are seen with the exact same look as the 'drama', and the characters.

What these things and the landscape are *not* is what is interesting about the scene: they are not décor (mud, mist, the river, the shifting lines of the horizon are interesting in themselves); they are not atmosphere (an impress of realism); nor are they metaphors (the gloom of Aldo symbolised by the gloom of the wintry river). In fact they are not directly functional to the drama or to its credibility. They simply are, a reality to look upon, neither more nor less important than the behaviour of Aldo or the outcome of the race.

That Aldo has lost his centre, or rather, more exactly, fails to refind it and becomes increasingly unbalanced, unable to make contact, to retain anything, is of a different order than the loss of centre and the pluralisation of centres induced by the film. If for a character the loss of certainty and fixity is a cause of awful terror, and if the imponderability of things and self becomes oppressive and destructive, that very imponderability is a method for the film, and the loss of fixity a distinct pleasure. Aldo may find himself with no way out in not finding a particular path to pursue, but for the film the closing off of things, their dissolution, is the source of new possibilities, the very condition for new things to arise, as with the momentary disappearance of narrative and character for the 'joy' of a colour, or a tone, or a shape and the duration of these.

One of the 'things' that helps to hold Aldo in place and that he loses hold of is Rosina. Virginia (the petrol station owner), Aldo and Rosina go to Ferrara to place Virginia's father in an old people's home. Rosina and the old man were particularly close. On the way back Aldo and Virginia make love in a desolate open space; they are observed by Rosina. It 'ruins' everything: Rosina is unbearably distressed; Virginia had found her father a nuisance, in the way, and finds Rosina equally an obstacle in being close to Aldo. Aldo sends Rosina back to Irma and Goriano. A series of presences cancel out one another only to be cancelled out in turn: the old man, Rosina, Virginia for Irma. At the precise moment that Rosina leaves and Aldo is 'free', he turns his back on Virginia and leaves as well as if he has lost in these cancellations even more of himself, and of others.

This emptying of persons, losing substance and becoming shades, is a familiar occurrence in all of Antonioni's films: the shadowy spectres in the desert at *Zabriskie Point*; the phantom double images in *Il mistero di Oberwald*; the stockmarket in *L'eclisse* turning men into shadows; Claudia in *L'avventura* mistaking Giulia for Anna on the rocks on Lisca Bianca; Giovanni, at the end of *La notte*, desperately and violently seeking to embrace Lidia after failing to recognise himself let alone her; and there is Claudia's happy comment to Sandro in *L'avventura* at the hotel room in Noto when he wants to go out into the town on his own: 'Tell me that you want to embrace my shadow on the walls': Claudia has replaced the lost Anna but her own presence is threatened by the return of Anna, and more tellingly, by an absence of feeling in Sandro, by the finding and, almost at the same moment, losing the pleasure of love, the certainty of having been found and identified.

Character, traditionally, is fixed in a landscape or an environment or a context, and much of the meaning of character and action lies in this fixity and centring. One of the persistent accusations by Lukacsian critics, like Aristarco, against Antonioni's works was that the multiplication of centres, the separation and equalisation of 'things' and character, emptied all things and events of significance, substituted a mere naturalism for a realism; realism, it was asserted, was the ability to make selections, to underline importances, to grade, order, represent and give sense to reality, the way Visconti did, whereas Antonioni's failure to fix character was deemed to be a refusal to indicate the meaning of things, a retreat from the real, an abdication of responsibility.

This critical insistence on definition, which implies a stability and certainty of relations, is precisely an insistence which Aldo asserted while the world slipped from under him and caused him to lose his balance. For these critics there was a single reality and a defined relation to it; for Antonioni realities are *only* relations and those relations are multiple. The narrative joy, in contrast to a misery often felt by the characters, is a joy in the presence of that variety and possibility, of discovering more and more realities, movements, and images of realities and their simulacra, of, in effect, finding new relations to reality.

LE AMICHE
The girl friends

LE AMICHE
A confrontation

At the opening of *L'avventura* the camera follows Anna walking, with great determination, in what appears to be an outdoors. This exterior turns out, retrospectively, to be the interior of her father's villa, but when she finally moves outside of its walls, it only seems to be another space enclosed by encroaching buildings, the march of Rome and its ugliness, engulfing and absorbing its peripheries and the villa with them. One of the effects of the scene – it is like the opening of *Identificazione di una donna* where the appearance of wall becomes floor once a figure enters it and yet that entrance by Niccolò flattens him visually onto the surface, and turns figure into pattern, absorbs him, literally sucks him into its flatness – is to upset perceptions: you believe something to be one thing only to find that it is quite another and this in turn is subject to a further revision and change of perspective as spaces enclose other spaces and become further modified and as perspectives on these become multiple. The opening of *L'avventura*: the view of Anna, of her father, of the chauffeur, of Claudia, of the camera, overlapping but not at all the same. It reverberates in the dialogue: the crossing of purposes, of intentions, of misunderstandings between Anna and her father as it will reoccur later between Anna and Sandro, 'making' love in his flat, but spaces and worlds apart. There is always this double aspect in Antonioni's films: not only are perceptions of things unreliable, but things themselves are – the villa is taken over by the city it sought to escape from and the city is losing its centre and direction as it spreads.

One of the pleasures of the narrative is to escape from the conventions of purpose and function. In *Il grido* it is no longer possible to specify exactly the central from the peripheral, the dramatic from the non-dramatic, the important from the insignificant; the wavering of definition permits the narrative an unaccustomed freedom to wander and find its interests, and, more important, to respond to those interests and changes of place and things; or, to put things rather differently, because the narrative wanders, and because it refuses to weight scenes, it causes the loss of a centre, or an origin, or an end.

Antonioni commented on the primary presence of landscape over narrative in some scenes in *L'avventura*, but for him the absorption, even erasure of narrative by the landscape revealed a new fullness: a sense of new events (for the cinema) and new appreciations. In any case a screen full of the ripples of water, of waves on rocks, of the movement of clouds, of shifts in the line of the horizon, of an infinity of sand, is not exactly empty.

> I felt the need to really break up the action, inserting shots into many sequences which might seem formalist and inessential, shots of a directly documentary kind (a gust of wind, the sea, the dolphins, etc) but which, for me, in reality, are indispensable because they 'serve' the very idea of the film.[6]

About the time he made *Il grido* Antonioni spoke of the need 'to surprise theory with facts, with film' and 'to confront the conventions of narrative with visual evidence', 'to overturn story with facts.' 'The cinema I like', he said, 'is one in which the images give a sense of truth.'[7]

Water, damp, moistness, humidity, rain, drizzle, rivers, the sea, swimming pools, fountains figure in most Antonioni films with their contraries: the desert, dryness, sand, rocks, shimmering heat. A dampness invades all of *Il grido* while the sea dominates much of Antonioni's next film, *L'avventura*; it is also important in later ones: the sudden rain at the party in *La notte* which seems to release Lidia from the oppression of relations, making her want to fling herself, joyously, into the pool, and then the rain as medium through which her silhouette can be seen as pattern in the car; the damp mist-fog of *Il deserto rosso*; the play of wetness and dryness at the desert house in *Zabriskie Point*, the release and pleasure of the storm at the opening of *Il mistero di Oberwald*, then the morning damp drying on the fields. In *Il grido* wet clings to everything: the air is always damp, the ground muddy, the banks slippery, there is a

LE AMICHE
An attempted suicide

perpetual drizzle and sometimes an enveloping rain which turns inside into outside – the rain comes into Andreina's small hut by the river, making it dripping, wringing wet – and there is the river itself whose presence is permanent in the film; Aldo and the film follow its course, pause on its banks.

Damp and humidity, which are aerial, atmospheric qualities, matters of weather, are distorting mediums through which figures and landscapes are perceived in the films, as if they are, for Antonioni, the necessary terms for visibility. What the weather affects is the shape and clarity, or the shapelessness, of objects (like Lidia in the car in *La notte*, the ships in the fog in *Il deserto rosso*) and its principal aspect is that it varies: mist to drizzle to rain. Weather is a phenomenon of the moment which can erase or alter a perspective or the shape of an object from an instant before, making things tenuous, fragile, changing. And it has other qualities: it turns depth into surface, it blurs the lines between things. In the mists along the Po, in *Il grido*, it is often difficult to distinguish, certainly to fix, the line between sky and river, river and embankment, land and sky, while the mist tends to bring figures in depth to the surface so that landscape seems to be only a patterned surface, and objects in it only marks on that surface, but ones that pierce it, emphasising a torn surface rather than any depth. There is a comment by Antonioni about peeling away the surface of reality to find not a depth but another surface and so on, ever tempted to strip away a further layer but going nowhere.[8]

Water presents itself as a false surface: below it there is only more water and below that only more again; and it is perhaps also the most variable and changeable of surfaces, a trap which sucks in light, colour, even objects. (Lidia's joy at the rainstorm in *La notte* makes her want to leap into the water of the swimming pool, to lose herself in a surface which closes up without leaving a trace, but she is grabbed by Fanti: 'Don't be foolish,' he says; and there is that moment in *L'eclisse* when the drunk who had lost his balance and drove Piero's car in the river is fished out, dead, his arm hanging out of the car, and the gash made in the water is covered over again; and there is Rosetta's suicide in the river by drowning in *Le amiche*, and the attempted suicide in the Tiber in *Tentato suicidio*; and the boat out on the lagoon in *Identificazione di una donna* and Ida's story of flinging herself into the sea and being swallowed by a whale, and the mystery ship and mystery sounds on the fantasy island in *Il deserto rosso*, coming from nowhere, disappearing into nothingness). The desert has a similar quality to the sea or a river, obvious when Locke is stranded in its emptiness in *The Passenger* and when the screen fills with the sand at Zabriskie Point, making everything disappear into its infinite surface.[9]

Barthes has remarked that Antonioni's interests are always with what is unstable and at the 'interstices' of things, where things quiver and risk losing their identity: the in-between of surface and depth, figure and ground, water and air, inside and out, fullness and emptiness, that moment when things threaten to disappear, to lose shape, and that equally wonderful moment when they come to take shape. Antonioni's fascination with surfaces is primarily a fascination with relations between them, along their extension, and with their power to engulf.

The documentary aspect of Antonioni's films, what Aristarco called, accusingly, his naturalism, has little in fact to do with a naturalism, certainly is not simply a matter of reporting objects found, things only *there*, met by chance, but the addition to these of a look, the work of including within the object the look that constitutes it. The presence of fog, mist, damp, weather as a moving phenomenon of the moment, to be caught as it changes into something else, shifts a value in light, creates a new shadow, is also a working upon objects and a construction of surface and of surface movement. Antonioni doesn't find surfaces but makes them and he does so against the grain of the illusionary depth of the cinema, the fictional interior spaces of

L'ECLISSE *(1962)*
The drunk

drama. Hence the marking of surfaces (graffiti, hoardings, pictures on walls, blotches, holes, grates, grills), the tearing of surfaces (the coming up of the car from the water in *L'eclisse*, Daria putting her hands through the waterfall fountain at the desert house in *Zabriskie Point*, a shaft of light piercing a black, blank darkness), the flattening-out of profundity, the seizing hold of depth in reflections in glass, in mirrors, reflected into other glasses, other mirrors. In the train corridor in *L'avventura* there is neither exactly exterior nor interior, nor substance of any kind; everything becomes absorbed in the windows of the train passing an changing landscape – the landscape, the characters, the compartment, the looks – as Sandro and Claudia seek simultaneously to hold on to each other and to let go, to remember Anna and cause her to disappear. And there is the dazzling sequence in *Zabriskie Point* of Mark driving his pick-up truck and picking up the whole world in its windows and its mirrors.[10]

As Anna walks out of the villa at the beginning of *L'avventura* to say goodbye to her father outside its gates, and as the place of the villa, of interior and exterior, of centre and periphery, shifts, the centrality of Anna also shifts. The background moves forward at a level with Anna herself (it is no longer her ground, or her context, but her equal) while Anna moves slightly back to join up with it. The realignment and confounding of figure and ground to the point of figures becoming lost in a landscape or absorbed in a surface, becoming themselves surface, not a substance, but an effect of light or a metereological consequence, is persistent in all of Antonioni's films, as in his collage-water-colour-photography-enlargement work of *Le montagne incantate* whose fascination is in the movement between lines, figure and ground, surface and depth as an effect of enlargement, and of the change from one medium to another, much like the effect of weather in his films, so that what moves and fascinates in the images is a movement of light and boundaries: 'I am interested,' Antonioni remarked, 'in the dynamics of colour. That's why I like Pollock so much. His paintings have an extraordinary rhythm.'[11]

Like Pollock's paintings, the compositions of many of Antonioni's shots and sequences are without any perspective space or central point of view; it isn't simply that things move, that 'reality' shifts, but the perspectives on it are also shifting or rather there is no single perspective from which things can be seen. This is a narrative as much as it is a visual effect: the equalisation of dramatic and non-dramatic scenes, the presence of a visual or background-landscape fascination coming forward to overwhelm the subject of the narrative, and the mirror images between narrative events, the threat of their becoming the same and losing their difference, dissolving into nothingness (like water, like the sands of the desert), all these figurations and techniques deny to narrative its classical props of centrality, hierarchy, progress and finality. As frames move around figures in a visual field, they move narratively as well, centres of narrative interest become displaced, or diffused and dissolved: Aldo's distress and loss is no more important, of no more interest than the outcome of a boat race, or a change in light and density, or rather it is the fact of the mutual coexistence of these points of interest, separate, only contingently related, that is the source of the fascination of the film, that it wants to interrogate and experiment with, whose possibilities it seeks to explore.

The events in *Il grido* – the break with Irma, Aldo's wanderings from place to place, woman to woman, along the stretch of the Po valley, his return to Goriano, and his death – occur within an autumnal and then wintry landscape, over a period of some months. If the film is filled with events which occur over time, the sense of the film is of a going nowhere, of a wandering in an abstract space to no purpose and where time, though it erodes things and above all Aldo's security and balance, is imperceptible. If space and landscape move forward to flatten and de-dramatise figure and character, time has a similar function: it is not a context for events, a duration which the story accomplishes and creates, but a quality of flux and change on the same level as the characters and the drama, as if by their side.

What Antonioni's time seems to lack is continuity. Often what occurs in his films, as in *Il grido*, is a repetition of things, the coming of the same, as if in the story nothing happens, which is precisely what marks a duration. In a more classical rendering duration is erased by the force of events; in Antonioni, the events, in their repetitiveness, their doubling, their mirroring, and often their emptiness (the event is 'only' a landscape, a reflection, not an event but its shadow) are erased by the force of time, by the imprint of duration.

Perhaps 'event' here is the wrong word. In fact it is not events which are lacking so much as their connectives, the progress and continuity of a story; Antonioni's films are filled with events, but the events are emptied of drama or the attributes of a story. It is precisely by severing connections that events are marked out, not as a pretext or consequence, but, in all their presentness, what Antonioni called 'the fact' against the conventions of narrative, the 'image' against the falsity of the plot.

This arresting of the narrative on behalf of the 'moment', the immediate present, which, in order to stand out, must be stopped from going anywhere, was one of the great achievements of the best films of Italian neo-realism and it was recognised as such by Antonioni. And, in his films, just as object, shape, line, colour, tone become noticeable, make their presence 'felt' because they are freed from their narrative function and subordination to narrative, duration is equally freed. And with it a new absorbing line emerges between space and time. What Antonioni observes is always a movement, a shifting in space and objects in space; but what is being watched is also the duration of that movement, in which something occurs, 'takes place', yet outside the narrative, where, formerly, classically, everything had taken place. Perhaps this is what accounts for the sense that some people have of Antonioni's films: that they are very long and that nothing happens in them.

On *Il deserto rosso*: 'Hardly have they left the shack when the fog becomes the protagonist, the fog that alters the outlines of things, dilutes colours, 'devours' the characters, removes them from sight, or, unexpectedly, brings them into view, and thus distils from them that sense of fragility, of shadowy beings swallowed by their surrounds and which at the same time fills their every gesture, their every expression with ambiguity.'[12]

This is the sense the film gives of the world it creates. It is also the sense of the world which Giuliana has: she regards something and it, and her, and her feelings alter, the colour of the world begins to move, the focus of objects change. But when she creates a fantasy, an unreal world, it is in technicolor with everything clear and precise and sharp: red sands, blue water, a laughing, bronzed, wet young girl, frozen in time.

Notes

1. Guido Aristarco, 'Il lungo coltello', *Cinema Nuovo*, 25 September 1955, and Guido Aristarco, '*Il grido*', *Cinema Nuovo*, 15 October 1957.

2. 'Questions à Antonioni', *Positifsitif* no. 20, July 1959, p. 9; Antonioni: 'rather than there being a documentary influence in my films, it seems to me more correct to speak of the narrative tendency in my documentaries.'

3. Aristarco, '*Il grido*'.

4. Aristarco, 'Il lungo coltello'. See Georges Sadoul 'Le poids de la solitude', *Les Lettres Françaises*, 10 December 1958, p. 6.
    The Sadoul is a review of *Il grido*. Sadoul makes the distinction between a novelistic cinema (in which he places Antonioni) and a dramatic one; the novelistic, for Sadoul, referred to contemporary modern fiction, like the French *nouveau roman*. Sadoul also, correctly, placed Antonioni firmly within a tradition of neo-realism, but one not interested in posing a critique or making a judgement, so much as observing an atmosphere and its effect within characters, the neo-realism of Rossellini; this was a subtlety well beyond Aristarco. Sadoul thought the comparison with Bresson ill-founded; and though Antonioni, in an interview in *Positifsitif*, did mention *Les dames du Bois de Boulogne* as a film which had impressed him, the film-makers that first came to his lips were Eisenstein, Renoir and Welles; he secondarily mentioned Rossellini, but Carné not at all. See 'Questions à Antonioni'.

5. Renzo Renzi, 'I quattro della crisi', *Cinema Nuovo*, 1 December 1957; also his 'Cronache dell'angoscia in Michelangelo Antonioni', *Cinema Nuovo*, May–June 1959.

6. Requoted in Guido Aristarco, 'Cronache di una crisi e forme strutturali dell'anima', *Cinema Nuovo* no. 149, January–February 1961, p. 46.

7. Requoted in Giorgio Tinazzi, *Antonioni* (Il castoro cinema, 1974), p. 29.

8. Michelangelo Antonioni, 'Prefazione', *Sei film* (Turin: Einaudi, 1964), p. xiv.

9. See Michele Mancini and Giuseppe Perrella, *Michelangelo Antonioni: Architetture della visione* (Rome: Coneditor, 1986), pp. 114–115, 117, 282–286.

10. Ibid.

11. Aldo Tassone, 'Michelangelo Antonioni', in A. Tassone, *Parla il cinema italiano*, vol. 1 (Milan: Edizione Il Formichiere, 1979), p. 39.

12. Cesare Biarese e Aldo Tassone, *I film di Michelangelo Antonioni* (Rome: Gremese editore, 1985), p. 127.

Chapter Six

In 1953 Cesare Zavattini, one of the 'fathers' of Italian neo-realism, produced the first of a series of film 'journals' whose stated purpose was to record everyday life and actions, the ordinary dailiness of life: shopping, working, courtship, leisure performed by ordinary people. There were to be no professional actors, nothing at all of the extraordinary or the dramatic except the small dramas of the everyday and the familiar made extraordinary and unfamiliar perhaps by being framed and quoted and represented, as if the ordinary were being seen for the first time. It was an idea that had appealed to the French surrealists and had informed their interest in documentary photography: to represent the distortions, the bizarre, the fantastic, there but unnoticed in daily life and ordinary occurences.

A number of interesting questions and problems were suggested by such a series: the notion of the everyday itself, of the typical, of the dramatic, and the problem of acting and self-representation. Zavattini, in one of the episodes he made for this first 'journal', whose subject was love in the city, chose an actual incident, a *fait divers* of the time, the story of Caterina Rigoglioso who in desperation at having no work, no money and no prospect of work abandoned her illegitimate child Carletto in a park in Rome, not out of lack of care for him, but on the contrary in the hope that he would thus be given care by a stranger or the authorities. Zavattini chose the real Caterina to play herself and to reproduce in exact detail, with the real Carletto, the story of the abandonment: the same words, the same gestures, the same park, the same encounters, the same kind of days and times.

The film 'journal' was called *Lo Spettatore* and this first number of it, *L'amore in città*. In fact, no further numbers appeared. It was to be, for Zavattini, a perfect expression-development of neo-realism: no more fiction, no more false drama, no more false acting. Real persons would act as themselves; their existences would not, as in ordinary films, be assumed fictitiously by another. Rather than only seeming to be true, *Lo Spettatore* would in fact be true: real places, real time, real events, real people. Zavattini:

> It is very clear that for neo-realism even the actor no longer has any rationale, any more than does the fictional subject. Neo-realism – as I understand it – requires that everyone act as themselves. For someone to act in the place of another assumes a preplanned story. Our efforts have been to show things as they are and not to invent fairy tales. . . . Of course

that means that we have to choose themes that automatically exclude professional actors.[1]

Each of the other episodes of *L'amore in città*, each done by a different film-maker and each illustrative of a typical instance of aspects of love in the city, were intended to put into practice Zavattinian realist ideas, and though all in their way did so, not only were they remarkably different in feel and attitude and style, but they seemed to conform more to the various film-makers' other films and concerns than they did to Zavattini's ideas, as the Zavattini 'real life' story of Caterina Rigoglioso seemed to conform more to the forms of fiction of other films that Zavattini had worked on, notably the 'neo-realist' De Sica–Zavattini films such as *Umberto D*, *Ladri di biciclette* and *Miracolo a Milano*, than to life itself.

Caterina abandons her baby out of love for it as Umberto Domenico had abandoned his dog in *Umberto D* . . . to save it; in *Ladri di biciclette* there is a circular round of losses and substitutions and abandonments for the sake of love, as there is in *Miracolo a Milano* and further back to the wartime *I bambini ci guardano*; *La storia di Caterina* not only has this same cycle of substitutions and losses but the same contradictory problems of love and desperation, humanity within the midst of the inhumanity of poverty, starvation, deprivation. What moves the narrative in every case is an almost fairy-tale structure of alternations of lost and found, lack and fulfilment, evil and goodness, hatred and love.

Zavattini's other fictions, which only tried to seem true, seemed more true than his representations of the actual story of Caterina which was 'true'. Caterina's performance as Caterina seemed more a performance, an act, than the performance of the actress who played the maid in *Umberto D*, or the performance of Emma Grammatica in *Miracolo a Milano*. Reality was indeed very strange; certainly less real-seeming than fiction.

The other subjects of this first *Lo Spettatore* number on aspects of love in the city were on the dance hall by Dino Risi, prostitution by Carlo Lizzani, the marriage bureau by Federico Fellini ('Can you find a wife for my friend who has fits and believes he is a werewolf?' 'Not a problem.'), ogling by Alberto Lattuada, and attempted suicide, called *Tentato suicidio*, by Michelangelo Antonioni and which is about 20 minutes long.

There is hardly an Antonioni film in which death is not a central concern; and there are many in which attempted or successful suicides are involved (*La signora senza camelie*, *Le amiche*, *Il deserto rosso*), or a suicide-like ambiguous pursuit of death and self-destruction (*Il grido*, *L'avventura*, *Zabriskie Point*, *The Passenger*, *Il mistero di Oberwald*). Suicide, which is a kind of imagining of yourself as no longer and an acting out of your own obliteration, is an imagining both of death and of yourself as an other; it is a situation in which identity is uncertain, the line between being subject and object quivers, and all meanings and their location are made ambiguous. *Tentato suicidio*, like *I vinti*, seems to have from a narrative perspective an 'impossible' subject. But all of Antonioni's films share this impossible, fleeting, almost from the onset, elusive lost subject: from the very first feature *Cronaca di un amore*, where Guido and Paolo imagine their lives as other by imagining the death of others, through *L'avventura*, *La notte*, *L'eclisse*, narratives in pursuit of bodies, identities, feelings which remain always unattainable, unpossessable, to *Identificazione di una donna*, in which problems of self, otherness, and the images of these are posed for the characters in the film and for the audience watching them. And this double dimension is also true in *Tentato suicidio* where identity, self-definition, the finding of a subject are problems for the 'actors' and for the spectators.

These Antonioni 'themes' always involve questions of acting and self-representation which are in part questions directly posed by the Zavattini *Lo Spettatore* project concerned with a reality beyond the falsity of performance, with true representation, with the elimination of falsity:

> Someone starving, someone down-and-out has to be seen as himself, with his own proper name, and not represented in some tale as someone starving because that is an entirely different thing, less effective, and less moral . . . characters need to be taken from life, the very same person needs to be chosen to tell the story that he in fact had lived: they and not the script must tell their story.[2]

Beside the Zavattini episode, it is those by Fellini and Antonioni that most directly treat the matter of falsity and performance. Whereas Zavattini confronts the notion of the false and the acted by proposing in their stead the self-evident nature of the real, the other two film-makers are less convinced, and more interesting. Fellini begins his episode on the pretext of a lie (the werewolf story) around which everyone else manufactures further falsities of feelings and intentions: the director of the marriage bureau, the girl willing to marry the werewolf, and the boy who first peddles the story and then, simultaneously, has to maintain it and wriggle out of it when faced with the apparent sweetness and 'sincerity' of the willing girl.

The Antonioni episode is extremely interesting: in relation to Antonioni's other films – the concerns with death, suicide, identity, obliteration – and specifically in relation to the Zavattini and hence to the practices and ideas of Italian neo-realism, in this case, centring on matters of acting, the true, the genuine.

The film places itself within a world in which truth is hard to find not only

LE AMICHE
Rosetta's suicide

because, as Antonioni notes, 'Suicide is so enigmatic a gesture . . .', or as the narrator of the film asserts, 'We always have such a sense of horror when faced with a suicide because to confront death so deliberately is always a mysterious thing and which has about it something of the absurd' – that is, not only because the motives and meaning of the act can't be fully known, but because these are not suicides, but attempts at suicide and thus have about them a quality of being false acts, feigned deaths, mere performances. There are four attempted suicides in the film. The last, Donatella, expresses the wish to be an actress. The narrator wonders whether this too (as well as the attempted suicide) may not be a pose.

André Bazin was enthusiastic about the Antonioni episode. Antonioni seemed able, in the impassivity and apparent objectivity of his approach, to make the real characters 'act' and to observe them, by virtue of the force of their desires, turning their reality into fictions. Bazin was not enthusiastic about the Zavattini episode which he found absurd. Zavattini attempted to ensure reality by reduplicating it in the reality of the actual Caterina, thereby losing the drama of the real, causing it to lose its fiction in the chimerical pursuit of a lost reality;

the effect of the Zavattini was that it was false; by allowing for the false, the effect of the Antonioni was that of truth . . . a truth defined by uncertainty, in ambiguity.[3]

There are a number of feigned suicides in Antonioni's films: Gianni takes an overdose in *La signora senza camelie* but not enough to kill him; Rosetta tries out suicide at the beginning of *Le amiche* then finally accomplishes it at the end; Locke's change of identity with the dead Robertson in *The Passenger* is a way of killing yourself, but remaining alive. In *L'avventura*, Anna's disappearance on Lisca Bianca might have been a feigned suicide like the shark attack she invented earlier when out swimming. In fact we never know exactly what happened. Giuliana makes two attempts at suicide in *Il deserto rosso* which though not faked are not successful either: one is at a time before the film begins, but which weighs upon the film and on her, almost without relief; the other is at the close of the sequence at Max's cabin when she drives to the end of the jetty stopping just short of going over it into the sea.

Even if the attempted suicides in *Tentato suicidio* were not feigned, but rather coincidental failures (the car against which one hurled oneself stopped; someone fished you unconscious from the water; the nurse caught you as you were about to throw yourself from the window), there is the other possible or extra dimension of an imaginary death in the desire of these attempted/failed suicides to tell their stories. To attempt a suicide is already to imagine and stage your death, to act it out (Locke in *The Passenger*, but, in part, also Mark flying to an appointment with death as a presumed other, the killer of a policeman, in *Zabriskie Point*); relating the suicide turns the action into a pretext for a story, a self-representation imagining yourself as other and imagining yourself as no longer existing. To imagine your own disappearance, as perhaps Anna does in *L'avventura* and certainly Rosetta does in *Le amiche*, adds to the actual attempt at suicide another perspective and another fictional dimension.

Guido Aristarco didn't like Antonioni's episode; he found it over-academic, intellectualist, formalist, what he called *elzeverismo* referring to the traditional high-culture page in the Italian newspapers.[4] Antonioni responded speaking of the seriousness of his concerns for the issue of suicide, the moral and psychological plight of the victims, and so on. On the other hand, Antonioni wondered at the need that some of the figures in the film had to make him believe that they truly wanted to die, had indeed tried to kill themselves, and would, in similar circumstances, try again: 'I'm convinced it isn't true. I am sure they were lying, that they were exaggerating for who knows what reason of vanity, or masochism.'[5]

At the heart of the real, the problem of acting, performance, credibility, fiction – aspects Zavattini seemed to assume would no longer be a problem and would disappear along with fictitious impersonations, fabled stories, contrived plots – made their entry. Rather than the substance of the real being the actual subject of the story as it is in the Zavattini episode, the subject in *Tentato suicidio* becomes the problem of the story itself, the uncertainty of what is true, not the substance so much as its representation, by those who lived that story and those, like Antonioni, who document it. Though none of this is made explicit – the film is exceptionally, elegantly understated, quiet in its intentions, restrained and modest in its approach – it was this aspect of it, rather than an easy assumption of the real, that seemed to merit Aristarco's criticism: that the film had not taken its model from reality but, inappropriately, from forms of modern fiction.

Aristarco had a notion of cinema as something specifically designed to capture an external reality; the great contribution of neo-realism, for him, was that it found its forms from the world rather than on the basis of other representations. Antonioni never accepted this difference. The question was raised regarding his use of a Pavese short novel, *Tra donne sole*, as the pretext for *Le amiche*, to which he responded:

> The novel is only a point of departure. I can't see any difference between a literary or theatrical text and an everyday event, between an idea a friend suggests and episode which you happen to witness or an idea that comes into your head. The work of re-elaboration is identical in every case. It may not seem right to you, but if you think about you will see that things are that way. It is a question, in every case, of reducing the idea or the fact to its essentials and then re-expressing them with means that have nothing to do with them originally. In the case of Pavese the reduction of the text presented enormous difficulties and sometimes the text directly got in the way.[6]

What was at stake between Zavattinian realism and the approach by Antonioni (Antonioni obeyed the Zavattini rules that there were to be no professional actors and those who experienced the events would relate them and act them out) was not popular reality as against modernist fiction but rather alternative forms of fiction. It might be argued on political grounds that one was preferable to the other (populist, closer to the people, simpler); but for Antonioni politics was involved in the unreality of realist popular forms, quite simply in that the idea of a direct unmediated representation of reality by means of the real (real stories, real people) always foundered on the reappearance within that reality of fictional forms, which in part provides the subject and the fascination of *Tentato suicidio*, along with, of course, the 'real' substance of the tragedy of these lives and the feigned or genuine attempts to end them: 'I tried to arouse in the audience a revulsion towards suicide by depicting the spiritual squalor of the characters. I was directly concerned with content, with the substance of the theme. Thus, I don't accept the criticism of "pretentiousness" [*elzeverismo*].[7]

Tentato suicidio begins not in the street, in the midst of life, as do the other episodes of *L'amore in città*, but in a film studio, in a place of artifice and construction. At first there is only a huge blank white screen strongly lit and shot at a sharp, distorting angle. About a dozen or more men and women dressed in heavy coats slowly file into the studio before the white screen. They pause and take up fixed, unmoving positions in silence. No one speaks. All are in shadow, like shades or silhouettes of themselves, as if without substance.

The scene recalls other scenes in later films by Antonioni, as well as instances from past films. One early film certainly: Antonioni's description of the documentary he never shot on mad people before the war: the bright lights, the lack of relation by the 'characters' to each other or to the background, the curious sense of disembodiment of the figures, action as a provocation by the camera, and a scene which is simultaneously artificial and horribly real; or the static, unnatural presence of the mad people encountered by Rosina on a Po-valley plain in *Il grido* and who try to touch her; and the student mimes from *Blow-Up*. The design of the setting of the scene of the suicides in *Tentato suicidio* placed before the backdrop of the white screen recalls early De Chirico paintings: the displacement of the physical by the metaphysical, the unreal perspectives, the depiction of figures in two dimensions, flat along the picture plane, featureless, in silhouette.

In 1948 Antonioni made a beautiful documentary short on the streetcleaners and garbage collecters of Rome: *N.U. – Nettezza urbana*. One of the fascinations of the film is the sense of unreality, almost non-existence of the streetcleaners. The cleaners have no presence for the passers-by in the streets. No one looks at them. No one talks to them. They silently sweep the street, empty dustbins in bare dawn landscapes as if they are more objects than persons, inanimate shades. People pass them by and argue, exchange confidences, toss out garbage, throw down papers, tear up letters as they stand beside the cleaners taking no more notice of them than they would of a bin or a lamp post.

There are scenes of a sweeper looking at his own reflection in a shop window before which he pauses. The reflection looks back at him; both are cut through by another movement and other figures as if sweeper and reflection were not there.

There is in this film, and certainly in the film studio opening to *Tentato suicidio*, a series of doublings: substance with shadow, person with character, the real with the artificial, reality with its image. The process of doubling has no starting point: it is not first the reality, then the image of it, first the substance, then the silhouette, but rather the tenousness of both, their intermingling, the fragility of the line marking them, the constant threat of obliteration and dissolution; it makes judgements on actions or the assigning of responsibilities difficult. Subject and object waver, their very existences at stake.

N.U. begins with a figure appearing out of dawn and ends with a figure disappearing into the dusk; in *Gente del Po* figures merge then disappear into the landscape, erased, as in *Il grido* or *Il deserto rosso*, by mist and fogs, or, as in the final shot of *Blow-Up*, by a trick of editing.

In 1940–41, Antonioni was enrolled for a short time in the directing course at the Centro Sperimentale di Cinematografia. He made his first film after only a few months:

> A respectable woman meets up with a shady woman who is blackmailing her with some letters she has managed to get hold of. The respectable woman gives the other one some money and in return receives the letters. The camera follows the woman as she approaches the blackmailer. You soon see that the respectable woman and the blackmailer are being played by the same actress. Nevertheless the movement of the camera is continuous. It is all done in a single shot. No one was able to figure out how I was able to do it. In fact, there is a break, but it is absolutely undetectable.[8]

The Zavattinian project to fix reality and assert its primacy comes adrift at the very beginning of *Tentato suicidio*: the image of reality overtakes reality itself; persons become shadows of themselves, dead, silent, aspects of a composition, then actors of themselves, as they, and the film, seek to grasp a reality through images and stories which end by further estranging them from themselves, which add to the mystery of their gestures, their actions and their motives, the mysteriousness and ambiguity of images. Antonioni: 'The very same things provoked different reactions, suggested different things. Looking at them in a new way, they took possession of me. Trying to understand the world through images, I began to understand images, their force, their mystery.'[9]

The various episodes of *L'amore in città* not only begin within a 'reality', rather than mark out a place from which to view it or even construct it, as Antonioni does in the film studio in *Tentato suicidio*; but they remain in that location, which, if it was a question of traditional fiction, would be the space and time of the fiction itself. Antonioni, to the contrary, marks out not only alternative locations for the 'story', but multiplies the places from which they are told and the narrative voices which relate and depict them. These places and devices assume an interest equal to that of the story itself, or, more exactly, are equally stories, not of a 'told', but of a process of 'telling'. For example, Rosanna, in the first story, tells her story from different positions and in different modes: as voice over to a series of images in which she is the subject, but equally as a direct verbal narrator, standing against a white screen, face on the camera, being questioned by the film's narrator. She is both subject and object of her own story and in decidedly distinct ways. In one instance she acts out her story. The marks of it as 'story', as 'depiction', in a present of a past, are very evident; even this is varied: the 'story' is sometimes hers as narrator, and sometimes it is taken over by the narrator of the film. There is not one but two voice-overs for the image, a double description and a differential status to the 'objective'.

In Zavattini's *Storia di Caterina*, once you enter the past world of Caterina Rigoglioso, duplicated in every detail, the present ceases to matter, or rather the past absorbs it. The only time is the time of the 'story', a reality whose stability depends on the fiction of it not being narrated, the Zavattini notion of no-more story, no-more actors, no-more illusions, i.e. the fiction of truth. When Rosanna speaks as a subject telling her story in *Tentato suicidio*, that activity of telling is itself filmed. She becomes the object of the gaze of the camera. In it her gestures often belie, certainly counterpoint, her words. It is not solely the story which is of interest, nor exactly the telling of it, but how they relate and how and in what manner the camera relates these 'facts' of telling.

The question involved in this suicide attempt and in all the others concerns the 'truth' of the gesture: did they really risk their lives? what is the motive for retelling the story? is the story true or invented? are they acting or genuine? if they are acting, inventing, lying, posing, why are they doing so? what status can one give to their images, either verbal or visual?

Sincerity is undercut by the acting out of sincerity, the wanting to seem true. At this point the subject divides: true/seeming to be true, real/feigned, and in such a way as to make any unified subject impossible, since nowhere, amongst no one, can a truth be stabilised, or a motive secured. It is exactly the situation with the attempted (feigned?) suicides: 'At the hospital the doctors knew that it was a faked suicide; she herself later explained that she only wanted to attract her husband's attention, make him return home.'[10]

There is hardly a single film of Antonioni's which does not involve, or is not primarily structured around an investigation, but an investigation which inevitably loses its way, becomes diverted, displaced; interest in it dissolves: Sandro and Claudia gradually, imperceptibly forget their search of Anna in *L'avventura*; Niccolò, in *Identificazione di una donna*, in pursuit of a subject for a film, or of a woman, or of her image, loses the track of these and their outlines; Thomas in search of a murderer in *Blow-Up* (or is it a body, or a woman, or his own surety, or his own identity?) hesitates between subjects and quests until the very reason for them disappears. There are variations on the investigation; instead of a search for something which is then lost, there is a search for nothing in particular, only something to be found, a fascination, or a feeling which is what is often at stake when characters seem to move through the world, almost aimlessly, wandering without purpose, except perhaps to discover one, which is true of nearly all of Antonioni's main characters, Lidia in *La notte* finding she has lost a love, Vittoria in *L'eclisse* finding the freedom of purposelessness as an opportunity to allow new things to appear, new objects and attentions to take place.

But it is a mark as well of the films, which, like the characters in them, encounter the world as it appears, find and lose interests, define subjects and end only to have these change and escape it; if the characters are in search of their identity, of lost loves, of desires, the films seem to be in search of their very subjects. In *Tentato suicidio* each of the suicides is in search of a self which eludes them whom they ceaselessly represent and try to possess, but who never quite gel with any clarity; and the film follows that search, but equally without success and often, as in all of Antonioni's films, finds itself in the course of the investigation, de-centred, with a new subject it hadn't initially sought (an image rather than a reason, the fascination of a gesture not the security of an explanation), discovering the edges moving to the centre, and the centre itself not holding.

In *L'eclisse* the subject of the film is always just out of reach; when you arrive at it, either it becomes something else, or rather than being what you sought, only creates another thing to find.

L'eclisse was made in 1962. It is part of a loose trilogy which includes *L'avventura* (1959) and *La notte* (1960) and which are perhaps Antonioni's best known films and on which much of his reputation was first established. Of the three films it has the thinnest story, but is the richest and most compelling to watch, as if the reduction and abstraction of events, their near obliteration, gives a space for other things to be observed and to happen: the stars, cloud formations, Verona from the air, the sounds of the night, a meeting place where no one meets, the meandering of the white line on a roadway, a car being pulled from the water, a casual look, the activities of the stock exchange. All of these events, contrary to the more usual place of events in films, are not central to any drama nor do they even have the usual sense of 'event'; they are fleeting, momentary, casual, 'insignificant', and their consequence, if any, for the heroine or her 'drama', is indirect and indefinable. They are at once imponderable and weightless, light.

The film begins with the banality of a break-up of a relation at dawn after a night of presumably fruitless, tiresome exchanges: Vittoria is ending her affair with Riccardo because it no longer works, no longer makes her happy, but there are no precise reasons for this loss of love, or none that she knows of. Vittoria wanders through Rome, encounters some friends, talks of Kenya, recovers a lost poodle, finds her mother at the stock exchange, casually meets a stockbroker, Piero. They play with each other, wander together, have a brief affair, and towards the close of the film make an appointment at which only the camera shows up to record their absence and, as a result of their not being there, the presence of other things: the coming of the evening, a bus, the headlines of a newspaper, a woman with a pram, a trotting horse being exercised, a drum with water slowly leaking from a hole, a lawn sprinkler pulsating, a building under construction, the sound of the wind and the sight of it shaking spring acacia blooms. In this absence the film ends.

What is lost in the ending is the customary fullness of narrative, the 'central' subject in the usual sense: the heroine, the lover, the love and the appointment which signifies it; what is found is the emptiness of that narrative within which there succeeds a train of seeming non-subjects, decentred objects, events

L'ECLISSE *The break-up*
Monica Vitti at the window

without a significance except that of the possibility ensured by the emptiness; had Piero and Vittoria met, these other objects and images would never have existed, or at least would not be seen, would instead be pushed to the edges of the narrative; the loss of the subject is less a loss than an opportunity.

The film moves by means of an assumption and discarding of subjects, of filling and emptying; at each moment what appears is either not what it seems, or ceases to be what it had promised: in the opening scene of languor, tiredness and separation in Riccardo's flat, a cloth, faintly moving, turns into an arm, then into the face of a man whose fixed gaze the camera follows . . . to nowhere. Neither the man nor the look centres anything or constitutes a subject. Between him and Vittoria there is no reciprocity of looking. The camera plays with objects in frames, pictures beside pictures, flattens depth, surprises looks in mirrors, wanders through the room finding images which are variously imponderable, decentred, displaced, upsetting notions of centre, of subject, or object; what fascinates is the movement, the oscillations, the changes all of which presuppose a refusal to fix anything in the narrative, or in the image, quite against the usual practices and satisfactions of a cinema aimed at fullness and centre.[11]

Antonioni's 1940–41 student documentary in which two separate characters in the narrative (the good woman and the bad woman) are one in the narration (they are played by the same actress) is re-echoed in *Tentato suicidio* not only for the multiplication of narrative voices and the differential modes by which the subject appears, but very concretely in images. (Like the startling shot in *The Passenger* when Locke puts his face directly up against the face of the dead Robertson, almost as if he is inquiring into it, and the two separate identities of alive and dead, Locke and Robertson, for an instant merge; and another scene in *Il deserto rosso* when Valerio asks his mother how much one plus one makes and reveals that the answer is 'one' as he places a drop of coloured liquid on a glass slide then places another drop of liquid over the first drop and the two merge into a single blot: it is a terrible scene from Giuliana's perspective; it further dissolves her very tenuous grasp on herself and on the world, and separates her from a love and connection to her little son).

In the last attempted suicide of *Tentato*, Donatella, the one who wants a career as an actress, is standing in her room, looking out of her window. Here, directly, is a re-enactment of the past. The narrator in the present describes her state of mind . . . in the past: 'Desperate, she shuts herself in her room and with an unconscious calm . . .' The camera depicts her going to her bed, and sitting down on it, then, abruptly, looking at herself in the wardrobe mirror, staring at her own face. She sits down once more, takes a razor blade from the bedside table, cleans it carefully (!), lies down on the bed, and then very slowly draws the blade across her wrist. This act is feigned – it is a re-enactment, a doubling, in fact a representation – and what we see is not her blood, but her scar. Here Donatella from the past meets Donatella in the present, Donatella the object of her own story confronting Donatella who relates it as a speaking subject: 'I cut as deeply as I could. Then I stayed here a half an hour, an hour, I don't remember . . . I dirtied everything. Then I put on a pair of trousers, a blouse and went out to find a chemist. But on the street I met two policemen who took me to hospital. I was given seven stitches.'

The meeting of yourself in the retelling of your story and the finding of yourself in a difference which is temporal and sentimental goes through each of the suicides. Not a single suicide is represented: we see the car and we see Rosanna but not the two colliding; in the case of Lena we see nothing at all; for Lilia, her suicide is re-enacted in her physical absence, from her perspective, but without her, the camera seeking to imagine her actions as she speaks. Lilia had tried to kill herself by drowning, walking into the Tiber, very slowly from its bank. Lilia remembers the tide taking her and the camera, as if following an imaginary body seized by the current (but from whose point of view?), moves towards the centre of the river, further and further out, towards a pier of the arch of a bridge across the Tiber, where the current is at its most turbulent. Was this how it happened? Is this Lilia seeing herself? telling a story? imagining?

On a rather different register, in part because it is stated and explicit (though the sense is not at all obvious), the present re-enactment of the past 'drama' of the suicides effectively dilutes and dedramatises that past if for no other reason than that of an altered perspective.

Each of the suicides in the present, in the position of telling their story, are relatively content with their lives. Donatella looks forward to a career; Rosanna broke up with her boyfriend, realised he was too egotistical, not for her; Lena too has adjusted, as has Lilia, and are intent on reconstructing their lives. The instability of love, which had apparently brought them to the edge of self-destruction, equally brought them away from that edge: their feelings changed. There was not one Donatella but two, not one set of feelings, but another. What had condemned them to attempt suicide was a fear of instability; what had saved them was that instability itself.

Why had these women come to tell their stories? The film offers a number of reasons: vanity, an insistence on their need to die, their own curiousity, exhibitionism. But . . .

They also came because they were aware that this moment of sincerity might be useful for them and for others to take a look at an action which is truly the only irremediable action anyone can take. Of one thing one can be sure . . . Many times, when the motive is that of love, it is a matter of a passing crisis. If the person wanting to suicide is able to overcome it, nothing is apparently easier than finding once again an appetite for living.

Tentato suicidio returns to itself and to its own beginning: the figures who had been only silhouettes and became characters, turn back into silhouettes against the white screen seen in the same distorted perspective at the opening of the film. Very slowly, as they had come, they file out until only the blank screen is left. The film meets up with itself, encounters its own narrative, its own past, which dissolves into the emptiness and abstraction of the white screen.

Antonioni always exhibits a certain restlessness with story and the narration of events, a kind of impatience with it, so that attention can often become errant, absorbed elsewhere as if, though still 'with' the narrative, he is also in search of something else. It might appear almost unseemly in the case of *Tentato suicidio*, with these poor young girls, somewhat threadbare, pathetic, not to be always listening, or to create, in the midst of their pathos, another taste and sensibility quite at odds with theirs and their stories. Not only does it happen, and not only does it further displace the narrative, dilute it, dedramatise it, decentre it, but these moments, in a way moments of distraction, are some of the most beautiful moments of the film, and, like the close of the film (though equally, of course, like the close of so many of Antonioni's films), are moments of abstraction, an emptying of meaning and narration, a silence and an obliteration.

When the camera imagines Lilia's attempt at drowning on the Tiber and moves out towards the centre of the river and then to the swirling of the waters around the bridge-pier, for an instant it seems as if it has lost its subject in a fascinated contemplation of the water itself, the shifting movability of it, its surface always closing upon itself, never being torn, as it would have closed upon Lilia had her attempt succeeded. When Lena answers the narrator's questions as she stands by an open window, looking out on a desolate urban landscape and inside opening on to the desolation of her home, the broken down, handed down furniture, the cots for beds for the two children, one of the children whining, a scene narratively speaking of squalor and sadness, it is none of this that makes its impress, but rather the window as a frame, the beauty of the light, the contrasts with the shadows in the interior, a metaphysical, insubstantial, unreal aspect to objects and things.

The silence and obliteration which adhere to Antonioni's moments of abstraction are like moments of death, beckoning with a beauty which simultaneously offers up an absolute of emptiness and of freedom, as when

Aldo falls from the tower or Locke, unseen, meets his death in the instant of a camera movement, or Mark joyously flies to die in his painted bird in the fictitious place of another, in an image, in the emptiness of the imagined place of the other.

If the women who attempted suicide in *Tentato suicidio* are not completely sincere in the sense that they acted, feigned a suicide and then represented that feint as genuine, acting it out, posing for a second time, it may be wondered where these representations and self-representations had their source. Where might these stories of disappointed love, abandonment, amorous betrayal, existential *angst* have originated? The stories present themselves as true and yet one has heard and seen them all before as if these women, 'real' women but nevertheless consummate actors, were not so much conforming to their own 'truths', their own specific stories, than conforming to images and stories of the way life might be. The result is that what is read is not the particularity of these lives, not even any longer characters, still less 'real' people, but the generalities of 'abandonment', 'betrayed wife', 'the lost generation'. Very subtly, the substance of these women becomes dissolved, lost to a world of images into which they irrevocably enter. The result is the exact reverse of the Zavattinian impulse: not the substance of reality, but its imprint.

It recalls Clara Manni from *La signora senza camelie*, made in the same year as *Tentato suicidio*. Manni gradually loses herself as she grows more like her images on the screen until that final image of her as melodramatic 'tragic' heroine, utterly sincere in her distress, and yet a sincerity in conformity with an image of sincerity; at her most desperate – she has resigned herself to a tawdry affair with Nardo, Gianni has refused her a part in a film of taste and sensibility, she has accepted the role of a sex queen in a crude costume spectacle, all her ideals and hopes unrealised and broken – her only way of expressing it is as an actress, in a cheap image of desperation, in a simulacrum of despair, to an audience of photographers taking her picture.

The 'characters' of *Tentato suicidio* emerge out of their own shadows, their silhouettes projected on the white screen in the studio at the beginning of the film to which they return at its close. They take shape, a story takes shape, meanings emerge, and then, in the end, dissolve.

There are moments in the film in which the sense of the stories and the squalor of the characters become peripheral to a visual design, to movement, to a graphic pattern, most strong perhaps in the Lilia sequence, the woman who attempted to kill herself by drowning. But such design and visual stress is perhaps most strong at the opening and close of the film when persons are no more than patterns, visual objects and not narrative subjects, when background is nothing more than the blank of a white screen (not a house, or a district, or a street, or a river) and though there are forms and movement, there are no significances put forward, no meanings posed.

What happens to Clara Manni in *La signora senza camelie*, and to these women of *Tentato suicidio*, of losing their persons first to a character and then to an image, of being progressively reduced to a picture just at that moment when they seem to be fully emerging within a story, is characteristic of all of Antonioni's narrative films, from the first, *Cronaca di un amore*, in which the detective is in search of an image he constructs of Paola and Guido, and they in seeking to escape that creation, fall back into it, to the last, *Identificazione di una donna*, in which Ida and Mavi are sought for to conform to the image of Louise Brooks pinned to Niccolò's wall, an image into which they dissolve, and also an image which itself dissolves into the masses of black and white which compose it.

It is 'like' what happens in *Blow-Up*. At the point at which the enlargement seems to be about to deliver up the sight of an unseen crime from the nothingness of dots and shadows, the design disintegrates back to the emptiness from which it had come to leave only the fascination and pleasure of the design itself.

The women in *Tentato suicidio* wear more than one set of clothes. There are the clothes they have on in the present from which they relate their past, and clothes they wear within the images made of them from the past. Lena is seen in the costume of 'Baby Sister' doing a caricature exotic-sexual dance in a grass skirt and Donatella, half undressed in her bedroom, while relating the story of her wrist-slashing, includes details of putting on a skirt, a blouse and going out to the chemist after having cut her wrists.

The clothes in part have a temporal, chronological function. They mark out a past and a present, the present of narration, the flashback of the narrated. In part they indicate character and class and environment. The clothes also have a certain symbolic value, for example the soft greys Rosanna wears sitting on the bench, pregnant, abandoned by her boyfriend, and the dark, heavy colours and textures of her clothes as she relates those events, indicative of a change in mood, a shift in sentiments. It is not unlike the division between the morning clothes Lidia wears in *La notte* and the black evening dress she puts on for the party divided by the scene of her bathing when her husband, Giovanni, hands her a towel apparently oblivious to her body and her nakedness.

None of this may seem remarkable. It is a standard narrative device for defining character, marking time, indicating atmosphere, signifying change. But in *La notte*, for example, Lidia and Valentina are wearing the same dress as if there was a different time to fashion than to feelings or character, and

ZABRISKIE POINT
Mark and Daria in Death Valley

also as if the women were interchangeable, as they are that night for Giovanni.
As dress comes away from person, so the attachment of person to body
becomes less: dress takes on a life of its own as texture, fold, colour, shine,
pattern, surface, geometry, tone, and it does so in relation to a body; the white
of Lidia's neck and shoulders, the softness of her skin, its hollows and
undulations are enhanced and worked on and made noticeable in the black
dress, which later, in complicity with Valentina, she takes off, to reveal both
a new Lidia and new patterning by the light in the room iridescent on her
underwear, her wet hair, the dampness of her skin, the towelling of it.

However much it may be a cause for regret within the terms of a narrative
that the suicides lose their persons to the clichés of romantic images, that Clara
Manni is lost to the melodrama of her own acting and that in these, what was
once called, in a quiver of advanced philosophy, 'alienations' of the person,
a real tragedy was being expressed, nevertheless the dissolution of the 'real'
into images enables an experimentation with the consequences of that
dissolution, an experimentation and joy with images themselves: hence that
movement towards abstraction in Antonioni's films in which dress often figures
prominently as artifice, materials and design which form images and illusions
of bodies (say within a world of fashion which has always fascinated

Antonioni), and as pure visual play. It is a play, however, which at any level
it is viewed always involves that line between pattern and substance, design
and meaning, landscape (ground) and story, a line ever renewed and cross-cut
in his films, and remarkably lucid and contained in the modest dimensions of
Tentato suicidio.

There is a temptation to continue almost endlessly with examples, for fear
that, without them, some of the forms I have suggested which contain them
might appear as self-sufficient or exhaustive, that the particulars might only
serve further to confirm the generality. It is precisely because this is not the
case that I want to multiply examples to prevent a reductiveness into possible
formula, or worse an explanation pretending to be comprehensive: all those
instances of fashion, of dressing, undressing, of the assumption of clothes of
another, Locke for Robertson, Claudia for Anna, Daria for Mark (the red shirt),
Sebastian for the King, the original for the model (*Cronaca di un amore*),
clothes without persons (for persons who have died, like Rosetta's abandoned
coat on the embankment where she commits suicide in *Le amiche*, or as in
Rosina's story to the old man in *Il grido* of the animated shirt, the shirt made
live), and persons without clothes, stripping bare, half nakednesses (Thomas
and Jane in the studio in *Blow-Up*), the performance of clothes, cross-dressing,
wigs, hair tied up, hair let down.
    I want to cite, almost without comment, three instances from Antonioni's
films.

Lucia Bosè was Miss Italia about the time that she took the lead as Paola in
Cronaca di un amore. The film has many sequences involving clothes, fashion
parades, the buying of clothes, undressing, being fashionable, from the very
first stunning image of Paola in white evening furs before the theatre, and a
shabby Guido regarding her from across the square. Bosè had made an
advertisement, circulated in national magazines, for Luxardo, for a raincoat.
The feel and sense of the image of her was of naturalness, freedom, looseness,
genuineness. This is exactly the reverse of her image in *Cronaca di un amore.*
In her first face to face encounter with Guido at the football ground she is
wearing a high fashion coat which he remarks on and which emphasises all
her artifice, all her work at seduction, at making a desirable image of herself,
for him, down and out, starved of elegance. It brings out the artifice in the
pose of naturalness behind the publicity photograph of her for the raincoat.[12]

There is a startling shift or rather transfer of identities in *L'avventura* between
Anna and Claudia which is marked in part by a transfer of clothes: Claudia
wearing the blouse of Anna who gives it to her as if offering not only a blouse
but her very body. It is that body, in a further transfer of bodies, the lost body

ZABRISKIE POINT
The lovers multiply

of Anna, the substituted-for-it body of Claudia (and also the body of the high-priced whore, exhibiting a tear in her clothes, a fetish, the hidden, revealed, who for a night becomes Claudia – or Anna?), that is at the centre of this film of lost identities and the dissolution of sentiments.

There is a lovely moment on Lisca Bianca when the lost Anna is being sought among its rocks and cliffs, with Claudia, in the dark blouse of Anna, standing very still against the rocks. In that moment there is a double confounding of identities: of Claudia with Anna, but also of Claudia with the rocks, of Claudia becoming that landscape, an inanimate object, not a figure in the landscape or against it, but one of its constitutents. Claudia is productive of a whole new set of relations here in the generation by her body and her clothes of shadows, of tensions, of outcroppings, of details. What 'happens' in that moment, the 'events' of the film, are the events of that light which pass along her body, of the outline of different masses, of the tonal varieties of black and white. Claudia, displacing Anna, is in turn displaced.

The third instance is from *Zabriskie Point* and it occurs at the point where nothing is alive, miles of sandy desert. Mark and Daria begin to make love, and as they shed their clothes, and turn around and over each other, in a dance of love, they merge with the landscape, become part of that point. At the same time, as they lose their person, their character, their features, as they become undifferentiated from their background and indeed from each other, as only bodies, not Mark nor Daria, not male nor female, other bodies, other images of bodies begin to dance and make love in imitation of theirs until, in this multiplicity and serialisation of their image, they become lost again, in a movement which can't be stilled and whose terms are that of joy and death, animation and objectification. The figures become in their dance of love like the desert, like its sand, chalky white, as if ghosts. But that figuration, like the bodies themselves, equally wavers and moves towards a new pleasure in the abstractions of geometry, and light, of line and arabesques, of textures and surface.

At the moment when the image is most narratively empty and seems to revert to a purity of abstract form, at that moment it becomes most visually full. It is as if the dead, the void have come alive.

Notes

1. The statement by Zavattini is from 1952; it is requoted in a review by Giulio Cesare Castello, '*L'amore in città*, *Cinema*, 15 December 1953, p. 339.

2. Requoted in Guido Aristarco, '*L'amore in città*, *Cinema Nuovo*, 15 January 1954, p. 27.

3. See André Bazin, 'Le neo-réalisme se retourne', *Cahiers du Cinéma* no. 69, March 1957, pp. 45–46.

4. Aristarco, p. 27.

5. Michelangelo Antonioni, 'Suicidi in città', *Cinema Nuovo*, 15 March 1954: the article is in the form of a letter/reply to Aristarco.

6. Requoted in Cecilia Mangini, 'Diventano amiche le donne sole di Pavese', *Cinema Nuovo*, 10 June 1955.

7. Antonioni, 'Suicidi'.

8. In Aldo Bernardini, *Michelangelo Antonioni da Gente del Po a Blow up a Blow up* (Milan: I Setti editore, 1967) p. 27; requoted in Carlo Di Carlo 'Vedere in modo nuovo' in Michelangelo Antonioni, *Il primo Antonioni* (ed. Carlo Di Carlo) (Bologna: Cappelli, 1973), p. 12.

9. Michelangelo Antonioni, 'Prefazione', *Sei film* (Turin: Einaudi, 1964) p. xvi.

10. Antonioni, 'Suicidi'.

11. See the analysis of *L'eclisse* by Jean-François Tarnowski, 'Identification d'un œuvre: Antonioni et la modernité cinématographique', *Positif/sitif* no. 263, January 1983, pp. 46–54.

12. Michele Mancini and Giuseppe Perrella, *Michelangelo Antonioni: Architetture della visione* (Rome: Coneditor, 1986), p. 374; but see, more generally, the discussion of clothes and fashion on pp. 359ff.

Chapter Seven

As The Girl (Maria Schneider) in *The Passenger* looks back, from the rear of the convertible, on the road she and Locke/Robertson are travelling, her arms spread out, like a bird, enveloped in the frame of the shot by the full-leaved trees by the roadside, the effect of the movement forward of the car and the sensation of the backward movement of the trees and landscape flatten both figure and ground, as if the girl were being projected onto the screen of the landscape, the figure turning into ground, being dissolved by it, fullness and depth becoming surface, substance and figuration turning into an image.[1]

One impulse of neo-realism had been to close a gap between language and reality so that the function of the former would be as a transparent glass for the depth and weight of the latter; if Antonioni's films are on the side of surface, neo-realism, on the contrary, always seemed on the side of substance, profundity, its famous depth-of-field, of single fixed shots, sculptured lighting, the clear definition of figures, objects and ground arranged in a deep space. What seems remarkable, visually, about the neo-realist worlds was their solidity, their order. It is not that Antonioni's turning to surface lacks clarity, but it does lack what neo-realism seemed to have in abundance: centre, hierarchy and, perhaps, as well, space, in the sense that Antonioni's explicit turning of the real into images, the absorption of the figure of Maria Schneider into a system of images into which her roundness, corporeality, three-dimensionality are lost, or rather transformed into two dimensions, seems most to do with time, fluctuation, and the uncertain, perpetual variability of light, atmosphere and pattern. It is not only that the figure tends to be derealised and dissolved in Antonioni's films into shadows and phantasms, tracings on a surface, but rather that space itself is dissolved, at least that 'classic' space of depth, perspective order and commanding view. Neo-realist space assumed a sense to the world, everything in its place, and all things perfectly legible.

By absorbing reality into images, by involving it in its fabric and patterns, reality begins to take on the same lightness of consistency, the weightlessness, the fragility and the rhythms of the images. The fogs, the mists, the rain, the drizzle, the waters, the clouds are not only mediums through which things are perceived and dimmed, the very condition of perception, but they are, in their changeability and perpetual reshaping, their lightness and their granularity, the qualities of reality itself. Language and reality come together, but in precisely the opposite manner to neo-realism. Rather than giving substance to things, Antonioni's images contrive to absorb reality, and to invest it with the lightness and insubstantiality of its visual language.

I want to multiply, even at the risk of repetition, some examples of this image-making, the vacillation of order, of centre, of substance, hence of subject, in surface, in reflections, on glass, on windows, on windscreens, on, as in the case of Maria Schneider, the landscape-become-screen. But first I want to remark on a consequence of this procedure, already perhaps present in some Japanese film-makers and notably in the films of Ozu.

Schneider stretched out against the screen of the trees, the figures in *Il deserto rosso*, standing before Max's hut, silent, unmoving, as in a still life, slowly made to disappear in a fog thick with particles and colours of industrial waste, Mark, in *Zabriskie Point*, being caught and held in the moving surfaces of his truck (the mirror, the windscreen, the bonnet), pushing inside to the outside and absorbing on its interior surface the light and movement of the outside (there is a similar scene in *Blow-Up* of Thomas driving his open Rolls Royce convertible through London), all these instances of image-making, de-realisation, de-substancing are akin to the *temps morts* and the moments of unmoored, dislocated images of objects already remarked on in Antonioni's films.

As these events (a drive through Spain, through Berkeley, through London, the stillness of the port periphery of Ravenna) lose their substance as 'reality', the 'reality' lost is the reality of a fictional world. These are no longer, in any narrative sense, events, still less aspects of a story subordinate to a logic of plot, or character, or motivation, but instead are places at which all those features common to narrative fiction are suspended, or more precisely, erased. It is not only the figure of Maria Schneider who is lost to

Figures dissolve into the fog
in IL DESERTO ROSSO *(1964)*

the background of the trees, or of Max and Ugo to the descending fog, but the very fiction itself is lost, at least for that moment.

The interest of what is shown is not fictional nor narrational; in fact, the scenes have none of these functions, none of these places, as if they have become pure signifiers, imposing themselves absolutely in the full force of their visual and abstract power, only possible by a loosening of all signified attachments including that to the fictional world. By producing an image without a function, Antonioni returns it, absolutely, to a real world, as if for the first time – though it is true also in a way of Ozu – the documentary ambition to truth has been realised, but only by means of the suspension of time, of story, of event, of history, and above all, of significance. The need to signify has always confounded documentarism and forced it, reluctantly, often unconsciously, into the stream of fiction.

In Ozu's films the most ordinary, everyday objects, a kettle, a hat, a glove, a broom, shirts hanging out to dry, framed on their own, outside of the flow of the narrative fiction, estranged from time, assume an autonomy and an unreality at the precise point at which they lose their fictionality and are placed in, if not a non-fictional 'real' time and space, at least in another world and space from that of the fiction which surrounds them and which these objects have suspended. Antonioni does a similar thing in the *temps morts* moments of his films, in the fixing of familiar objects in a look so intense that the objects lose their context, stare back at us, and in the instances I have described, of which there are many, when figuration is dissolved into an image outside of the boundaries and confines of the fiction.

To the side of the fiction, freed from its time, without the context of significance that fiction bestows, these 'real' objects and 'real' images assume a metaphysical character, as if in the documentary real, where fiction comes to a halt, what appears is not reality but a simulacrum of it, its phantom. Only

fiction, it seems, has the ability to bestow substance, to make 'real'. Antonioni's objects and beings are most light, most ethereal, most phantasmagoric and insubstantial when they are removed from a fictional world which has given them body into another world of images and 'writing' which liberates their soul.

In 1972, at the invitation of the Chinese goverment, Antonioni made a nearly four-hour documentary on China, *Chung Kuo Cina*. The film was produced by Italian state television. Antonioni was in China for only a brief period of eight weeks during which time he shot the film (30,000 metres in 21 days) with the help, co-operation, and also supervision, of the Chinese. It was the period of Mao's Cultural Revolution.

A year later, the film, and Antonioni, were condemned by the Chinese with great violence and persistence. Posters of Antonioni appeared along the streets of Peking defaced with swastikas; the Chinese press accused him, simultaneously, of being the lackey of Mussolini and the lackey of Brezhnev. In an instant he became a figure to be hated by 800 million Chinese: 'an insult to the Chinese people', 'a terrible anti-Chinese event', 'this apparent documentary in the service of international reaction', 'an openly anti-Chinese, anti-communist and counter-revolutionary work'; 'instead of working to strengthen the ties between the Italian people and the Chinese people, he has shown his hostility towards the Chinese and, using contemptible means, has taken advantage of his visit to China to attack and slander the nation and its people'.

The principal accusation against Antonioni was that rather than speaking of 'the achievements of the new China', he 'maliciously created images which disfigured and deformed it'; Peking, in his film, it was said, appeared as an old decaying city of narrow streets, with women whose feet had been tied, 'a suffering, miserable people, as if from a time before the Liberation'; in Shanghai, the Chinese pointed out, rather than showing the large, new factories, Antonioni concentrated on artisanal production, insisting that Shanghai was 'a city made by capitalists in the nineteenth century'. Antonioni was 'a worm who spoke for the Russians', who demonstrated 'extreme hatred' for China, from 'out of the pack of imperialists and social imperialists.'[2]

At the close of his preface to the published script to *Chung Kuo Cina*, in a small essay entitled 'Is it still possible to make a documentary?', Antonioni relates:

> I remember once, at Su Chow, I wanted to shoot a scene of a marriage. My interpreter told me that at the moment in Su Chow no one was getting married. 'All we need,' I said, 'is a boy and a girl in order to reconstruct a marriage scene.' My interpreter could only repeat that no one was getting

married at this time in Su Chow. I reiterated that it would be all right to feign a marriage. He concluded however that it would not be right to feign a marriage given the fact that no one, in reality, was getting married.

Thus, the film does not contain the scene of a Chinese marriage. There is nothing in the film composed as it might have been in a studio.

Perhaps the interpreter was simply ingenuous, but I wanted to recall this small incident because it seems to me typical of the importance one might give to the image and to the manner of its formation. The Chinese have a very terrestial, concrete, *visible* notion of reality.[3]

Antonioni travelled through China accompanied by his Chinese hosts. What was shot was a matter for discussion and of negotiation. For the most part, nothing that was shot was not shot without the approval of the Chinese. Antonioni related only one incident of conflict between himself and the Chinese when he used his camera to record a free market in a village in Hunan, an unofficially tolerated but officially prohibited practice; he didn't go on with it, finally stopped in the face of the obvious, extreme displeasure of his hosts, who while not preventing him from filming made it clear that they didn't like it. 'Everything I did in China was done in complete accord with the people who were there to accompany me. Usually there were eight of them. In Nanking there were fourteen. Thus I never did anything that wasn't allowed and I never shot anything without their being present.'[4]

Antonioni has maintained that at the time he made the film the Chinese had approved of it and liked it enormously when it was completed. It was only a year later, he pointed out, and as a result of internal conflicts in China related to the Cultural Revolution, that the film came to be condemned.[5]

All this may be true, but there is something decidedly perverse in his filming in *Chung Kuo Cina*: a wandering off from the subject; a losing of interest in a significant detail for the seemingly insignificant; a neglecting of a political possibility for an aesthetic, graphic pursuit, a wisp of colour, an atmospheric feel; a look held, seemingly interminably, on a wall, for its textures, its compositional quality, but only for an instant on a factory, on the Revolution, on the officially sanctioned.

Rather than following the flow of traffic in an early morning going to work, he followed the slow, methodical, controlled gestures of someone doing Tai Chi, a disciplined conflict with an imagined shadow, arms and fingers stretching out to touch a phantom opponent; an entire nation was hurrying to its work, and Antonioni paused on a silent, unreal play of shadows, moving in unheard rhythms, an exercise the regime wanted to abolish as a residue of the past, of ancient superstition, but perhaps because of this and because of its shadowy, unreal existence, it is something difficult to get hold of and therefore stamp out. In the main Tien An Men Square in Peking, Antonioni began a lengthy shot pursuing cyclists, crowds of people, the few buses which went by, but his camera soon wandered off to end the shot on two large pillars whose surface was covered with columns of writing, none of which, at least to Antonioni, or to a Western audience, had 'meaning', 'signified'; it was writing divorced from all function except as design and as a surface effect, a kind of graffiti but not to express a message, rather an activity of work on a surface, a transformation of the pillars, as Antonioni had transformed the body of Maria Schneider, into the flatness of an image.

The film opens in Tien An Men Square. It is worth recalling that opening, especially poignant after the recent massacre of students there in July 1989 and the subsequent systematic persecution of 'dissidents'.

It is a normal, eventless day, a day like any other in Tien An Men Square. The camera watches knots of people, the face of a young girl with long braids, uneasy at being photographed, but very calm, with an extraordinary gentleness. The camera moves to other young girls, to soldiers, to students queueing at little stalls with white umbrellas on one side of the square; people taking

Graffiti-covered wall
in CHUNG KUO CINA *(1972)*

photographs of each other and photography booths – this is the object of the queues, to have your picture taken. The camera observes a group of cyclists, a group of soldiers. This opening conveys the entire sense of the film: dailiness, ordinary lives and the graceful rhythms of every day, things not easily grasped or ever completely formed by a politics, certainly nothing at all dramatic, and a camera watching this surface, finding not a purpose, or a centre, or a subject, but multiplying these and in so doing decentring itself, or rather, more to the point, opening itself to observation, to tracing and caressing things. What is preserved is beyond the reach both of a politics and a precisely aligned narrative: gestures, habits, looks.

The narrator:

Tien An Men Square, one day in May. We began our brief trip to China from today by placing our camera here. The song you have just heard, 'I love Tien An Men Square', is sung by children in every school in China. For the Chinese this great silent space is the centre of the world, The 'door to heavenly peace' is the heart of Peking and Peking is the political centre of China. And China is 'Chung Kuo', the country of the centre, the ancient kernel of world civilisation. It is a square of parades, of speeches, of displays. The Chinese People's Republic was proclaimed here, and here the waves of Red Guards passed in the Cultural Revolution. But we preferred to come here on an ordinary day, when the Chinese came to take pictures of each other. It is they, the Chinese, who are the protagonists of our filmic notes. We don't pretend to try to explain China: all we hope to do is to observe this great repertoire of faces, of gestures, of habits.

Chung Kuo Cina is a film about a China seen but not known, observed, but not explained and that is its wonderful power and its secret happiness.

The camera moves, runs, turns, moves back, slows, pauses, follows, meets, attends, seeks to gather, finds a detail, loses itself in a movement; there are fields which attract it, causing it to pursue something, others which seem to be of no interest at all, and from which the camera turns away. Antonioni, as he said, was respectful. He followed his Chinese guides, never created, except in that one instance in Hunan, stolen, still less forbidden images; he kept always within the permissible, obeyed the rules of the visit. Yet those rules, the limits they imposed, the confines they created, a kind of wall between the legal and the illicit, seemed never to hold, came to be imperceptibly negated as if the political and social rules which had made these limitations were without power, were empty, ineffectual. The head of a local Party committee and his deputy leave a small house and walk down a path; the camera stays to frame a man seated, immobile, between trees. As the two continued their walk, now flanked on either side by two large walls, the camera once again stops, delays to focus on the large figures of writing on the white walls, the Party officials are left to go on, unnoticed for the immobility and emptiness of the wall; the entire scene is decentred.

Toward the end of the film the camera pauses in a working-class area of Shanghai. It is wet, raining, only a few passers-by with umbrellas. What is noticeable is the luminosity of the street, the pavement in the rain, the emptiness of the scene. The camera suddenly rushes along the street, but following nothing, until it reaches the banks of a river where a boat is tied up and where some fisherman, in a long line, are etched against the heavy, opaque water. A political discussion is being filmed and the camera drifts off to explore the room: the bed, the bare walls, the fireplace, the few bits of furniture.

Visibility, as his Chinese hosts defined it, very slowly falls away. The substance and order of things are no longer full, sure, self-evident. Colour is drained. It is difficult to find a centre to the images. The camera seems to be motiveless, following designs irrespective of what is being demanded of it, subjective, impulsive. It is not work which is filmed, not production, but moments of stillness, of inactivity, of quiet, private gestures which are often beautiful, but always illegibile and to that extent hidden, secret, and above all outside of any control, any politics, any institutionalisation, like the Tai Chi sequences at the beginning.

Antonioni not only creates 'illegal' images within what is permissible by moving just to the side of what confines the legal, just at the edge of visibility, precisely at the point when the Party chairman leaves the frame and the camera turns its gaze to a wall, to an empty expression, to a frozen gesture; but the image of those images, the lengthy duration of a gaze, the dissolution of a subject, all these are illegal, perverse gestures which imply a different politics (hence a different film) to that demanded by a politics committed to power and control.

The narration of *Chung Kuo Cina* concludes:

> China opened its doors to us, but it remains, nevertheless, a remote world, for the most part unknown. We were not able to do much more than glance at it. There is an ancient Chinese saying which goes:

> 'You can draw the coat of a tiger
> But not his bones.
> You can draw the face of a man,
> But not his heart.'

Antonioni, in China, watched something he couldn't hope to know, nor did he even try. The film is not a documentary of China but a documentary of

Antonioni looking at China. Its subject is that looking or, more precisely, as Antonioni phrased it, glancing, a look at effects on a surface, not probing, but something gentler than that, lightly touching, like a caress, and, like a caress, attentive to what is glanced, felt and to the feelings it gave to him, which he remarked on later as tender, moving. Antonioni was very hurt by the Chinese reaction, the violence of it, the hatred in it, the rejection of his touch, of his appreciation, of his love.[6]

Antonioni's films are often filled with shots of hands moving, groping, reaching out, in search of something which only becomes clear when it is found and sometimes not even then. It is most obvious in sequences of love-making: Giuliana's twisting, turning, seeking hands in *Il deserto rosso*, her fingers spread in pain and in ecstasy, searching for something solid, on the bed, in the body of Corrado; Vittoria, in the opening to *L'eclisse*, letting her hands and her eyes caress the surfaces of objects, even touching the air stirred by the fan in the quiet, heavy atmosphere of an all-night end of a love affair; Lidia, in her walk through the outskirts of Milan, in *La notte*, passes her finger over surfaces, picks up a crying child, and watches, horrified, at the violence of the gang fight, the naked bodies, smashing into each other, the very contrary to the feel of her look and her touch on the world, as the violence of the struggles at the Rome stock exchange so visibly clash against Vittoria's gentle, happy, wondering caresses in *L'eclisse*.

The instances are in fact innumerable. Two, perhaps three, are very remarkable: Claudia, at the close of *L'avventura*, extending her hand to a crying and remorseful Sandro on the terrace of the hotel at dawn in Taormina, a movement which only finds itself in the course of its own progress. Claudia does not extend her hand in a caress (what it becomes), but simply extends it, uncertainly, gropingly, as if seeking to discover itself, the sense of its own movement, a direction, being attentive, painfully, to that movement, but even more deliciously to the air, the atmosphere, the silence, the dawn, the quiet sobs of Sandro. The qualities in this movement of attention, tenuousness, softness, and an acute, indeed exquisite observance of things and of self, an intense sensuality, are the same qualities which characterise the movement of the camera in *Chung Kuo Cina*, its walks, runs, glances, pauses, its look and its touch, as they are the qualities of Lidia's walk, not only through Milan, but everywhere in *La notte*, at the party, at the night club, at the book launching, and, finally, in the park, assaulted, grabbed, pounced upon by Giovanni, so desperate as no longer to feel her. The violence of Giovanni's act recalls the violence of Sandro's remark to Anna, in *L'avventura*, before she disappears on Lisca Bianca, 'And didn't you feel me the night before?', and also, in *Il deserto rosso*, Corrado's inability to keep up, to caress the intensity of feelings of Giuliana who can touch things with her hair, her eyes, with all the surfaces of her body, where he can only tear, push, strip, take, anxiously seeking to possess something which, necessarily, eludes him.

The other instance are the Tai Chi sequence in *Chung Kuo Cina*, the touching, tentative outlining of an imaginary body, a phantom double, which is made and remade at the tips of the fingers, in a slow arc through the dawn light, in a motion which takes shape and which is also, like a caress, searching, sensitive, exquisite. The camera in *Chung Kuo Cina*, and hence its images, are like these movements of Tai Chi, a movement of delicate imaginings, seeking not only to find the body it traces, but to find itself in the course of its own touching, that glancing which simultaneously finds and loses itself along a surface and in the emptiness of light and air.

The third instance is in *Identificazione di una donna* and has perhaps less obvious reverbations in other Antonioni films than the two instances just mentioned. It involves two scenes, one in which the action is out of sight, and the other in which that sight is restored by Mavi telling Niccolò what had happened and which neither he nor the audience with him was able to witness. On the way to the aristocratic party Mavi is stopped on a spiral staircase by one of the guests; it is the fact of the spiral and the wall which blocks the view. All that is left for the audience is the wall. Later, when she recalls the scene, it involves the claim by the guest that he is Mavi's father. The proof is the similarity in the shape of their hands. What is shown are the hands, stretched out, in close-up, lining up against each other, establishing an identity.

The revelation of the hidden view reveals very little indeed. It doesn't matter hardly at all to the narrative, who is Mavi's father. An aspect of the scene relates to the frequent figuration by Antonioni of uncovering a surface

CHUNG KUO CINA
The Tai Chi sequence

to reveal not a depth but only an other surface (perhaps one reason that his most favourite surfaces are water and desert sands; no matter how deeply down you go, how much you pierce it, it is always the same, reduplicates its surface, covers over the gash); and it relates too, in the film, to the fruitless quest for identity (for certainty), the interchangeability between the real and its reproduction, a person and their image. But there is another aspect. Mavi's identity is beyond her, escapes her, is outside of her reach. It is her hands which betray her, which tell a story despite her will and her consciousness; hence for Antonioni their privileged place, the hand which moves the camera, which seeks to find the reasons for its own gestures, its corporeality, the rationale of its movements, which moves, and which documents that movement. Making a film is a way of finding out, but it is the body, the eye, the hand, which tells.[7]

The Chinese attack on Antonioni was hurtful, vulgar, vicious, disgusting . . . yet, it wasn't unfamiliar. Umberto Eco tried to understand the attack as a failure to understand Antonioni by the Chinese, for historical reasons, for reasons of political desires and ideological commitments. Eco's understanding was enclosed within a structure of east and west, of mutual incomprehensibility; he even, though only lightly, touched a notion of an oriental world that couldn't be ever fully known, would remain mysterious. His task, eminently rational, clear, praiseworthy, was to make the Chinese attack credible and thereby to show just how far they misunderstood the Antonioni film, how distant it was from their needs and their sensibilities and their history.

A decade earlier, Eco had written a lovely short piece on *L'eclisse*, about

IDENTIFICAZIONE DI UNA DONNA *(1982)*
Mavi on the spiral staircase

the incomprehension by a student of the film, a student of course taken as typical, and there, in that article, Eco once again sought to make Antonioni clear, to explain the reasons for his strategies of incommunicability, of reserve, of aestheticism and the reasons the student perhaps could not read these.[8]

The two articles, both extremely interesting, a decade apart, are very much the same, not only for the structure of the argument, the interest in misunderstandings, and above all the interest in paradox (perhaps 'there' in both the Antonioni instances, though also placed there by Eco for a love of paradox), but also because there is not such a wide gap, in substance, between the Italian student of 1962 and the Maoist Chinese of 1972, at least not as Eco shapes these.

In fact, charges of imperialism, fascism, revisionism and lackey of Brezhnev apart, the Chinese were criticising Antonioni for presenting an over-subjective China, of ignoring political achievements and social progress, of concentrating on the insignificant, of presenting images primarily for their beauty not their content, of draining China of its colours, of its brightness and hope, of dissolving contexts, of unmooring figures, of favouring the perennial and the traditional against the historical and the new, of making the most stable structures, the Nanking Bridge for example, not secure and frontal and glorious, but distorted, assymetric, imbalanced, out of true, shaky; and though it could be argued, as Eco does, that the Chinese had misread Antonioni's intentions, turning his sweetness into malice, his appreciations into hypocrisy, his love into hatred, criticisms of this kind had been levelled at Antonioni from his early years as a film critic on *Cinema*, have been repeated for nearly every film he has made (were the Chinese any less civil than the Cannes audience in 1960 which hissed and shouted at the screening of *L'avventura*?), and continue to be levelled at him today.

And it doesn't only come from a vulgar left, or even a reactionary right. There is no substantial difference, except perhaps of tone, between the Chinese criticisms of Antonioni for *Chung Kuo Cina* and the American criticisms of him for *Zabriskie Point*. Seymour Chatman's discussion of *Zabriskie Point*, in his rather stodgy book on Antonioni, could have easily appeared in *Renmin Ribao* and Eco might have written an article on it, pointing to the confusions, the misunderstandings, the paradoxes, not now between east and west, or communist and capitalist, but America and Europe, or something like that, and it would have been equally wonderful as his other two articles were and filled with sweet reason. The American criticisms of *Zabriskie Point*, which were nearly universal, were in their way as vicious, as stupid, as uncomprehending, as insulting and certainly as vulgar as anything the Chinese might have composed.[9]

Chatman is a student of narrative rather more than he is a student of film. His book on Antonioni centres on the four films of the early 1960s which Chatman thinks are Antonioni's very best: *L'avventura, La notte, L'eclisse, Il deserto rosso*.[10] They are best because they most embody Chatman's ideas of what a modern narrative should be. The films before these four were to Chatman insufficiently free of conventional notions of plot, character, motivation, so that, for example, *Cronaca di un amore* confusingly mixed elements of detective fiction with modern elements of distancing and objectification; Chatman was satisfied on neither count. The conventions were disappointed, while the new was insufficiently realised. The films after these four (with one or two exceptions) he regards as a decline: in these the narrative experimentations of the early 1960s are left behind for a visual play which, however stunning, has no narrational purpose or reason to exist. The later films seem to him to come apart at a junction between the narrational and the visual, between real substance and what seems to be only decoration, between the full and the empty, meaning and its negation.

In these terms, for Chatman, *Zabriskie Point*, and even more so, *Il mistero di Oberwald*, are two of the worst films Antonioni has made. He dislikes

Zabriskie Point because it is merely, pointlessly beautiful; narratively it is badly acted, unrealistic, inaccurate (no 'real', 'true' American could accept it), unlikely, over-contrived. For him, its narrative ineptitude in fact emphasises the emptiness of its visual beauty: 'Narrative so dominates one's experience of a fiction film as to control one's final reaction to it. Indeed, the more physically beautiful a weakly plotted and acted film is, the more pretentious it strikes us.'[11]

Il mistero di Oberwald was shot on video then transferred to celluloid; all colour mixing and optical effects were created at the moment of shooting on the television console and with the video camera; the colour is stunning, but unrealistic, excessive, out-standing. Chatman's criticism of *Il mistero di Oberwald* and the considerable experiments it made with colour, with film and video images, and the extension in it, by means of colour additions and television colour mixing, of Antonioni's fascinations with image dissolution and image change over time, is along similar lines to his criticisms of *Zabriskie Point*:

> Since these effects are so subtle, it is a shame that Antonioni did not attach them to material worthy of his usual subtlety. Settling for simple heroes and villains can only banalize the use of colours to characterize them, no matter how clever the process itself is.[12]

True, Chatman doesn't call Antonioni a lackey of Mussolini, and his remarks are a cut above those of Stanley Kauffman, John Simon, Charles Samuels, but this is a very tired line, used repeatedly against Antonioni and at the heart of the Chinese criticism: namely, that Antonioni strayed from what was significant, showed only the peripheral, the trivial, and by doing so ended up in error, pretence and lie.

The Chinese wanted 'legal' images which could be politically used, institutionalised. The images Antonioni presented slipped outside of any traditional political grasp. But here I think is where narrative and politics may come together. Chatman wants complicated meanings, but meanings nevertheless; he wants vision and narrative to be integrated; he wants a perspective from which to see; and he has an agenda which says how things ought to be combined from which he can judge and prescribe. Antonioni, in these late films, and *Chung Kuo Cina* and *Zabriskie Point* are here exemplary, begins to dissolve the very substance of film narrative by making the sight and images one sees rigorously objective, yet unstable, impossible to seize; and this is achieved primarily by work on images, one of whose aspects is to give the image, as an image, autonomy from the subject, as earlier Antonioni had disengaged figure and ground, object and use, and had denied the functional time and space characteristic of most film fiction.

It was one thing for Chatman to watch Giuliana or Anna or Claudia or Vittoria lose their hold on reality, doubt their perceptions within a frame that never doubted its ability to present such insecurity as in the films from *L'avventura* through *Il deserto rosso*. But it is quite another thing for the audience (and Chatman) to lose hold and to do so at precisely the point when Antonioni's fictions (or documentaries) cease to employ a subjective camera (from within the fiction and from the perspective of characters) and to use, in an apparently older, more classical tradition, an objective camera in the technical sense of the camera held by the author of the film, from a place outside the fiction, divorced from any perspective within it, but at the same time without any presumption of possession, of knowledge, of dominance. Antonioni's look in that sense is blank, open, distanced, even, as his critics would have it, 'cold'.[13]

What is interesting about Antonioni's films after *Il deserto rosso* is a more rigorous objectivity which allows him a much greater subjective freedom, neither narration nor camera any longer so tied to character and story. It is one of the pleasures and the discoveries made in making *Chung Kuo Cina* and it was perhaps the fact of the documentary which helped Antonioni move in that direction. The objective view in late Antonioni is not at all classical: it neither dominates, nor centres, nor controls, nor provides guidance. It is a gaze at risk watching its own fictions, its own documentation, its very looking, but neither the looking nor what is looked at, or rather the combination of the two which gives birth to an image, can provide any anchor, a certainty to grasp; it begins to move, to slide away at the precise moment that you think you have it, threatening not only the subject, the narrative, but subjectivity itself with extinction, with formlessness. These are moments of the most intense, most exquisite joy.

Notes

1. The image is discussed at some length in Mancini and Perella, *Michelangelo Antonioni: Architetture della visione* (Rome: Coneditor, 1986).

2. *Renmin Ribao* Commentator, 'A Vicious Motive, Despicable Tricks – A Criticism of M. Antonioni's Anti-China Film "China"', (reprinted in) *Chinese Literature* no. 3, 1974; see also Umberto Eco '*De interpretatione*, or the difficulty of being Marco Polo', *Film Quarterly* vol. 30 no. 4, Summer 1977; and Gian Maria Guglielmino, 'Violento attacco cinese alla "Cina" di Antonioni', *Gazzetta del Popolopolo*, 31 January 1974, p. 6.

3. Michelangelo Antonioni, 'E ancora possibile girare un documentario?', in Michelangelo Antonioni, *Chung Kuo Cina* (ed. Lorenzo Cuccu) (Turin: Einaudi, 1974), p. xvi.

4. In an interview with Gideon Bachmann ('Antonioni After China: Art Versus Science', *Film Quarterly* vol. 28 no. 4, Summer 1975, p. 30); this interview is one of the most interesting Antonioni has ever given, and especially interesting for *The Passenger* and an understanding of the 'documentary' impulse involved in its making, or perhaps, more accurately, the impulse

for 'objectivity' which informs not only *The Passenger* but above all *Identificazione di una donna*.

5. Guglielmino, 'Violento attacco'.

6. Bachmann, p. 30.

7. Mancini and Perella cite frequent examples both of hands and of stairs in Antonioni's films; I have relied on them for focusing my attention.

8. Umberto Eco '*De Interpretatione* ', and Umberto Eco, 'Antonioni "impegnato"', in Carlo Di Carlo (ed.), *Michelangelo Antonioni* (Rome: Edizioni Bianco e Nero, 1964.)

9. See, for example, John Simon, Joseph Gelmis, Martin Last, Harrison Star, Al Lees, 'Antonioni: What's the Point?', *Film Heritage* vol. 5 no. 3, Spring 1970, pp. 26ff; and as well Harry Medved and Randy Dreyfuss, *The Fifty Worst Films of All Time* (New York, 1978), pp. 277–282; Charles Samuels, 'Puppets: From *Z* to *Zabriskie Point*', *The American Scholar* no. 18, Autumn 1970; Stanley Kauffman, '*Zabriskie Point*', *The New Republic* no. 162, 14 March 1970; Gordon Gow 'Michelangelo Antonioni's Film *Zabriskie Point*' *Films and Filming* no. 21, 1975.

10. Seymour Chatman, *Antonioni, or The Surface of the World* (Berkeley and Los Angeles: University of California, 1985).

11. Ibid, pp. 167–168.

12. Ibid, p. 211.

13. Bachmann, p. 30.

Chapter Eight

The Passenger (1975) was the third film of a group of three English-speaking films Antonioni made for Carlo Ponti/Metro-Goldwyn-Mayer; the other two were *Blow-Up* (1966) and *Zabriskie Point* (1969). The films are different from preceding Antonioni films in a number of ways: they are in English; they are set outside of Italy; the main character is male, not female; and they have a more 'objective' narrative style and camera than the other films, more on the other side of the fiction, documenting it, refusing to share perspectives with the characters or to enter within their fictional world. The narration is at a greater distance from the narrative than previously and for that reason more free.

The Passenger is the story of an Anglo-American journalist, David Locke, in crisis: his marriage, his work, his life no longer engage him; he seems outside himself, regarding himself almost with disinterest, a self that no longer belongs to him, or he has ceased to care about, or wants to shrug off. He is in the Sahara covering an African guerrilla war; at his hotel he meets Robertson, who physically resembles Locke, but seems otherwise more 'within' his own life, not like Locke, the object of his own observation, and unlike Locke a man of action, not a professional onlooker. Robertson dies suddenly of a heart attack and Locke, spontaneously, decides to take on the identity of the dead man and to live this 'other' life: Robertson's appointment diary is all set out, plane tickets, names, locations. Locke takes them over: clothes, objects, appointments, fate.

Assuming the itinerary of Robertson's life, Locke goes to London, Munich, Barcelona, rural Spain; he meets a girl who travels with him; as Robertson he is pursued by Locke's wife anxious for news of Locke. Robertson, as it turns out, was a gun runner for the African guerrillas. Pursued by Locke's wife (who could reveal Locke's 'true' identity, that Robertson is Locke), by the police, by the African government (wanting to kill him in his guise as Robertson), Locke keeps an appointment Robertson made in a small hotel in Spain; it turns out to be an appointment with death, with two assassins sent by the African government.

Among other things the film is about not being at home, wandering, losing context and identity.

None of Antonioni's characters ever seem at home. They are on the move, in houses which belong to others or appear to belong to others, in places of passage like hotels, bars, restaurants, hospitals, in unfinished places, in flats or houses which are also offices, or offices which function, for the moment, as homes.[1]

At the opening of *The Passenger*, in the African town at the fringe of the Sahara, no one seems to recognise Locke or acknowledge his presence, as if he wasn't there for anyone, or that he and they inhabit different worlds, different universes. Some make contact with him then abandon him. The camel rider passes him in the emptiness and nowhere of the desert. Locke greets him but the camel rider doesn't respond, carries on past him. A boy appears in the Land Rover, then disappears. A guide begins to lead him to the guerrilla camp, then he too disappears. The project itself vanishes. The Land Rover gets stuck, lets him down. That sense of bodies unmoored, unlocated, happens again in the appearance (but only to the camera) of The Girl in the Bloomsbury park, in the same shot with Locke/Robertson but seemingly in different spaces, as when they try to join up at the roof of the Gaudi building in Barcelona, appearing and disappearing, being led astray in false spaces.

Clara, in *La signora senza camelie*, after she is married, spends her days wandering around an unfinished home; it is doubly not hers: never completed and not to her taste. She is out of place, in the wrong identity, in the wrong marriage, not in her world but in Gianni's world. For most of *Le amiche*, Clelia is trying to have her fashion salon decorated for the opening, it too, like Clara's home, uncompleted and something alien, a false, other identity which she seeks, but which also repels her, another Clelia which doesn't quite fit this Clelia, a body which is not yet fully a character, which hasn't found itself; like the salon, it remains unfinished. Fictions need characters, not simply bodies.

There is often the sense in Antonioni's films of fictions which haven't yet completely materialised, that aren't fully formed, as if the film, like the body of Clelia (or Clara, or Locke) were still searching for itself: its character, its fiction. That sense of a fiction which hasn't yet arrived is most strong in *The Passenger*. It has to do in part with a narrative pretext: Locke uncomfortable being Locke assumes the identity of Robertson whose body he finds and whose story he then seeks. But Locke never identifies totally with Robertson: he is always watching himself in this body of an other. Locke seems never himself, more an idea than a person, a figure who is not real. The fiction he is in seems something observed by him from outside of it, only an object of his gaze. The entire film has a sense of estrangement, of a great distance between its events and their observation. It is made even more strange by the fact that as Locke looks at himself 'from the other side', the record of that look is 'on this side', interior to the fiction. While the fiction is made an object of a glance, the glance returns as the object of itself.

In *L'eclisse*, Vittoria and Piero play at love, not at home, where they are always uncomfortable, but in Piero's office. There, they are not at home with

Locke abandons his Land Rover
in THE PASSENGER

themselves: they kiss each other, but watch the kisses, make promises, but as an 'other', never intending to keep them. Reminiscent of this scene, but more strongly of the self-estrangement/self-observation in *The Passenger*, is Giovanni's failure to recognise himself in *La notte*, not only in the final scene when Lidia reads out to him his own love letter to her which he no longer recognises as his, but throughout the film, as Giovanni loses all substance, to become an image of a dead self . . . to Lidia, at the book launch, to the industrialist Gherardini, to himself.

The studio of Thomas in *Blow-Up*, of Sandro in *L'avventura*, are also their homes. The desert house in *Zabriskie Point* is also an office, a place not to live in but to hold meetings at; and in it a whole complex of houses is planned, a desert development made of simulacrum, model houses – houses, which, like the one from which these others are planned, seem only toys lived in by fake people and which you can blow up; and the people are like the houses: mannequins, fake, toy people, doubles which are not them but are not anyone else either.

Niccolò's flat in *Identificazione di una donna* was completely furnished by his ex-wife. He lives in it, but it seems still to be 'hers'. When he returns

Piero's apartment in L'ECLISSE
where he is not at home

to it, the burglar alarm goes off, rejecting him, repelling him like an intruder in his own house. The fear of his ex-wife remains, left behind to haunt him. Niccolò can't find his key, tries to avoid setting off the alarm, but immediately he acts, he records his actions in a notebook, as if he had become a character not only in this, but in a future fiction, and like Locke, an 'other' to himself. When Ida comes to the flat to see Niccolò in 'his' surroundings, he tells her that nothing there is his. He can't find things: he had been searching for nearly six months for mislaid postage stamps for his nephew; he finds unrecognisable objects, stares at doors he is afraid to open. He is more at home 'nowhere': in hotels, in a hired boat, in the flats of others, out in the emptiness of the Venice lagoon, in the car, in a rented temporary house.

Piero's family house in *L'eclisse* is filled with shadows and presences which have no existence for him: odd objects which belong to no one, ancestral portraits of persons he no longer recognises; he offers some chocolates to Vittoria – the box is empty. Like Niccolò, Piero is a stranger in his own house. When Vittoria returns to her old room at her mother's, that too seems not hers, to call up an alien, other, strange Vittoria. It is like the teenagers in the French and the Italian incidents of *I vinti*, out of context at home, displaced, not recognised; the images which their parents have of them, and they of their parents, don't correspond to actions, to gestures, to selves. Clelia in *Le amiche* does not any longer belong to the Turin from which she fled, nor completely to the Rome to which she escaped; she wanders around her past in Turin, but only recognises it as not hers, as does Lidia, in *La notte*, in her long splendid walk around the periphery of Milan. *Il grido*, with its emphasis on wandering, rootlessness, is the story of Aldo expelled from his home, realising it was never 'his', seeking another, never finding it, instead inhabiting places that are not even properly habitations, shacks, store rooms, or places which expel him in other ways: a roof leaks, doors come unhinged, holes in the wall are blocked with newspapers.

In Antonioni's early documentaries people live in moving houses (boat cabins in *Gente del Po*) or makeshift houses: in *N.U.*, a derelict shuts himself up at night in a flower seller's kiosk in Piazza di Spagna.

Antonioni's houses seem to be houses of no one. In *Identificazione di una donna*, the rented country house to which Mavi and Niccolò escape is being sucked into an empty void at its centre, disintegrating; its real inhabitants are bats who fly at them, frightening Mavi; the fireplace won't draw, the wood is wet, the paper damp, as if it has been cursed.

When Locke/Robertson in *The Passenger* returns to his London house he confronts his own absence, all the marks of his not being there (more evident in the European release print where he finds an obituary of himself, a letter to his wife from her lover, some papers in the safe – incidents cut from the American, English-language version). Earlier he had changed his identity with the dead Robertson in an hotel room somewhere in Africa, as, later, he dies in an hotel room somewhere in Spain, keeping an appointment which was not his but Robertson's, in an anonymous place, a place of passage, belonging to no one.

Locke/Robertson never has a home. Not only is he always in hotel rooms, rented cars, third-hand cars, cars that break down, that reject him, refuse to do his will, be 'his' (the abandoned Land Rover, the American white convertible), waiting in bars, phoning from bars, sitting in restaurants, but he is in the guise of someone else, a rented identity; he inhabits the body of a dead man, the life of a corpse, a body not 'his'. He is never anywhere nor anyone, always in passing, between places, between identities.

The estrangement between characters and their contexts, bodies and fictions, which is a constant in Antonioni's films, is doubled over in *The Passenger* by the gaze of the narrative upon its own fiction as it unfolds, as if the body of the film was estranged from the fiction included in it, hence that sense in *The Passenger* of a fiction and the fiction being watched, but these two positions,

these two perspectives never meeting, no more than the body of Clara in *La
signora senza camelie* joins up with the characters offered to her. In *La signora
senza camelie* (and in most of the other films) it is only the character who
seems strange, a kind of shadowy phantom double of herself, but in *The
Passenger*, the entire fiction assumes this character of estrangement from itself.
It is an odd sensation: a fiction made unreal by the film which registers it, not
only doubled characters in an Antonioni film, but a doubled film: the fiction
and the record of it.

Setting up the penultimate shot
for THE PASSENGER

In *The Passenger* the most dramatic sign of this estrangement and doubling
of film and fiction is the penultimate shot sequence.

The shot sequence is seven minutes long and took eleven days to set up
and complete. The shot – this is a bare description – begins as a track from
inside the hotel room towards the window facing the square at the Hotel de
la Gloria where Locke/Robertson is lying on the bed. The shot moves to the
bars on the exterior side of the window, seems to pass through the bars, and
then pans 180 degrees around the square until it returns to the window looking
inside from the outside through the bars at Locke/Robertson, now dead,

murdered, during the time the camera accomplished its itinerary around the square.

There were a number of reasons why the shot proved so difficult and took so much time to accomplish. Light was a factor. The shot needed to be taken in the evening towards dusk to minimise the light difference between interior and exterior; since the shot was continuous it was not possible to adjust the lens aperture at the moment when the camera passed from the room to the square. The problem of time of day – the scene could only be shot between 5.00 and 7.30 in the evening – was compounded by atmospheric conditions: the weather was unsettled, windy, nearly cyclonic. For the shot to work the atmosphere needed to be still to ensure that the movement of the camera would be smooth; Antonioni tried to encase the camera in a sphere to lessen the impact of the wind, but then it couldn't get through the window. There were further technical problems. The camera ran on a ceiling track in the hotel room; when it emerged outside the window it was picked up by a hook suspended on a giant crane, nearly thirty metres high. A system of gyroscopes had to be fitted to the camera to mask the change from a smooth track to the less smooth and more mobile crane. The bars on the outside of the window were fitted on hinges. As the camera came up to the bars they were swung away at the same time as the hook of the crane attached itself to the camera as it left the tracks. The whole operation was co-ordinated by Antonioni from a van by means of monitors and microphones to assistants who, in turn, communicated his instructions to the actors and the operators. As things turned out the camera could only take a spool of 120 metres which was insufficient for the length of the shot; the camera needed to be modified and the giroscopes readjusted for a larger 300 metre spool.

The people of the town had watched all the preparations for the shot; when at last it was completed they cheered 'as if a goal had been scored at a football match.'[2]

The shot is an 'objective' shot in the sense that what it sees is seen by no one in the film. The camera leaves Locke lying on the bed, his eyes closed, to go its own way; the only perspective is the perspective of the camera. When the camera enters the square to accomplish its 180-degree pan in a continuous movement back to the outside of the window looking in, it passes a number of figures and events, and records some sounds: a driving school car, a few birds, an old man calling a dog, the dog, two old men talking, a young boy who throws stones at the dog, The Girl, a Citroen, a black man and his companion who get out of the Citroen and walk in contrary directions, a police car, and the police and Rachel who rush to the hotel entrance, the departure of the Citroen, the reappearance of the driving school car. The camera glances by these events; none of them are central, nor given any weight, nor emphasised: the killers who come and go in the Citroen are of no more concern to the camera than the small boy who throws stones at the dog, or the old men who are talking. It is the same with the sounds heard: a door opening and closing, a car backfiring (or is it a shot?), the sound of a trumpet, voices, a dog barking, the whistle of a train, a clock sounding. None of these have any particular significance, or order, or hierarchy. They just are and the camera does no more than register them.

What is true for this shot is in part true for the entire film, though elsewhere it is less marked and less noticeable. It happens sometimes in minor ways: The Girl and Locke/Robertson are sitting eating and talking at a restaurant by the roadside; for a time the camera watches them, listens to their words. But then it ignores them for the traffic as the camera quickly pans to left, then right, then left to pick up cars as they speed past in front of the couple.

After changing his identity with Robertson, Locke, now Locke/Robertson, is first seen in a small square in Bloomsbury, in London. The Girl is also there reading a book on a bench in the foreground of the shot. She is only a body, not yet included in the drama of the fiction. The camera notices her, but blankly. She and Locke/Robertson are part of the same shot, but not yet, apparently, part of the same fiction.

Just before the long penultimate shot of the film, The Girl and Locke/Robertson are in the hotel room. She is looking out of the window into the square and he is lying on the bed. He asks her what she sees: 'A small boy and an old woman are discussing which street to take . . . A man scratches his shoulder, a little boy throws some stones. It is dusty.' The camera sees what she sees, but not with her, rather by her side, over her shoulder. There are two views of the same; a single set of objects, but a double perspective.

The camera watches the fiction as it unfolds, but independently as a separate presence. It is neither before the fiction, in the sense that these events have been pre-arranged, nor exterior to the fiction, in the sense that it knows these events and dominates them. There is nothing anterior to the fiction for the camera, nor outside it as an idea or thought which the film then illustrates. As the events take place the camera becomes aware of them.

One function of this autonomous but non-dominant narration is to seek out meanings, not to proclaim them. Hence, it has always been permissible for Antonioni's camera, like his characters, to wander away from a centre, until the entire notion of centre and periphery, significance and non-significance, ceases to have much meaning. This independent and seemingly im-pertinent narration was very clear in *Chung Kuo Cina* and very difficult for the Chinese to accept; it is still clearer in *The Passenger*.

There is a further yield to this form of narration. In *The Passenger* the narrative remains open; the camera regards it as it is formed. Without a finality known in advance everything is potentially crucial, but nothing definitely so.

Because the narrative is not fixed, and the narration reticent and unknowing, the narrative potential (and narrative energy) is all the greater. There is a sense in *The Passenger* of the narrative never wholly eventuating, but the consequence is a multiplicity of possible narratives, as in detective fiction in which any number of stories, any number of suspects remain possible until one, in the end, is chosen. Antonioni indefinitely suspends that choice.

An aspect of the documentary tradition is not that it presumes to tell the truth, nor seeks to be objective, but that fundamentally it doesn't fully know and in that sense is not in complete possession of its narrative; the sense of such documentaries is not the presentation of a known, but the investigation of a not-known and part of the technique of that investigation, given the uncertainty of the camera, and of the narrator, is to remain both reticent and external in relation to the events, often coming upon as they take shape, and for that reason not dominating them.

Such documentarism informed Italian neo-realism, or contrarily, is one of the reasons it is often assigned a realist-documentary inheritance the signs of which are the shot-sequence, an uninterrupted temporality, an unfragmented space and a narration-at-a-distance. In many of Rossellini's early films an 'event' erupted within the narrative which was waited for, yet unexpected, in timing and in sense, when it came. The narrative 'waits' but it is not clear what precisely for until the event happens. The Rossellini 'event' reversed the preceding narrative sense in the film, as if a miracle has occurred or a conversion: Carmela's sacrifice for Joe in *Paisà* (1946), the sudden understanding of charity in the monastery sequence in the same film, or the suicide of Edmund in *Germania, anno zero* (1947).

This last reference is interesting in relation to Antonioni: Edmund wanders, lengthily, through the rubble and ruins of a destroyed, bombed Berlin; he looks, he is looked at, but it is impossible to read anything in his regard, and the regard of the camera, though attentive, even affectionate, is inexpressive. In an instant, but with no particular prior motivation, Edmund jumps from a building and takes his life, not unlike Aldo's fall from the tower in *Il grido*, which similarly is observed, and then recorded but not anticipated by the narrator. The logic of the acts is clear, but only afterwards; before there had been other possibilities, only one of which was the death/suicide.

In so far as Antonioni relates to Italian neo-realism and perhaps most of all to Rossellini, it is partly here in this reticent narration and the documentation of objects, events, figures on the other side of the camera without immediately functioning as the signs and objects of a pre-known, pre-organised narrative. But there is another element in common as well with, if not neo-realism, certainly Rossellini: the documentation of the 'writing', the presence of the camera seeking to find, and waiting to find, its subject. In the case of Rossellini the subject is more certain and the apprehension of it relatively unproblematic; in Antonioni, the uncertainty and slippage of the subject becomes the drama of the narrative.

The seven-minute shot in *The Passenger* registers an external reality in which it itself is included. While watching the cars, The Girl, the dog, the old men, it also watches itself watching them, observing not only their movement, but its movement, not only what is outside it, but what fascinates it, what it imagines and turns into images. It is not, as Antonioni commented, a thought illustrated by a sight, but a thought in the process of formation which includes a reflection on its own thinking: '. . . the undulating, just perceptible movements of the camera . . . I was trying unconsciously to find the same movement our imagination makes when it tries to give birth to an image.'[3]

There is nothing substantially different between the camera passing through the bars of the window and circling the square before the Hotel de la Gloria and it looking at a sight by the side of The Girl, or being diverted by the traffic, or, in the hotel room in the Sahara, leaving Locke to observe an insect on an electric wire. Not once in *The Passenger* is the camera 'in' the fiction: it never adopts the 'classic' technique of moving in and out between subjective-character views, nor views outside characters, but which, nevertheless, remain dominating views overseeing the narrative. As a result the spectator is neither bound to the fiction by being caught in an identity with a character view, nor by being bound in an identity with a narrational view. The freedom of the camera from the necessity to determine, to control and possess the narrative, its freedom simply to look, 'objectively', doubles over for the spectator, equally free, positioned in a place of objectivity and non-necessity.

The Passenger serialises doubles to an infinity, turning round each other, like a spiral around a void. The doubling is not so much of bodies, or even characters, but of positions.

Locke, the television-reporter interviewer, always on this side of the camera, looking at the world on the other side, changes his identity with Robertson, the gun-runner, making events which Locke habitually reports. Robertson is selling guns to African guerrillas whom Locke is trying to find to tell a story about. When Locke becomes the 'other', assumes the identity of the dead Robertson, goes outside the window, as it were, to become part of the reality which before he only looked at, though felt estranged from, he finds himself looking at himself, elsewhere, as the 'other'. The one Locke has become two, subject and object, or rather he is now in two positions, neither of which are clear and which tend to supplant each other, or turn round each other as Locke pursues himself in the guise of not-himself.

THE PASSENGER
Maria Schneider as passenger

Like Locke, the camera assumes a double position: it moves, it looks, as a subject, but at the same time it is an object of its own regard; it turns around the square and looks at itself turning. And just as the camera ends by registering its own movement, and the duration of its look, so too the audience finds itself in a similar position, looking at that movement of the camera, but catching, as it does so, its own reflection.

Antonioni remarked to an interviewer: 'This is a film about someone who is following his destiny, a man watching reality as reported, the same way that I was watching him, in the same way that you are pursuing me. You could go back and find another camera watching me and another watching the other camera. It's surrealistic, isn't it?'[4]

Chung Kuo Cina was made in 1972; just after it, and before *The Passenger*, Antonioni had prepared the script for another film, *Tecnicamente dolce*. He had searched out locations in Brazil, and had begun casting, but in the final stages, before production, Carlo Ponti decided to drop the project. *Tecnicamente dolce* has certain resemblances to *The Passenger*: it is the story of a reporter who seeks to escape his identity by going where the rules of the world seemingly don't apply, the Amazonian jungle – 'T changes his skin like a snake' – and where he meets his death. It is impossible to know how the film might have been realised, but it does seem to have those elements of duplication, as in *The Passenger*, between the reporter as an observer of himself as 'other' and the camera as an observer which takes itself as its own object.[5]

In any case, for the unrealised *Tecnicamente dolce* and the realised *The Passenger*, the experience of *Chung Kuo Cina* was crucial; it suggested a technical means for ordering fiction which, while always present in Antonioni's work, had never completely been realised. That means was the 'objective' camera in the narrow sense of a camera which never adopts a subjective, character perspective.

In China Antonioni found himself before a reality he could not hope to understand, but only see from the 'outside': 'To look at it and to record what passed under my eyes.'[6] This view is a familiar one from his other films: not to presume to know the feelings of his characters, knowing no more than they and often less; not exactly describing so much as watching, being interested, but from a distance, 'on the other side' of the fiction. But the China film is different from his other films by the fact that that distance is never crossed, that the camera rigorously maintains itself as exterior to the sight it sees. It is not simply that Antonioni refuses to judge or to assume a knowledge he doesn't have, to be a narrator in the more conventional, dominant way, but that he refuses ever to enter into the world, or the perspectives of those who pass before his camera.

The 'otherness' of China in the film is not a function of its exoticism, but rather of a technique of objectivity, of never bridging a gap between the camera and the reality before it, not even to give it a name or assign it a significance. China has the same strangeness that characters and objects do in other Antonioni films as a result of disengaging them from a story, denying them their fiction, leaving them bare as bodies, or as things, which is what bestows on them their often metaphysical, unreal quality; but while in these other films scenes or characters lose their 'fictionality', become strangely, simply 'objects', in the China film (later in *The Passenger*) the entire film assumes this character of objectivity and otherness. It is as if a narration has been achieved which no longer narrates, in which there is no longer a narrative, or if there is, it is elsewhere, something observed, not told.

Until the China film there was often a division in Antonioni's films between narrative and vision in the sense that the narrative was often suspended or deflected by sights which were not only 'beautiful', but seemed to have no narrative rationale, or the narrative tended to dissolve or become uncertain as figures or objects blurred into fogs, mists, drizzle, sand, dust, smoke. In *Chung Kuo Cina*, in *The Passenger*, in, perhaps above all, *Identificazione di una donna*, vision and narrative join up, not by means of beautiful images – there are no *belles images* in *Identificazione* – but by a narrative technique of objectivity tied to the camera in which the narrative itself seems to disappear and another narrative takes its place, no longer as a story narrated, but as a sight seen.[7] It is in this sense, I think, that *The Passenger* is a documentary of a fiction rather more than it is a fictional narrative.

Until *Blow-Up*, but perhaps also including *Zabriskie Point*, Antonioni played a kind of hide and seek with his fictions, sometimes wandering from them, but also going inside them, usually by the traditional method of adopting a position which was also that of a character. Pasolini praised and criticised Antonioni for it in his essay, 'Cinema di poesia'; Pasolini cited *Il deserto rosso* and the adoption by the narrator of the position of Giuliana who was neurotic and whose grasp upon herself and upon reality seemed uncertain.[8] It permitted Antonioni, according to Pasolini, to present images purely for their abstract beauty, for their colour, their shape, while at the same time offering a realistic alibi for them as the sight of a neurotic: distortions of reality had the justification of being seen by a distorted subject.

It is this 'subjective' camera, on the inside of the fiction, that is no longer used in *The Passenger*; the sense, in other films, of an uncertain, tenuous reality, had been achieved by direct work on the images of reality, of making the sight of things ambiguous. Though it could never be directly argued that such work always had a narrative rationale, the fact that characters in Antonioni's films felt themselves or felt the world to be unreal, unstable, out of reach, was consistent with images of landscapes and objects divorced from character and difficult to read with any certainty.

If Antonioni denied any certain meanings in his films, the meaning of incertainty itself arose and seemed to have, in part as a result of perspectives which were those of characters, and of images whose motives were subjective, very definite narrative justifications.

'Objectivity', the viewing of the fiction from the outside, shifted the subject of his films from that of images seen to, more directly, the act of seeing itself. Antonioni no longer needed a narrative excuse for what he viewed. The narrative was elsewhere. He was not involved. Earlier, before *The Passenger*, 'in' the fiction, he sometimes chose to wander from it (towards beauty, to follow a flock of birds, to fix his eye on a colour, to become fascinated with an object); but always he was forced to return, to pull back and by so doing encounter the necessities of the narrative he had only a moment previously seemed to escape.

In *The Passenger*, and absolutely in the penultimate seven-minute shot sequence, Antonioni seemed to have found, and certainly more completely than his character did seeking to elude his history, a new freedom and joy: 'I have never quite felt this liberty.' 'I have replaced my objectivity with that of the camera . . . the liberty I have achieved in the making of this film is the liberty the character in the film tried to achieve by changing identity.'[9]

Notes

1. See the section on homelessness in Michele Mancini and Giuseppe Perrella, *Michelangelo Antonioni: Architetture della Visione* (Rome: Coneditor, 1986), pp. 133–212.

2. Michelangelo Antonioni, 'La penultima inquadratura', in Michelangelo Antonioni, *Professione: Reporter* (ed. Carlo Di Carlo) (Bologna: Cappelli, 1975) between pp. 75–76; there is an English translation of this in *Film Comment*, July–August 1975.

3. Requoted in Fernando Trebbi, *Il testo e lo sguardo* (Bologna: Patron Editore, 1976), p. 51; the book is entirely devoted to *The Passenger* and is one of the few really interesting books on Antonioni.

4. Renée Epstein, 'Antonioni speaks . . . and listens' *Film Comment*, July–August 1975, p. 7.

5. Michelangelo Antonioni, *Tecnicamente dolce* (ed. Aldo Tassone) (Turin: Einaudi, 1976).

6. In Gideon Bachmann, 'Antonioni After China: Art Versus Science', *Film Quarterly* vol. 28 no. 4, Summer 1975, p. 29.

7. François Aude et Paul-Louis Thirard, 'Entretien avec Michelangelo Antonioni', *Positif/sitif* no. 263, January 1983, p. 22.
   AntonioniAntonioni: 'I have tried to eliminate 'beautiful images'; if they are there it is not by intention.'
   ThirardThirard: 'I think they are there!'
   AntonioniAntonioni: 'All the better.'

8. Pier Paolo Pasolini, 'Il cinema di poesia', in his *Empirismo eretico* (Milan: Garzanti, 1972); the entire book was translated in 1988 as *Heretical Empiricism* edited by Louise Barnett and published by Indiana University Press; the particular essay can also be found in English in Bill Nichols (ed.), *Movies and Methods* (Berkeley and Los Angeles: University of California Press, 1981), pp. 66–70.

9. Bachmann, p. 27; See also Alberto Ongaro, 'L'Europeo intervista: Antonioni', *L'Europeo*, 5 March 1975.

Chapter Nine

Antonioni (1964):

We know that beneath the represented image there is an other image more true to reality, and that beneath that one, still one more, and again a further image beneath that one, until you get to the true image of reality, absolute, mysterious, that no one shall ever see. Or perhaps, one will arrive at the decomposition of any image whatsoever, of any reality whatsoever. The abstract cinema would then have its rationale for existing.[1]

Il deserto rosso was made in 1964; it was Antonioni's first film in colour. And, if *Il mistero di Oberwald* (1980) can be thought of as an exception, which I believe it is, *Il deserto rosso* is the last film of Antonioni's with a woman as the central character. In theme it is like the trilogy of films beginning with *L'avventura* and which includes *La notte* and *L'eclisse*: an erosion and *malaise* of feelings minutely observed in the gestures and exchanges within the couple; it is like these films too in its narrative: a reticent narration, a reduction of 'event', an investigation of feelings, but at a distance, without drama, without even, strictly speaking, plot. But the feel and sense of *Il deserto rosso* is different from these other films; though it retains a narrative subject, colour appears as a subject in its own right, connected to the narrative, but also autonomous from it, an area in which the narrative loses itself in abstraction, and a new subject, the colour, the 'writing' of the film seems to displace it.

Except for one or two moments in the narrative, the camera seldom leaves the central character, Giuliana, the wife of Ugo, an industrial 'manager' of a factory complex in the industrial periphery of Ravenna which appears in the film as a collection of silos, chimney stacks, turbines, power generators, steam, smoke; it is a vaporous, discoloured, unreal landscape in which nature seems out of place, dying, overwhelmed.

Giuliana, as it turns out, had attempted suicide, was hospitalised, and now, though strictly speaking 'cured', is still visibly shaken and disturbed, subject to neurotic anxieties and fears, which are manifested as an acute sensitivity, in her very body, to the environment, to colours, sounds, a touch, a look. She is not unlike the heroines of past films, Claudia, Lidia, Vittoria; but her looks and her feelings, though as intense as were the looks of these other women, are less balanced and what she sees and feels can't be handled; she can't adjust to them. She meets Corrado, an associate of her husband's, who

IL DESERTO ROSSO *Giuliana and Valerio*
cross the polluted landscape

becomes interested in her, and yet the interest is oddly dissociated from her
so that together with him she seems most isolated, as with her husband, and
terribly, painfully with her little son, Valerio.

The film follows her, and Corrado, wandering in the pollution and
discoloration of the Ravenna industrial landscape, and the pollution and
sickness, emotionally, of those who work in it, made manifest in a dirty, mean,
salacious suggested orgy in a broken down shack on an estuary. Corrado and
Giuliana have an afternoon of passion – she runs to him, as a refuge after
feeling estranged and pushed to one side by Valerio. But it doesn't calm her.
The only place of peace for her in the film is an invented fantasy on a magic
island of pink sands, in technicolor, at one with the sea, with nature, with self;
but it is a fable and she returns to the real world in which colour is drained,
no longer primary, nothing at all clear. In the end she learns, apparently, to
cope. She and Valerio are wandering in a steamy, vaporous deserted landscape
outside the factory walls; coloured smoke is belching from chimney stacks,
there is a scream of machinery, the very earth emits fumes, gases, as if
fermenting.

Valerio: Why is the smoke yellow?

Giuliana: Because it is poisonous.

Valerio: Then if a bird flies through it, it will die.

Giuliana: Yes, but the birds know about it now and they don't fly through it anymore.

After Giuliana and Corrado make love in the hotel room, the entire room takes on a rose-pink tint, the same colour as the sand on the Sardinian beach in the fairy tale Giuliana composes for her son. The scene is an extreme example of something which occurs in many places in the film. In Giuliana's shop, where Corrado pays her a visit, the colour of their spaces is completely different, or, more precisely, the tones are different: Giuliana is in a clear, open, even light; Corrado is in a darker light, the background is discoloured. Two things seem to be happening at once: depth in the image is reduced so that figure and ground are flattened into the same plane; and, the colour of the walls and its light seems to overcome and absorb the figure, equalising figure and ground into surface.

This same division of space into colour patches and the absorption of figures into their own particular space and colour and surface are very noticeable in other interior scenes: in the home of the technician in Ferrara, in Max's hut, in an early scene in Giuliana's house during the night when she is overcome by anxiety. As her anxiety is heightened and then dissipates, the tones in the room shift.

It seems, in these instances, as if the film hesitates between the image serving a function in the narrative, and the image detaching itself from the narrative, becoming purely pictorial, as if these patches of colour were simultaneously narrative signs and purely relations of colour. But the fascination of these images is that they are neither completely the one nor the other: the narrative seems to fade out, as the colour of it fades in, or it is the reverse of this, in either case a kind of shimmering effect between significance and its loss.

When Giuliana and Corrado leave her shop and go out into the street, the page of a newspaper floats down along the side of a building to the ground where it is 'caught' and held by Giuliana's foot. 'What do you know, it's today's paper,' she says, and lets it go. For a moment the narrative is halted as the paper descends along the wall bringing forward in its movement the sense of that movement itself, the effect of it on the colour and texture of the wall, the feel of the air, and then the narrative returns, in Giuliana's intense yet distracted remark.

IL DESERTO ROSSO
The newspaper

In 1942, Antonioni wrote a lovely article on colour for the journal *Cinema* : 'Suggerimenti di Hegel' ('Suggestions from Hegel').[2] It welcomed colour to the cinema for the expressive possibilities it offered; and it called for the use of colour, not simply as a rendering of external reality, but for its ability to transfigure nature, to render reality by unreal means, as Antonioni remarked to Godard more than twenty years later speaking of *Il deserto rosso* :

> *Godard* : When you begin or end certain sequences with quasi-abstract forms of objects or details, do you do it in a pictorial spirit?
>
> *Antonioni* : I feel the need to express reality in terms that are not completely realistic. The abstract white line that enters the picture at the beginning of the sequence of the little gray street interests me much more than the car that arrives: it's a way of approaching the character in terms of things rather than by means of her life. Her life, basically, interests me only relatively . . . [3]

In 1949, Antonioni quoted Matisse to Samuel Goldwyn: "'There aren't fixed colours for objects. A poppy can be grey, a leaf black, and the grass isn't always green nor the colour of the sky always blue." . . . Mr Goldwyn . . . the law of the beautiful doesn't lie in truth to nature.'[4] In the 1942 article, what was interesting about colour in the cinema for Antonioni was that the cinema, unlike painting, moved; the suggestions he took from Hegel related to that quality of movement.

Hegel spoke of colour as a kind of echo and it is an echo effect, or precisely a train of reverberations, that Antonioni noticed in the cinema. The changing of a tone, being caught up and carried over elsewhere, in a play of tones created for example by the passage of clouds over the valley in John Ford's *Stagecoach*, or at the opening of Carl Koch's and Jean Renoir's *Tosca* when the galloping of the horses in the silence of the street is picked up in the billowing of the white capes of the riders in the black of the night. Colour – though for Antonioni these films were 'in colour ' – would increase the range of the echo.

It is precisely this kind of echo that happens as the page of newspaper floats down towards Giuliana's foot, but not only between colour and atmosphere, wall and paper, a discoloured green and a discoloured grey-white, but between these abstract and pictorial qualities, and the narrative sense of Giuliana's frozen, distracted attention. But the mechanism is not one of simple reinforcement, colour and movement in the image forming a commentary on Giuliana's character, or her psychology. It is the echo itself that is the subject. The wall alters as the newspaper floats by it, like the changes in the valley over which the clouds sweep in *Stagecoach*, but the wall also alters with Giuliana's attention, as she seems to alter by the fact of attending to it; it is as if the streetscape and Giuliana are equally, but independently, objects for the camera.

The echo is not narratively irrelevant, but rather narratively something new. What *Il deserto rosso* observes and simultaneously establishes are relations between character and things, but in a way to see character not as etched against things, foregrounded before landscape, but as things them-selves, objects in a landscape, or, more precisely objects and landscape. The flattening out of depth in the film is not primarily motivated by plastic considerations so much as by narrative ones, or rather – and this is what is new – it establishes a relation between landscape and character in which both exist on the same plane, displayed along the same surface. There is no difference in the film, Antonioni told Godard, between the 'plastic' and the 'psychological'; they were exactly the same thing.

> *Antonioni* : . . . I dyed the grass around the shed on the edge of the marsh in order to reinforce the sense of desolation, of death. The landscape had to be rendered truthfully: when trees are dead, they have that colour.
>
> *Godard* : The drama is no longer psychological, but plastic . . .
>
> *Antonioni* : It's the same thing.[5]

Giuliana wanders uncertainly around her unfinished, unrealised shop before patches of colour which redefine each other as they are looked at, establish echoes and variations which are re-echoed within Giuliana; that in turn is the subject of the regard of the film which is equally sensitive to this variability, to a continuum of substitutions and shifts and movements between figure and landscape, volume and surface, and which it documents.

The film is not a commentary on colour, nor exactly does colour function as narrative commentary, nor is colour simply aesthetic effect. It is rather a relation and caught up in that relation are not only Giuliana, other objects, other characters, frames, surfaces, but the camera as well. On the one hand, Antonioni has established a narrative; on the other, and because it is a narrative which isn't closed, which avoids explanation, which shuns context or finality, which cancels drama, the narrative is there primarily as a field to be observed and identified and interrogated. Implicated and present in the regard directed towards the narrative (and its objects, and its colours) is that regard itself; things are felt and questioned by the camera as Giuliana feels and questions the world as it comes to her, as she encounters it, and just as her look alters the world, the look of the camera alters, 'before our very eyes', the look of the image. It is at this point that things slip, explanations falter, the look and the narrative simultaneously hesitate.

After Giuliana's 'attack' at home, which closes with Ugo making love to her, a discoloured, mottled green-grey surface fills the screen. It is difficult to identify the sight immediately since there is neither a narrative reference point (the cut to this new sight has no motive nor exact cause) nor a visual one. This often happens in the film and only retrospectively do things reveal themselves as wall, or industrial waste, or water, when a figure or object enters into that space or along its surface to form a relation which identifies it.

In a scene in *Il deserto rosso* which recalls Antonioni's remark about the uncovering of an infinity of surface levels of 'reality', the wall in Via Alighieri where Giuliana has her shop only becomes wall with the entry at the lower part of the image of a white patch which reveals itself as a car as Corrado emerges from it and then reveals the wall as a wall of a building in a Ravenna street. But something else happens as well: the white patch of the roof of the car changes the compositional structure of the image and alters the tonal relations in the wall colours. The 'appearance' of a narrative figure, Corrado and his car, does not erase the plastic 'subject' of the wall, its colour, the shift in composition; indeed, it helps to form it.

There are scattered references to colour in a number of articles Antonioni wrote between 1935–49 when he worked as a critic for *Corriere Padano* and later for *Cinema*. On the whole he took the position then that he would take later for *Il deserto rosso*, that colour while not to be employed naturalistically or merely as functional to the narrative, nevertheless ought not to be mere technical display, but be linked to events and to the drama.

It was not clear exactly what these links between colour and narrative ought to be; Antonioni used the term 'poetically functional' which seemed a kind of balance between an expressive use of colour within the narrative and one in which colour alone became the subject, or, at the very least, in which fantasy and imagination in the use of colour would not be restricted by a need to directly render narrative events. This comment, for example, by Antonioni, in 1945, on Olivier's *Henry V*:

> Painted backdrops abound in the film, damp green landscapes with cardboard castles: all of this belongs to Shakespeare. They are inspired, as English painting was at that time, by Dutch and Flemish artists, but it eschews all realism. Influence doesn't become an end in itself, but rather poetically functional under the stimulus of a free inventiveness. . . .
>
> If the film, for other reasons, never quite reaches a very high artistic level, its use of colour is enough to render it fundamental in the history of the colour film.[6]

BLOW-UP *(1966)*
The photographer and his model

There wasn't the slightest hint then of any dissolution of the narrative, of rendering it abstract by means of colour; on the other hand, given the novelty of the process in the 1930s and its enormous potential, Antonioni's enthusiasm was often expressed for a use of colour independent of narrative, though not independent of its ability to make objects and landscapes stand out, as if being seen for the first time. Though some of Antonioni's formulations may now seem vague, there was less equivocation in it than it was an attempt to give colour and objects, but also 'technique', a narrative presence equal to that of character and drama, and even a degree of autonomy from these more usual narrative aspects, and thus it was an attempt, I think, to begin to redefine narrative for the cinema.

It was for these reasons that Antonioni could often appreciate not only minor but often extremely mediocre films for the possibilities they suggested rather more than for their overall actual achievements. For example, these comments by Antonioni on an American film by James Hogan in 1938:

> The colour allows us to see the ocean directly, from up close, in all its varied aspects: at dawn, at midday, at dusk, by moonlight, clear as glass, thick and dark like ink, calm, angry, garlanded by foam at the tips of its waves. The inner life of the Ocean, colour by Technicolor . . . and except for some sunsets worthy of a *crepuscolare* painter of the nineteenth century, things are done extremely well: beautiful greenish-blue tones, suggestive horizons bleached milky white in the haze . . . a sudden tragic darkening of the waves . . . in short, a realistic range of tints completely convincing, without a trace of exaggeration. The trouble begins when the the characters, moved by the needs of a confused drama, enter the cabin.[7]

In a 1940 film review, Antonioni compared the way in which colour was used in *Tom Sawyer* (1938) (the film was almost certainly Norman Taurog's *The Adventures of Tom Sawyer* made in Technicolor) to its use in *Follie di Hollywood* which is probably Irving Cummings' 1939 film *Hollywood Cavalcade*. Antonioni preferred the Cummings because in it colour is not mere effect but integrated with the narrative events; at the same time it is not simply a function of those events, 'quite the contrary'.[8]

There were a number of articles Antonioni wrote at the time which referred to technical innovations other than colour (sound, television, 16mm) but in similar terms. He argued against any naturalist, realist use of technique, while at the same time rejecting an avant-gardism and pure experimentalism which would see technical matters divorced from narrative and dramatic concerns. The kind of cinema that Antonioni tended to favour, or rather the notion of technique that he supported, was one in which a 'technical' aspect of film, like colour, was both a subject in its own right, but also tied to the sense of the narrative; or, more precisely, 'narrative' for him had as much to do with traditional elements like character and drama as it did with the colours of the landscape, the cold of the atmosphere, the quality of the light. What is important here is that these technical elements are not mere functions of a narrative referent.[9]

In 1940, Antonioni published a treatment for a film called *Terra Verde* based on a story in the *Corriere della Sera* by Guido Piovene. (Piovene was a journalist, essayist and novelist; his major works of fiction appeared in the 1940s, among which an epistolary novel, *Lettere di una novizia*; one of the outstanding qualities of the novel was its descriptions of the Veneto landscape, and particularly its colours; Piovene had also written an exceptionally favourable review in the *Corriere della Sera* of Rossellini's *Un pilota ritorna* on which Vittorio Mussolini had collaborated and which was in part scripted by Antonioni.) The story takes place in a mythical Greenland. It is an ecological fantasy and concerns the progressive change in the climate of the island from temperate to near arctic conditions, the ensuing destruction of its culture and way of life and the emigration of its peoples to warmer lands to the south. At the end of the treatment, Antonioni discussed the colour of the projected film:

> No one should ignore the use we expect to make of colour in our film: not exhibitionism, nor decor, but rather the needs of the narrative; in it colour will determine not only the climate, but the psychological movement, the drama, which involves – visually – the changing of colours, their gradual loss of vividness . . . very white or red veined tiny pebbles, the sea made up of the most beautiful colours, like the colours of minerals collected in a museum: those reds, those unreal greens, sulphurous yellows, those forgotten silver whites in the sunshine, distant reefs in colours which change according to the hour and the time. . . . Green fields quivering with the colour of apricot or of pink in the light, fields of wheat, expanses of pale blue flowers, skies cut by rainbows: things which, when seen on the screen, will make one say: 'it's false', but it is precisely in this falsity that the truth of the far north rests, whose landscape sometimes takes on the tonality of an impossible palette. And then the terribly sad fading of all this, the excessive clarity of the air, the final burst of the flowers, of ornamentation before the advancing whiteness glances by things with its stellar reflections. All joyfulness, life itself disappears with the fading of colour. . . . Days which last for twenty-four hours, nights which fall at eleven in the evening, a sun which lightly touches the water without setting or which remains in wait a little beneath the burning horizon, tinting the overhanging clouds red, while the sea is of the purest steel making one dizzy: these are – it is said – truly apocalyptic scenes.[10]

In the introduction to the script of *Il deserto rosso*, two similar stories are told, one by Antonioni, the other by the cameraman, Flavio Nicolini.[11] Antonioni's story, 'Il bosco bianco' ('The white wood'), is about painting the woods outside of Ravenna a grey, dirty white to achieve a sense he had of the wood as he passed it each day: the slow loss of its natural characteristics, the fading of its green, its inevitable death from industrial pollution; he wanted to give the woods that colour of death, to register a transfiguration, by unnatural means, it is true, but in order to render 'reality' more accurately. The terms were similar to those expressed in his articles on colour in the 1940s. But, in the event, when all was ready for shooting, and the woods, at great effort, suitably painted the grey-white Antonioni wanted, the sun shone very brightly the next morning and the sequence had to be abandoned. All that is left of this 'image' of the white woods is his description of it.

The diary of the cameraman is the diary of efforts to achieve colour effects contrary to the 'real' colour of things, and over and against all the variables which alter colour, so that any variables or rather variations in tones in the final images in the film would be those wanted, rather than simply accepted and suffered. There were essentially two kinds of problems: distortions for effect on one level, for example the use of filters dictated by the need for artificial fog, unsuitably altered; on another level, the colour of faces, which then required the use of coloured lights to return the faces to a more natural hue, and just at that point, real cloud appeared which forced an alteration in the whole sequence of controls, or the sun came out after days of cloudiness and ruined a painted woods; this was the second problem, the contingencies of weather, of light, of temperature all of which were inter-related and all of which affected each other: the coming and going of winter clouds, altered temperature, varied the light, changed the colour.

The story by the cameraman, perhaps more than the one by Antonioni, is very detailed about all the difficulties involved, demanded, and overcome, in achieving precisely the image wanted: the right colour, the right tone, the correct line and design, against not only the conventional nature of things, but against the contingencies of nature itself.

There is a politics of a sort in the relation of Giuliana to Corrado; when they speak his words are abstract, divorced from things, made up, already empty; but when she speaks they are always in relation to things, as on the rig when she says that if she were to go away she would have to take all the things that she was attached to, all the things she loved. He on the other hand, on the subject of leaving Italy for Chile, at first talked about the industrial equipment he would take; and as for personal things, they were an afterthought: 'only a few suitcases.' Giuliana feels the world and all its objects, its colour and its light through her hair, her fingertips, the surface of her eyes.

There is a key to the film in the cameraman's description of the difficulties of filming due to the contingencies of weather and atmosphere and the sight of Giuliana (and other Antonioni women) as they move through the world, touching it, feeling it, absorbing it. Antonioni's concern, his care for form and structure in the image is not strictly a formal concern, and yet it is also more subtle than ordinarily might be thought of as a narrative one. To place a figure or an object in an image is to place it in a relation to the world, to the air around it, to the things you can see, and to the things that are invisible, so that form here, the precise manner in which a colour invests an object, or the way a figure is flattened against a plane, no matter how 'pictorial' or 'plastic' that image is thought to be, and, no matter how insubstantial the reality seems which is represented, all the 'meaning' of these images resides precisely in their 'form'.

What is so sweet in both the Antonioni and cameraman stories is that in order to establish a form at the heart of which is an oscillation, an unsteadiness, a hesitancy, a lack of resolution, and which concerns relations of persons to colours, both of whom shift and change, Antonioni faced with that variability, with a subject the terms for whose realisation always threatened to escape him, had to invent the most devious means to fix contingency.

The reviews in Italy, generally, for *Il deserto rosso*, were not initially favourable. Critics were disturbed by the juxtaposition of the beauty of the images and the apparent emptiness of the narrative, or of the dressing up, in magnificent colour, of tawdry, rather old ideas:

> What is the use of having reached the limits of colour if it is placed in the service of superficial ideas, of a story without any narrative developments . . . of characters for whom we cant feel either sympathy or compassion, and of rather mediocre performances?'[12]

In these kinds of criticism there was the sense of aesthetic and formal means as aspects of cinema distinct from meanings and narrative, or rather of form having only the function of 'rendering' the narrative, quite contrary to what Antonioni intended, not only in *Il deserto rosso*, but in all his films. In an interview with Enzo Siciliano, Antonioni remarked that poets use images in the same way as film directors use them in their films. It recalled a Crocean notion of the unity of the arts and of poetry as a generic term which crossed over different substances of expression. Siciliano asked him to elaborate on how poetic images in literature and images in film were alike. Antonioni responded: 'From an expressive point of view. For example, my first films were accused of calligraphism. But, in fact, I was looking for the right images for what I wanted to say; calligraphism, it seems to me, is the the exact opposite of what I try to achieve . . .'[13] 'I read in some reviews,' Antonioni commented, '"the colour was beautiful, but the theme was weak." How is that possible? If

IL MISTERO DI OBERWALD *(1980)*
Monica Vitti as the Queen

what you see is beautiful, it can't be said that what lies behind it is ugly.' [14]
The comment has the sense of his reply to Godard, that between the 'plastic'
and the 'psychological' there was no difference.

Criticisms from some on the Left took the position that the 'modern'
cinema was a cinema of political commitment and Antonioni's concern
'merely' with formal colour and pictorial effects not only divorced characters
and emotions from any concrete context, but was idealist, romantic, and from
a contemporary point of view, irrelevant . . . reactionary.[15]

There were a multiplicity of factors in *Il deserto rosso* which determined the
colour of things and the colours of the images: light, atmosphere, movement,
temperature. In that sense colour had to be thought of as a relation, not as an
absolute, and the film on the whole could not be regarded in any sense as
about colour, or colour taken to be its principal subject however outstanding
the colour effects. To render the colours he wanted and to fix them amidst all
these uncertainties, Antonioni, as the cameraman noted, exercised intense,
careful control not only on the elements for taking a scene, but on the colours

of the scene itself: he painted the grass, the buildings, objects, or, as he related, an entire wood.

Antonioni wrote an article in *Cinema* in 1940 on the supposed artistic threat that the invention of television posed for film. The medium was then relatively primitive. To Antonioni, what differentiated television from film was the immediacy of television; but that immediacy disqualified it as 'art': it was too tied to the moment, unlike film in which the image could be worked on both before filming and after. For that reason Antonioni concluded that television was not a threat to the cinema, nevertheless it seemed to have some advantages in its limitations: the ability to adapt to the unforeseen and the immediate, the possibility of responding to the moment.[16]

In 1980, Antonioni made *Il mistero di Oberwald*, based on a Jean Cocteau costume melodrama, *L'Aigle à deux têtes* (*The Eagle with Two Heads*) originally a theatre piece later made into a film by Cocteau. (The initial choice was Cocteau's *La Voix humaine* which Rossellini had adapted as a vehicle for Anna Magnani in *L'amore* in 1948; it was eventually rejected by Antonioni, in part because of the earlier Rossellini treatment.) Antonioni's film was financed by RAI. Antonioni shot the film on magnetic tape and then had the tape transferred to celluloid. The work is somewhere between film and television: it exploits the seldom used possibilities of video not available in film for direct editing, for immediate colour changes. On video Antonioni could render colours immediately, mix them, remove them, correct them, transfigure them as they were being shot, as if he were painting, rather than, more traditionally, filming; he could adjust the quality and relations of tonalities and have the results to read instantly on a television monitor. The gap between event and its reproduction, characteristic of film, didn't exist on video tape: he could seize the moment, play with the contingencies of light and perspective and atmosphere that had been so much a problem for him in *Il deserto rosso*.

The formal experiments in the film, not only with colour, and with the variability of shapes and objects, but with the instability of the image itself, and the play between what is fixed and moving, the attempt to just touch things and in that touch convey their fragility, relate to other Antonioni films, and most directly to *Il deserto rosso* ; but the subject is uncharacteristic: a film in costume, melodramatic, wordy, overblown, artificial, theatrical in the most obvious way.

The film takes place in a dreamlike German castle in Oberwald. The Queen is staying there. On the day of her wedding with the King (long before the film begins), when he was only twenty-five, he was assassinated; she has remained a widow, a virgin, private, alone with herself, and veiled, ever since. She takes no interest in the political affairs of the kingdom but is the centre of intrigue, spying, plotting. On a stormy night, when the film opens, the royal police are in pursuit of a young man who has penetrated the castle walls and whom they have wounded. The young man, Sebastian, is a poet and an anarchist, come to assassinate the Queen. He crashes, faint, near death, through a door in her room on which is the full-length life-like image of the dead King. Sebastian and the King look exactly alike; he is the absolute double of the King. Rather than betraying her assassin, she hides him and restores him to health, appoints him her reader and they fall in love.

Until the appearance of Sebastian and the refinding of love with the body and person of Sebastian who precisely resembles the image of her lost love the King, the Queen had had no face (it was veiled), no apparent interests, no taste for life; she lived an existence between life and death, between presence and an absence from herself. In appearance, and in fact, she was like a shadow, a ghostly shade. Sebastian restores her: gives her body, substance, life, and convinces her to resume control of the kingdom, to change things, to wrest power, which is rightly hers, from the connivance of the Queen Mother, and from the Chief of Police, Count Foehn. She initiates his plan, but

Sebastian and Count Foehn
in IL MISTERO DI OBERWALD

her enemies initiate theirs which involve the capture and execution of Sebastian. To free her, he takes poison. When she learns about it, she deceives him, says that she never loved him, only used him. In anguish, he shoots her. At the last moment, he dying of poison, she of his bullet with the royal troops awaiting her outside the castle, they crawl towards each other reaching out only to die just before they touch.

If the costume, the setting, the melodrama is foreign to Antonioni, there are elements in the story that are not: the shadowy existence of the Queen; the changing of identity, of Sebastian for the King, of the Queen from a life which was dead, to another filled with love and desire; the playing with doubles and death; mock and real suicide; the instability of character, the instability of desire. In fact, at the level of these 'themes', but also in the manner of their realisation, there is much in common between *Oberwald* and not only *Il deserto rosso* (the colour), but *The Passenger* (changing identities), *Zabriskie Point* (the appointment with death), *Identificazione di una donna* (the uncertainty between the real and images, between self and objects, the difficulty in 'fixing', identifying).

Antonioni never liked Cocteau; to Antonioni he was romantic, excessive, melodramatic, verging on kitsch and the tasteless; at best he thought Cocteau was 'clever, fanciful, but limited'.[17] In 1945, Antonioni unfavourably reviewed a film by Jean Delannoy, *L'Éternel retour*, based on a Cocteau script:

> The intention was to bring the tale of Tristan and Isolde to the screen. Everything seemed promising when the film began in a sumptuous castle with its dreamlike, haunting atmosphere, with characters just outside the limits of the real, for example, above all, a dwarf who it seemed would be the centre around which the entire film turned. Instead the whole thing collapsed: realistic modes mixed with the fairy tale and the result was simply bad taste. Cocteau lost a crucial fight; make no mistake he isn't stupid, but he certainly demonstrated the impotence of his efforts in bringing to the screen talents, admittedly very modest ones, that can be appreciated in his literary works.[18]

When Antonioni remarked, in 1950, referring to the fluidity of his camera in *Cronaca di un amore*, his breaking of the shot/reverse-shot rule in dialogue scenes, his remaining with characters after an action was complete, an entire strategy which began to redefine screen time, narrational positions, the idea of drama, the terms he used were terms about freedom, about liberating himself from the common, the conventional, the usual and traditional. Later, in the 1970s, he described his work similarly, as the finding of a new liberation, in the finding of new techniques of narrative perspective and the 'objectivity' of the camera in *Chung Kuo Cina* and *The Passenger*. *Oberwald*, or rather the

A strikebreaker is escorted to work
in IL DESERTO ROSSO

Cocteau on which it was based, precisely because it was so alien in style to Antonioni, afforded him a similar freedom.

> To play more freely, I've chosen a story I have no relation to . . .[19]

> What a sense of lightness I felt faced with events without any of the complexity of the realities we have become accustomed to. What a relief to escape from the problems of a moral and aesthetic commitment, of the need to express these. It was like rediscovering a forgotten childhood.[20]

> I thought of *L'Aigle à deux têtes*, not because it seemed a work that appealed to me particularly but because it seemed as good a vehicle as any for trying out television cameras, which for years I had wanted to do. . . . The play offered me a chance for an intellectual non-commitment. It's a novelettish story, this tale of an anarchist who infiltrates into the queen's castle and ends by killing her for love rather than ideology. Of course I don't give a damn about this queen and the anarchist. . . . I've tried to be neutral.[21]

Many of the colour and light effects in *Oberwald* are not dissimilar from those in *Il deserto rosso*, either visually or narratively, though *Oberwald* displays its effects more openly. In some dialogue scenes in *Oberwald*, between the good Queen and the evil Count Foehn, or between Foehn and the good anarchist Sebastian, each is coloured in a different tinted patch of light, blue for Sebastian, purple for Foehn, in natural colours for the Queen, in an intense blue-violet for Foehn, or she, once again, in a natural tint, and Sebastian, standing right beside her, but whose colour drains away, completely bleached and whitened, as if the lack of community, the different universes of these same figures, in the same fictional space, are worlds apart. These effects are also present in the dialogue scenes in *Il deserto rosso* in enclosed, interior spaces in which figures inhabit different colour tints, though side by side (one of the most involved, the most riveting of these scenes, is in the flat of the worker, in Ferrara, between Corrado, Giuliana and the worker's wife), but the effects are less obvious, less 'dramatic' in *Il deserto rosso*.

Just as mood shifts colour in *Il deserto rosso*, or, alternatively, creates moods, this too happens, with considerable flourish, in *Oberwald*: the Queen and Sebastian, in love, gaze out at the landscape from a castle window through a telescope; the landscape changes with great drama from green to rose to pale green to blue to yellow to violet and suddenly the perspective that seemed to have determined these colours, or helped to determine them, is revealed as false: the Queen and Sebastian are in the field, amidst the flowers and colours they had, or seemingly had, been watching from the window. They declare their love and the landscape lightens to a blue-pink combining the customary colours in which Sebastian had been tinted with the soft colours associated with the Queen: it becomes the colour of love, this daylight, soft brightness in contrast to the grey, black, wet, dark reds of death and the night. When Count Foehn touches a rose, it darkens, seemingly dies to his touch; in the courtyard, a rich brown-red pool of blood from slaughtered chickens and floating in it, one white feather; as the image fades out, the red turns black.

An aspect of these effects is uncharacteristic of Antonioni: the obvious narrative function of colour, and the drama of it, the clash of characters, perspectives: Foehn is bad, the Queen is good; Felix is good, Edith is bad; Love vs Death, Truth vs Deceit, Doom colouring everything. But despite this 'melodrama' of colour there is a free play with colour which depends on it being unrealistic, and their narrative effect so obviously manipulated and artificial that it emphasises not the functionality of the colour but its autonomy and narrative independence. If, in other Antonioni films, the narrative is emptied, drained of substance, in *Oberwald* it is so excessively drawn as to be cancelled out in another manner; and in its place colour presents itself as the subject of the film, though less in relation to narrative than to objects, lines, figures and the sense of the solidity and sense of the image.

One of the principal interests of Oberwald depends on the quality of magnetic tape: the ability it offers to respond instantly to mood, to light, the chance to play with objective changes in relation to subjective feelings; for example, not only can external qualities be immediately transfigured, but they can be subjected to a *series* of transfigurations, and, as in the set of images from *Le montagne incantate*, one image of the set can be selected without thereby erasing the shadows, traces, silhouettes of other images, absent, not chosen, yet imperceptibly 'there'. For example, in the alterations of the colour of the landscape looked at by the Queen and Sebastian, 'naturalistically', in the sense of having a narrative motive, these can be understood as registering changes of mood, the joy, the brightening, the arrival of love, and equally they can be given the motive of the registering of change itself, the passing of clouds, Hegel's echo; but/and it is also the document of alternative images, of possible, multiple meanings, of a play with a range and therefore the cancelling out, again as with *Le montagne incantate*, of any fixed sense, or fixed representation. The interest in the series of landscape transfigurations in *Oberwald* is not in the 'beauty' of any given image, or group of images in the series, and least of all in their direct narrative function (the colour of love), but rather in the transitions, in the movements, in the not-being-fixed and in the multiple range of displacements and substitutions which they generate.

This work in *Oberwald* recalls effects in *L'eclisse* and *Blow-Up*, in particular the close of *L'eclisse* and near the end of *Blow-Up* when the films return to a place previously inhabited, but now empty, except for the presence of that emptiness, hence the trace and feel of absence: the things and objects which displace the couple at the end of *L'eclisse*, but recall them; and the park in *Blow-Up*, empty of the couple, of the body, and Thomas' studio, by then even empty of the image of that couple whose very imprint he has lost; and finally, at the very end of *Blow-Up*, the emergence of a sound and shapes from the miming of them in the tennis match, and simultaneously the wiping of the photographer from the screen.

Oberwald is like a film made of ghosts: characters are in unreal colours, inhabit patches of tinted phantasmic light, leave after-images as they move, appear in two places at once, 'here' in substance, 'there' as a trace; things are both 'real' and not (the alternative colours and tints of the Queen, of Sebastian, but even of the dead King's portrait, green/blue, turning to sepia, fading back to green/blue); a shimmering of light on the movement of water against a wall, the light itself, a torch, moving with the wind, making colour appear and disappear along the wall, changing tones, returning them so that there is no longer wall, but a range of walls. The entire film has this ghostly feel to it: at once a film and the trace of a film, the shadow of itself. Part of that sense rests with the use of magnetic tape: its ability to alter colour, to create shadows, to transfigure, and the extra graininess of the film image as a result of the transfer from tape to film, the chromatic variability, the loss of detail.

The process recalls *Le montagne incantate*: the video 'finds' an image in 'reality', 'there', but only so with the application of a process; it makes something new appear, and at the same time the transfer, which is a kind of enlargement, results in a graininess and chromatic variation which varies the image once more (however strict the colour control). Over and above then the serialisation of images within the space of the fiction (the colour of love in the landscape, or the gallop of joy and liberation through the woods by the Queen), superimposed upon that series is a series contained in the film as a whole in its relations to a reality recorded on tape, altered, then transferred to film.[22]

The 'play', the freedom in *Oberwald* is with the serialisation of image relations, with a direct violation of 'reality' (its conventional, naturalist representations), and with the ability, for the first time, 'to really write a film while shooting it', only possible for Antonioni with video which freed him from the time gap involved in film and of any dependence on laboratories for the final rendering of an image.[23] The 'writing' of Antonioni is a writing which

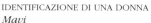

IDENTIFICAZIONE DI UNA DONNA
Mavi

approaches painting: in the move towards abstraction, in the dispersal of the subject, but also in the corporeality and immediacy of it, almost a physical thing; and with Antonioni that 'writing', which is delicate, which skims a surface, lightly, caressingly, is the very opposite even in abstract art of the hand which marks, shapes, makes an incision; *Oberwald* is the closest in all his films to approach that kind of rendering which his harshest critics thought to damn him with: the rendering of the calligrapher.

In *L'eclisse* or in *Blow-Up* there are traces in empty scenes of a lost presence; in *Oberwald* this effect seems directly attached to the 'writing', the shooting, so that it is more than the trace of the absent figure that remains, but of the hand that traced it, the touch itself, as if the camera had captured the wake of its own movement.

The Cocteau melodrama depends on a naturalistic rendering to be effective; Antonioni drained it of that naturalism, and emptied it of the sentiments and the emotions which are central to it. The 'narrative' of *Oberwald* lies elsewhere than in the play by Cocteau, or rather *Oberwald* proposes a somewhat new notion of narrative. In so many of Antonioni's films narrative was a process which tended to move towards dissolution, to an indeterminacy; factors both in the narrative and in the construction of images were responsible. In *Oberwald* image and significance are one and the same (but separate from the 'drama'), and rendered in an almost bodily manner, directly, so that, unlike *Il deserto rosso*, Antonioni could immediately respond to his own movements and to the movements before him, to each image as it was being formed, and in such a way as to bring the figurative fullness of narrative and the figurative emptiness of abstraction together.

What *Oberwald* 'tells' is a certain way of forming an image, of watching and reacting to that formation, of playing with variability, of risking certainty, of establishing a range of possibilities, of opening up a series against all strategies of closure: the film is not the rendering of the Cocteau, nor precisely its transformation, but rather the document of its formation. And this is not formalist, nor abstract, but a way of reacting to things and to images.

Antonioni's remark that *Oberwald* is not merely pictorial, but dictated by concerns for narrative needs to be taken seriously; and along with it the assertion that he had no feeling nor sympathy for the drama of Cocteau. The idea Antonioni expressed in relation to *Oberwald* of writing in film concerns the confounding of a distinction between narrative and abstraction, figure and image, and perhaps as well writing and painting, which, for that moment at least, seemed to be served by the superimposition of techniques from television upon cinema.

The image of things in Antonioni's films is not received 'directly', but through a regard which is marked and made evident; in the later films, it is a look doubled over between the protagonist and the camera. The object that is looked at incorporates the vision which constitutes it; in that sense perception and representation are not divided, but rather overlap; the subject of the image becomes that overlap. It is the split between 'reality' and 'image' which Antonioni emphasises and simultaneously condenses in the external, objective yet self-regarding look of the camera in which the look becomes the object of its own gaze.[24]

The representational codes of the cinema tend to privilege volume over surface, the figure over the image. Narrative devices are important in this balance: if the shot of the wall outside Giuliana's shop in Via Alighieri in *Il deserto rosso* had had a consequential motive in the narrative, its reality as wall might have been immediately clear. For a moment, before the appearance of a figure to retrospectively read and relate it, it was unidentifiable except as an image of, if not nothing, nothing very precise. It is not simply that the narrative was suspended in a *temps morts* (Ozu does this frequently in his films but there is never any problem about reading what it is that is represented – washing on a line, a courtyard, a garden, a hospital, a seascape – only perhaps a problem in deciding its narrative place), but it is rather that figuration itself is suspended, the entire volume and depth in which things take place in narratives seems momentarily absent and in its place appears the 'emptiness' of a surface image, unmoored, unidentifiable, narratively blank, a kind of eclipse of narrative into abstraction.

The wall materialises out of nothing both narratively and visually, but when it does its other status as image remains: while one part of the pressure of the scene is towards the construction of 'facts', of 'incidents', of lending support to character and action, and sustaining these (a chain of events: Corrado parks his Alfa on a street outside Giuliana's shop, they meet, they talk), another part of the scene moves towards dissolution, nothingness, an abandonment of character, a dead time without action: a discoloured surface; movement along the wall which changes its light intensity, alters volume and density; character becomes only an object figured in a landscape, like the momentarily immobile Corrado and Giuliana beside the fruitseller. Here the narrative is suspended not by the removal of character or figure, but by freeing them from any narrative function and equalising them with the landscape.

The landscape, though, has another quality, hard to define, or rather its quality is that of being enigmatic, slightly unreal and therefore disturbing: silent, unpeopled, a grey ghostly tinge as if it were a street in which nothing lived, and it itself insubstantial; the perspectives seem out of true as in a De Chirico or the ghost town Sandro and Claudia encounter in *L'avventura*. If this street isn't there and this town isn't there, what of its inhabitants? Corrado and

Giuliana? The sense of everything being a phantasm reacts back on the regard of these, as if that too was insubstantial, the subject disappearing as it encounters a world without substance.

Most narratives move forward consequentially, causatively, and within pre-determined structures. Antonioni's films are different from this; they seem to move, or rather to oscillate, not between event and event, but between narrative and its absence, between the fullness of story and activity, and the emptiness of an image, as if it were not only hopes and desires and perspectives within the fiction that were threatened with being lost, but the very fiction itself. The fragility and interest of the films are precisely here, in the tenuousness of the narrative and the feeling that what is being represented is less a thing or a substance, or an idea, than an intermediate zone, a line between the appearance of things, and their loss and which can't precisely be spoken. It is what gives many of Antonioni's films a shadowy, phantasma-goric feel, not quite completely 'there', as if a reflected trace of itself.[25]

Felix and Edith, in *Il mistero di Oberwald*, are discussing the fact that the Queen always appears veiled; Felix recounts that once, by chance, he had seen the Queen's face: 'It was pale, light, as if detached from her body.' As he speaks, the scene he evokes in words is faded in as the original image and the place from which it is spoken begins to fade out; but then, as the one image begins to appear and the other to disappear, both are held simulta-neously as an unreal, not completely formed time and space. The sense of incompleteness, of a wavering, a-not-quite-appearing/not-quite-disappearing event, is similar to the sense and the devices of the painting-collage-photo-graph-enlargement series, *Le montagne incantate*, in which serial superim-posed images form or leave their traces between the various processes and within them – the temporality and the arbitrariness, for example, of 'stopping' the enlargement and 'fixing' an image; it is the sense as well of the uncertain reality involved in the enlargement series in *Blow-Up* to the point of the complete dissolution of one figure until another figure, hence another image, begins to take shape. These effects are persistent in *Oberwald*: the passing of the night and the coming of the dawn first signalled by a blue patch of light moving towards the Queen covered with a white blanket sleeping on a chair and, as dawn begins to spread its light, the figure beneath the blanket disappearing until all that is left is the blanket whitened by the light of dawn like a kind of shroud; the dissolving of the discolorations on the wall behind the Queen and Sebastian to become the image of landscape and then returning to wall again; the Queen, her back to the camera, facing a wall from which her own ghostly image, from another time, is projected forward.

A central mechanism of Antonioni's films seems to be this oscillation between figuration and its decomposition rather than any forward movement. In part this is because of the uncertainty, the shadowiness and the tenuousness of what is represented; there is nothing that sure to go forward. While there are scenes in which there are definite occurrences and a chronology for them can be mapped out, an itinerary drawn, the continuity of the film does not lie in a fictionalised line of events, but rather in the continuous appearance and disappearance of the narrative itself and of the objects, characters, events which constitute it.

Thomas searches the landscape for clues in BLOW-UP

In the *montagne incantate* series, as in the enlargements in *Blow-Up*, not only is there no pre-determined final image – the series is always open, potential – but the image finally arrived at has the character of being both arbitrary (or at least subjective) and temporary. In that sense origin and finality are compounded while the pure contingency of image and choice suggests a multiplicity of possible other images, or other stories, other sequences. The images that are set in train, even if sequential, are not consequential; their linearity is only a vectorial line which disseminates contingency and multiplies signs.[26] These signs, these events, appear as 'found' events in the world (the found images, for example, beneath and alongside the painted images in *Le montagne incantate* series, as these are photographed, then enlarged), rather than contrived, and whose appearance and whose succession is casual.

It is for this reason perhaps that Antonioni's films appear to be so distant and so other; the films, like the objects and images within them, present problems for identification, something to interrogate, and to 'find'. The structure of oscillation which superimposes itself on the vectorial succession of events and objects in the films is both context and evidence of the problem of identification and decipherment. Since things lack the final determinations of a closed structure of events, and since the entire binding of events in a plot and in a drama are loosened to the point of disappearance, the entire film, and any image in it, is threatened with indeterminancy: hence the oscillation as central to Antonioni's films and the problem the films pose of fixing a reality, of seizing upon a substance which seems so insubstantial, whose very presence is in doubt.

Identificazione di una donna is Antonioni's most recently completed feature; it was made some time ago in 1982. The 'story' of the film involves the film director, Niccolò, in search of a subject for his next film (a film to be centred on a woman); simultaneously he is in search of a woman in his life. He encounters two women: Mavi (upper class) and Ida (an actress, socially unpretentious). And as things turn out he loses them both.

Though the women are different in class, in attitude, in gesture, in look, they are same in so far as they function as substitutes for one another. Niccolò loses Mavi, and Ida simply replaces her, not unlike Claudia replaced Anna in *L'avventura*. But these women also approach each other in another way. When Mavi is lost to Niccolò – she simply disappears like Anna had – Niccolò searches for her through images: stories from her friends, a photograph in a magazine, a card left at a florist, phone calls to her home, to her mother. The reality of Mavi doubles over with the image of her while the quest by Niccolò for 'her' becomes confounded with the quest by him for his film, as if not only reality becomes multiplied and doubled in images, but the images themselves begin to proliferate, duplicate. Ida, for Niccolò, is in exactly the same position: the image and the reality intermingle so far as to unsettle both, and to allow either to become the substitute of the other.

In one scene in the film Mavi guides Niccolò in the mechanics of her pleasure: to caress her between her legs with her underwear on, then to remove it, kiss and lick her sex, masturbate her with one, then with both hands. While he does so, he watches her, and while he watches her, she watches herself in a mirror, coming before her own reflection. Niccolò, in many ways like Lidia on her walk through Milan in *La notte*, walks through the world encountering things and watching those encounters, trying to

identify them and wondering what they are. In the love-making scene he is
both 'there' with his hands between Mavi's legs, in a fictional 'reality', and not
'there', watching it from outside, composing it, witnessing the reality giving
place to an image of it, and he himself being overtaken in that transformation.
The film, in that way, is like *The Passenger.*

The dispersal of the characters of Mavi and Ida into their images, the
uncertainty of subject caused by the shifting terms of Niccolò's 'life' and his

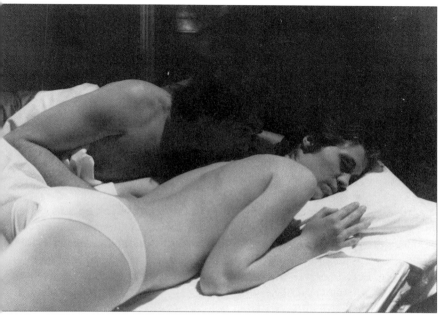

IDENTIFICAZIONE DI UNA DONNA
Niccolò and Mavi

'imaginary', the actual instability of things and persons (since so easily
displaced, cancelled, substituted) have to be connected to a narrative structure
in which the range of displacements is greater than the Mavi/Ida transfer. The
entire film consists, narratively, of a series of encounters by Niccolò with casual
and contingent events. His attitude towards these is essentially interrogative:
he asks questions of things and people, seeks to decipher relations, an object,
a menace, a sound, a shape. But what occurs, in this forward movement of
contingent events without a pre-determined sequence and hence 'meaning',
is a perpetual substitution of subjects within the line of the narrative: not simply

Ida for Mavi, or even the image of Ida for Ida, but a serialisation of 'others': a strange shape on a tree, the birds which fly out of the emptiness of the country house, the odd menaces, the spying, the pursuits, stamps, the sun seen through the telescope, a phone call . . . all, like the women, found objects with no particular import, there only because encountered and, because encountered, tempting to identify, to use.

After a time, Niccolò's itinerary, from woman to woman, object to object, results in greater and greater unclarity. The more objects stand out in their particularity, the less they seem to be connected with anything: it is precisely a narrative connection which is missing. As Niccolò's world becomes more opaque as it slips away from him, the film as an object to identify equally seems to lose outline, almost appearing as formless, with a sense of a vectorial but not consequential linearity, a kind of absolute casualness to the point where events lose all pertinence.

One of the reasons for this – already noticeable in *The Passenger* – is that the knowledge of the narrator, hence of the spectator, is at the same level as that of the main character. As Niccolò encounters a woman or a shape, so does the narrator, and for both the same problem arises: what is it? where does it fit? what to make of it? how can it be identified? The narrator has one additional object to decipher, the film itself, as an aspect of the reality of images and stories in which the narrator is caught.

The move in the film towards formlessness and abstraction of the narrative by primarily narrative means is not itself a formalist experiment, still less some 'meaning' of despair. Rather it is the setting up of a non-determinate, open narrative, hence the establishment of any number of stories, in any number of directions. What moves Antonioni is not, indeed is never, the desire to say something, but rather the desire to narrate, and it is to keep this possibility open that his narratives tend.

At the end of *Identificazione*, Niccolò decides to make a science fiction film, as suggested by his young nephew Lucio after Lucio has seen some Russian stamps commemorating the cosmonauts. Niccolò imagines the film in a dialogue with Lucio: it will concern an astronaut aboard a space ship made of an asteroid flying to the sun to observe it. In the final image of the film the asteroid craft, with its rear exhausts making it seem as if has dark glasses on, disappears into the glow, the emptiness, the incandescent empty centre of the sun, whirling around in a spiral, turning on nothing at all.

The final word is Lucio's: 'E dopo?' ('And what next?')

Notes

1. Requoted in Giorgio Tinazzi, *Antonioni* (Il castoro cinema, 1974) p. 4.

2. Michelangelo Antonioni, 'Suggerimenti di Hegel', *Cinema*, 10 December 1942, pp. 702–703.

3. Jean-Luc Godard, 'Night, Eclipse, Dawn: An Interview with Michelangelo Antonioni', *Cahiers du Cinéma in English* no. 1, January 1966, p. 28.

4. Michelangelo Antonioni, 'Il colore non viene dall'America', *Sequenze* no. 1, 1949, p. 30.

5. Godard, p. 28.

6. Michelangelo Antonioni, 'Film di tutto il mondo a Roma', *Film d'oggi* no. 20, 3 November 1945.

7. Michelangelo Antonioni, '*Isola delle perle* di J. Hogan', *Corriere Padano*, 23 April 1938. (The film is most probably *Ebb Tide* made in 1937.)

8. Michelangelo Antonioni, 'Lo schermo. Del colore', *Corriere Padano*, 2 January 1940.

9. See in this regard Michelangelo Antonioni and Gianni Puccini, 'Due lustri di sonoro', *Cinema*, December 1940 (on sound); Michelangelo Antonioni 'Elzeviri a passo ridotto', *Corriere Padano*, 23 July 1938 (on 16mm); Michelangelo Antonioni, 'Allarmi inutili', *Cinema*, 10 April 1940 (on television); Michelangelo Antonioni, 'Parole di un tecnico', *Cinema*, 25 December 1940, pp. 459–460 (on sound); Michelangelo Antonioni 'Povertà', *Cinema*, 25 September 1939, p. 205 (on narrative structures).

10. Michelangelo Antonioni, '*Terra Verde* (Sunto per un film)', *Bianco e Nero*, October 1940, pp. 971–972.

11. Michelangelo Antonioni, 'Il bosco bianco', pp. 9–13, and Flavio Nicolini, 'Dal "Diario"', pp. 27–37, in Michelangelo Antonioni, *Il deserto rosso* (ed. Carlo Di Carlo) (Bologna: Cappelli, 1978).

12. Giovanni Grazzini in *Gli anni sessanta in cento film* (Bari: Laterza, 1977), p. 110; see also Goffredo Fofi in his *Capire con il cinema* (Milan: Feltrinelli, 1977), p. 33.

13. Enzo Siciliano, 'Che leggono i registi: Il rifiuto d'Antonioni', *La Stampa* no. 168, 5 August 1972.

14. Quoted in Tommaso Chiaretti, 'Affettuosamente incolore', *Cinema 60* no. 45, 1964, p. 21.

15. See especially Edoardo Bruno, 'Deserto rosso', *Filmcritica* no. 146, June 1964, pp. 359–360 and Armando Plebe e Edoardo Bruno, 'Per un cinema italiano di tendenza', *Filmcritica* nos. 156–157, April–May 1965 .

16. Michelangelo Antonioni, 'Allarmi inutili', *Cinema*, 10 April 1940.

17. Requoted in Chatman, p. 202.

18. Michelangelo Antonioni, 'Film di tutto il mondo a Roma', *Film d'oggi* no. 20, 3 November 1945.

19. Quoted in Paolo Cervone 'Antonioni scopre l'elettronica', *Corriere della Sera*, 30 June 1981.

20. Michelangelo Antonioni, 'A quasi confession', *Il mistero di Oberwald* (Rome: RAI, n.d.).

21. Requoted in John Francis Lane, 'Antonioni and the Two-Headed Monster', *Sight and Sound*, Winter 1979–1980.

22. See the Biennale di Venezia catalogue of Antonioni's images of watercolours and collages enlarged from photographs of them in the *Le montagne incantate* exhibit of 1986 and

especially the contributions of Ida Panicalli, Paolo Portoghesi and Tullio Kezich. With regard to television/film relations in *Il mistero di Oberwald*, see Massimo Fichera, 'A new way of production' in RAI *Il mistero di Oberwald*. There are some interesting remarks as well in Keith Griffiths, 'Antonioni's Technological Mysteries', *Framework* nos. 15–17, Summer 1981; Vittorio Giacci 'Un film di fantasmi: *Il mistero di Oberwald*', *Filmcritica* nos. 307–309, September–November 1980; Carlo Di Carlo, 'Nei colori di Antonioni un futuro già cominciato', *L'Unità*, 3 September 1980; and Carlo Di Carlo, 'Antonioni parle de son nouveau film', *Image et Son* no. 351, June 1980.

23. See Aurora Santuari, 'Aurora col colore spiega "Il mistero"', *Paese Sera*, 30 August 1981, from which the statement about writing and filming comes; see also, for some technical matters involved in the transfer from tape to film, the section entitled 'Some technical production aspects' in the RAI booklet on *Il Mistero di Oberwald*.

24. See Lorenzo Cuccu, *La visione come problema* (Rome: Bulzoni, 1973), pp. 125–126.

25. See Michele Mancini and Giuseppe Perrella, *Michelangelo Antonioni: Architetture della visione* (Rome: Coneditor, 1986), p. 124.

26. See Lorenzo Cuccu, '*Identificazione di una donna*: prima ipotesi per la definizione dello stile', *Bianco e Nero*, January-March 1983, pp. 116–117.

Afterword [1]

Antonioni:

> I especially love women. Perhaps because I understand them better? I was born amongst women, and raised in the midst of female cousins, aunts, relatives. I know women very well.
>   Through the psychology of women everything becomes more poignant. They express themselves better and more precisely. They are a filter which allows us to see more clearly and to distinguish things.[2]
>
> I have always given great importance to female characters since I think I know women better than I do men . . . They are more instinctive, more sincere.[3]

In *Chung Kuo Cina*, near the beginning of the film, there is a sequence of a birth by caesarean section. The woman is anaesthetised by acupuncture. It is the only sequence in the documentary that could be called 'dramatic'. Most of the film has an eventless quality. The film seems decentred, out of true, and China, and the Chinese, though carefully observed, are observed in moments that are often still, private, self-absorbed; the observation, however kindly, is at a distance: delicate, non-intrusive.

This manner of observation holds for the caesarean section sequence, at once the most private and intimate, and the most public. There are two subjects to this sequence. One is of the woman giving birth, the acupuncture anaesthetic, the incision and so on, and the entire series of events from the initial acupuncture needle to the emergence of the baby. It is a small narrative: linear, causative, self-contained. It is as much the fact of the birth as it is the form of a narrative succession that gives the scene its drama and its sense. The other subject takes place alongside or within the narrative one and, though connected to it, intimately, is also autonomous from it, and seems at times to overwhelm its narrative subject. It is difficult to put it into words or to ascribe any particular sense to it; it involves the sight of the taut, round, swollen surface of the woman's belly, the insertion into that surface of the long acupuncture needles, the marking out of the place of incision into the surface, its being painted yellow-red-green with disinfectant, the cut into the distended smooth surface of the belly, the opening of the gash, revealing not so much a depth, but a new surface, the breaking of the water, and then again the shift in the surface with the appearance of the baby's head, and the change in it with the baby removed.

The scene oscillates between the figuration of the birth and this visual abstraction of the change in a surface; there seem to be at least two births – of a child coming out of a depth, and of surface emerging within a surface, appearing, changing, disappearing. It is a familiar occurrence in Antonioni's films: a new figuration taking shape within an original one, eventually making the first disappear, and, at the same time, the dissolution of any shape whatsoever into the informality, the uncertainty of abstraction.

I want to mark out a few things about these images: the oscillation between figuration and abstraction; the fascination with surface; the instability, the tenuousness, the fragility of things represented. The presence of these qualities is not intended as marking philosophic points, so much as a practice which opens up the possibility of a multiplicity of shapes taking shape, of a variety of surfaces being formed, so that the dissolution of the figure and of a defined subject is in a way the precondition for new and interesting, and heretofore non-existent, unknown things to appear.

There is a shift in Antonioni's work, evident in 1964 with *Il deserto rosso*, and very clear after 1968 with *Blow-Up*, from female to male protagonists which is connected to a shift in techniques of narration. On the whole the shift in the sex of the protagonists is an aesthetic and structural matter; the change in the position of women, a considerable change from being a subject to becoming an object, is not one, in the case of Antonioni, that easily lends itself to ideological or social conclusions. Just as figuration oscillates with abstraction in Antonioni's films, fullness with emptiness, drama with its eclipse, the ability to hold on to defined meanings, the very desire for these is made difficult, if not impossible.

The change from female to male protagonists, which is accompanied by a change from a subjective camera and narration to a rigorously objective camera and objective narrative position, is also a move towards a more complete and comprehensive dissolution of the subject and the appearance of a more fully abstract film within the narrative. In these late, 'male' films, political, sociological, even philosophic conclusions are less easily concluded, less securely held, than they might have been in the earlier 'female' films, the very great ones such for example as *L'avventura*, *La notte*, *L'eclisse* and out of which a whole host of existential meanings were generated, not, happily, by Antonioni, but certainly by critics, and especially by some on the Italian left, of the alienation-under-capitalism kind.

Giuliana, in *Il deserto rosso*, is extremely neurotic and so on edge, so unstable in relation to objects, colours, figures in the world as these appear to her, as

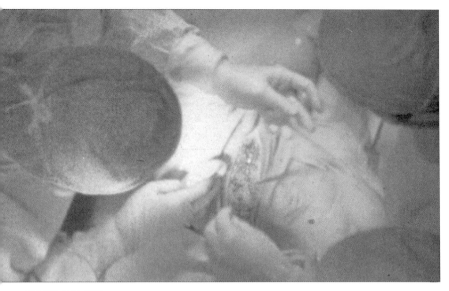

CHUNG KUO CINA
The caesarean

to be experienced with an intensity which literally overwhelms her: she feels the world not only with her fingertips, senses it with her eyes, her ears, but with every turn of her body, with the ends of her hair; and so strong is that sensitivity to sounds and colours and shapes and to their variability and unsteadiness as not only to unbalance Giuliana, but, to a degree, to unbalance an audience.

One of the reasons for this is technical and it has been most ably described by Pier Paolo Pasolini: it has to do with the use of a subjective camera so that for large sections of the film the camera and the narrator see and feel from the same perspective as Giuliana, or, more precisely, it is the only perspective, at those moments, which the film offers. (Though the scheme essentially holds, the situation is somewhat more complicated than Pasolini suggested: though the camera is often subjective, that subjectivity and subjective look is in turn 'objectively' regarded; Giuliana's subjectivity is more an 'object' observed than a subjectivity to identify with.) There is nothing uncommon or especially noteworthy about this fact or the alternation between subjective and objective perspectives which the film practises and which makes Giuliana sometimes the object of the look of the narration, and sometimes the subject coincident with that look. What is notable is the practical consequence of this in this particular film and for Antonioni: it enables him, as Pasolini pointed out, to have a realistic alibi for an abstract, primarily visual sensibility. Because

Giuliana is neurotic, unbalanced, the world appears to her distorted, and however horrible that might be from an individual, psychological perspective, however oppressed and imprisoned Giuliana might appear, her visions, as visions, are exceptionally beautiful, like the taut belly of the woman in the China film as a surface interesting for itself, quite apart from either the process enacted upon it or the eventual birth of the baby from within it.

Not only is Antonioni able to displace the psychological or dramatic subject with one that is either eventless or whose events are primarily graphic and visual – the changing light on a wall, the variations of a surface, a shift in focus, the fading of subjects in a mist – but he is able to do so in such a way as to drain all or most of the emotional charge from within the narrative event, to make the event eventless, to dedramatise the drama. There are two means to this in *Il deserto rosso*: Giuliana's subjective gaze which 'distorts' and 'abstracts' reality, including her own reality (she is the principal subject 'lost' in the film and which she struggles to recover); and the taking of that subjectivity as an object as the camera moves between subjective and objective positions.

Il deserto rosso, the last of Antonioni's 'women's' films, is only an extreme instance, and the most exciting, of what is present in all the films which precede it (with the exceptions perhaps of *I vinti* and *Il grido*), namely the adoption by the narrator of the position of the female protagonist and the alternation between this perspective and an independent, 'objective' one. Some of the most beautiful scenes in Antonioni's films of this period involve the subjective camera from the perspective of the female protagonist and yet a subjective camera which makes the subjectivity seen its object: Lidia's walk around the periphery of Milan in *La notte*, Vittoria's flight to Verona in *L'eclisse*, the sequence in search of Anna on Lisca Bianca in *L'avventura*, and before that, in the same film, Claudia's wait while Anna and Sandro make love. But none of these move so far as *Il deserto rosso* does towards the dissolution of figuration and indeed, of the sense of narrative itself, as this last film does with a woman as the main character.

Why choose women as the viewing centre of the films? Antonioni's answer is that women are better filters of reality than men, hence they see with greater sensitivity and such sensitivity is tied up for him with a tenuousness and gentility and intelligence as if looking were a caress, a kind of touching, not a seizing hold, certainly not a grasping for use, possessive, instrumental; it is the men who are like this in his films and they are, as a consequence, empty and insensate: Sandro in *L'avventura*, Giovanni in *La notte*, Piero in *L'eclisse*, and the frighteningly numb Ugo, Giuliana's husband, in *Il deserto rosso*.

Thus the move away from sense, from figurative fullness towards abstraction, is involved with a certain way of seeing which is Antonioni's, and a way of seeing of the women he represents; it is his look and the look of his women; its aesthetic yield, the exquisite visual beauty of the films, and their open narrative possibilities, is immense.

Antonioni's views about women or about the world are not particularly interesting, indeed, they are rather banal. But Antonioni is not a social philosopher. He is a film-maker and in the concrete terms of his films, of shooting, framing, lighting, colour, gesture, of moving a camera, of establishing objects, of telling a story, the qualities he gives to women and the qualities of vision he takes for himself have considerable aesthetic consequences and what is a cliché translated into social terms, is anything but a cliché in the activities and operations of the films. These film practices alter the way one looks, the shape of things, their movement, their stability, their duration, the space which surrounds objects and persons, and so thoroughly, and in such a complicated manner that the activity itself cannot be translated or reduced to discursive statements, statements for example about 'alienation', or even about the 'nature' of women, or their sensibilities.

From 1968 onwards the central characters of Antonioni's films are male and the camera and the narrator become, over time, completely 'objective', no longer viewing with the eyes or from the perspective of any character (*Il mistero di Oberwald* is the one exception to this). This objectivity is most pronounced in the China film, in *The Passenger*, and comprehensively and wonderfully in Antonioni's last film, *Identificazione di una donna*.

At the centre of *Identificazione di una donna* is Niccolò Farra, a film-maker, in search of a subject for his next film. He believes that before he can find the subject of the film, he requires a character around which the film might take shape and that character ought to be a woman. In the 'women's' films the central character was a woman; in this film, the main male character is in search of a woman, or the image of woman, as the centre of his film; women are still at the centre, but at a greater distance, and principal objects rather than central protagonists. In the course of the film, that is within the reality of the narrative fiction, Niccolò meets two women, Mavi and Ida, with whom he has brief affairs; Mavi disappears and the affair with Ida ends when she finds herself pregnant by someone else. The reality of the women and the images of them which Niccolò makes and projects are confused; the reality often dissolves into an idea and the ideas, like the women, can't be secured, are unstable in relation to Niccolò.

If the presumed or hoped for centre of Niccolò's film is a woman, that centre never coheres, never fully takes shape; but since Niccolò is a presumed other centre of the larger film, he and it never completely cohere either since his subjectivity is so tied to the subject of a woman he seeks but never finds, and is as uncertain as the exterior objects and persons he encounters.

The film then is doubly decentred: in the fiction that is sought within it, and in the fiction that it is, as if simultaneously one is watching two narratives in search of something which is never found and which is not even clear, but on which, nevertheless, their own narrative shape depends.

The great difference between this film and the 'women's' films is that in the latter there are abstract effects, but in this it is the very film itself which seems tenuous, on the point of dissolution. Lidia, Vittoria, Claudia, even Giuliana, despite the extremity of her neurosis, are centres and through them they can filter the world. Niccolò is not such a centre, nor is Locke in *The Passenger*. The narrative never looks with their eyes, never lends itself to their perspective. They are as much objects and as much images as the objects they encounter, or imagine, the women they meet and lose, the images of them they desire and marvel over, and which elude them.

The camera in *Identificazione* is always with Niccolò in the film, beside him as it were, looking as he looks, encountering as he encounters, like him facing the exact same problems of identification, of sorting out reality from its simulacrum, desire from the other; but while it doubles with the position of

IDENTIFICAZIONE DI UNA DONNA
Niccolò and Mavi

the central character, it never assumes that position. It is in that sense objective, both because it stands outside, and because it makes no judgement, at least not beforehand. The camera and the narrator face things precisely when Niccolò does and are in the same position as he in seeking to make sense of the world, of trying to find its centres, define its objects, bestow on it some value and meaning. And like him, it faces the difficulty of sorting out its subjectivity from the objects around it, reality from images, centre from periphery, meaning from insignificance. In this way the film takes itself as its own subject, and one that, by the very nature of this structure, can't be resolved.

In the 'women's' films, more so than in the later, more objective films, the couple in crisis was of principal concern: the men were limited in their vision, insensitive, seeking to grasp something of the world and of themselves, and of the women they encountered; but the world, and the women, and their own selves as well were resistant to that kind of approach; the women, to the contrary, were open, lucid, honest, interested more in looking than in seizing hold. The crisis of the couple was in this cross purpose of sight, of rigidity on the one hand, of flexibility and understanding on the other.

What was wrong in these films, and Pasolini perhaps inadvertently pointed to it, was that the sharing of what Antonioni imagined was a female perspective was an alibi which enabled him to have a perfectly clear narrative while at the same time escape it in a series of departures into the abstract, and what Pasolini named as the beautiful. Curiously, the one certain thing in a changing and uncertain fictional landscape was the women at the centre of it, for they could, in the films, perceive the multiplicity and variety and even incomprehensibility of the world while the men lacked that facility and became therefore the victims of the world and of their need to possess it: the startling example is Aldo in *Il grido*.

The advance in the late films is the giving up of what Pasolini named as Antonioni's subjective alibi, of no longer assuming, as he did then, that not only did women possess a particular and enviable truth, but he possessed the truth of their having it, and hence that mechanism for identifying with it, the subjective camera.

Curiously, it is in the conversion to a completely objective camera, in the sense in which I have described it, and, in the process, turning women fully into objects, that Antonioni liberated himself from not only an aesthetic but a social alibi. Women had a privileged place in the 'women's' films, outside of contradiction, and, I believe, outside of a certain problem; turning them into objects was not to make of them objects to be possessed, but rather objects, along with self, to be identified, and that, as things turn out in the film, is no easy, or even ultimately attainable end.

This new place alongside his main male character Niccolò, the film-maker, is a far preferable one to the position Antonioni assumed in his films of the 1950s and early 1960s. He has made the problem of women more clearly a central problem of desire and subjectivity in the construction of fictions, and has turned fiction, as well as women and self, into similar objects caught up in fictions and imaginings, not completely knowable, which has permitted him the liberty of an excursion into a more complete, more comprehensive and primarily narrative-discursive abstraction where before the narrative still held sway and it was in the visual quality of things that shapes, rather more than fictions, dissolved.

One of the great achievements of *Identificazione* is to have made its entire fiction, including the fiction of its construction, the object of itself, as if the film were a lens, and thus making, if not for the first time, at least convincingly for the first time, a documentary of a fiction, and in which women, along with men, have, if not their rightful place, a place free of any condescension, or, what amounted to the same thing, free of the fiction of subjectivity.

Notes

1. This Afterword is a revised version of a paper delivered at a conference on 'Women in Italian Culture' at La Trobe University, Melbourne, Australia, held between 30 June and 2 July 1989.

2. Georges Sadoul, 'Michelangelo Antonioni come je l'ai vu', *Les Lettres Françaises*, 26 May 1960, p. 7.

3. Requoted in Giorgio Tinazzi, *Michelangelo Antonioni* (Il castoro cinema, 1974), p. 14.

Bibliography

There are only a few major, important works on Antonioni's films: Lorenzo Cuccu, *La visione come problema* (Rome: Bulzoni, 1973); Giorgio Tinazzi, *Michelangelo Antonioni* (Il castoro cinema, 1974); and Michele Mancini and Giuseppe Perrella, *Michelangelo Antonioni: Architetture della visione* (Rome: Coneditor, 1986). There is some interesting material to be found in Carlo Di Carlo (ed.) *Michelangelo Antonioni* (Rome: Edizioni Bianco e Nero, 1964); and in a two-volume collection of short essays on Antonioni also edited by Carlo Di Carlo, *Michelangelo Antonioni: identificazione di un autore* (Pratiche, 1983–1985).

The Tinazzi is intelligent and interesting and the Cuccu simply superb; to both these books, the Cuccu especially, I owe a major debt.

The Mancini and Perrella is in two volumes, well illustrated and expensive; it has an English text alongside the Italian one. However, the translation is inaccurate, unreliable and in places incomprehensible, which is especially unfortunate since the book is not only the most stimulating and interesting on Antonioni, but one of the finest film books written in a long time.

These three books, despite the difference in their treatment of Antonioni, proceed from a similar position, or rather problem, namely the oscillation in Antonioni between figuration and abstraction, narrative clarity and experiment with narrative, not only beyond the conventional, but beyond where most other film-makers have attempted to be. Their general approach is productive and exemplary.

I found little material of any value in English on Antonioni. There is one short essay, however, written twenty-five years ago, which has not been bettered for its insights and for the elegance and intelligence of its formulations: Geoffrey Nowell-Smith, 'Shape Around a Black Point', *Sight and Sound* Winter 1963/64.

The most interesting material in French are two essays by Pascal Bonitzer, 'Désir désert' in *Cahiers du Cinéma* nos. 262–263, January 1976, and 'Il concetto di scomparsa' in the *Michelangelo Antonioni: identificazione di un autore* collection; there is a fine essay by Alain Bergala, 'L'exercice et la répétition' in *Cahiers du Cinéma* no. 342, December 1982, on *Identificazione di una donna* which is used by Lorenzo Cuccu at the beginning of his splendid essay on the film and which develops many of the ideas in his 1973 book; finally, there is an interesting essay on *L'eclisse* by Jean-François Tarnowski, 'Identification d'une œuvre: Antonioni et la modernité cinématographique' in *Positif* no. 263, January 1983.

Nearly all of Antonioni's own writings and his interviews are interesting; he was a fine critic and his exchanges with others are modest, precise, intelligent, never pretentious or careless. Among his two most interesting interviews (both in English) is the one with Godard, 'Night, Eclipse, Dawn' published in *Cahiers du Cinéma in English* in January 1966, and another, just after the China film, done with Gideon Bachmann, 'Antonioni after China . . .', *Film Quarterly* vol. 28, no. 4, Summer 1983.

This bibliography only includes works consulted and is not exhaustive.

Antonioni's writings, essays, interviews
I have listed screenplays and fictional works by Antonioni separately.

'Colpi di sonda. Cinematografo: soggetto e regia', *Corriere Padano*, 28 March 1935.

'Machaty e il suo "notturno"', *Corriere Padano*, 30 June 1936.

'Documentari', *Corriere Padano*, 21 January 1937.

'Per un teatro dello Stato', *Corriere Padano*, 18 February 1937.

'Dell'educazione artistica', *Corriere Padano*, 2 March 1937.

'Universitari alle prese con il passo ridotto (rassegna di documentari)', *Corriere Padano*, 7 April 1937.

'Consigli', *Corriere Padano*, 3 June 1937.

'Quaderno di appunti', *Corriere Padano*, 27 July 1937.

'L'ultimo Pabst (*Mademoiselle Docteur*)', *Corriere Padano*, 21 September 1937.

'*Sangue gitano* di H. Schuster', *Corriere Padano*, 5 November 1937.

'*Orizzonte perduto* di F. Capra', *Corriere Padano*, 6 November 1937.

'*L'uomo ombra* di W.S. Van Dyke', *Corriere Padano*, 7 November 1937.

'*Marcella* di G. Brignone', *Corriere Padano*, 11 November 1937.

'*Settimo cielo* di H. King; *Amanti di domani* di R. Riskin', *Corriere Padano*, 12 November 1937.

'*Accusata* di T. Freeland', *Corriere Padano*, 14 November 1937.

'*Cuor di vagabondo* di J. Epstein; *Angeli della strada* di M. Fric', *Corriere Padano*, 17 November 1937.

'*Aurora sul deserto* di W. Dieterle', *Corriere Padano*, 18 November 1937.

'*Nina Petrovna* di V. Touriansky', *Corriere Padano*, 19 November 1937.

'*Mayerling* di A. Litvak', *Corriere Padano*, 20 November 1937.

'*Una donna qualunque* di F. Nugent; *La corriera del West* di E. F. Cline', *Corriere Padano*, 23 November 1937.

'*Senza perdono*, di G. Marshall', *Corriere Padano*, 25 November 1937.

'*L'idolo del male* di H. Edwards', *Corriere Padano*, 30 November 1937.

'*Il signor Max* di M. Camerini; *Il principe e il povero* di W. Keighley', *Corriere Padano*, 2 December 1937.

'*Felicità Colombo* di M. Mattoli', *Corriere Padano*, 3 December 1937.

'*La danza degli elefanti*, *Corriere Padano*, 8 December 1937.

'Assente: l'intelligenza!', *Corriere Padano*, 17 December 1937.

'*Il Conte di Bréchard* di M. Bonnard', *Corriere Padano*, 1 January 1938.

'*Vittima sommersa* di W. Clemens', *Corriere Padano*, 6 January 1938.

'*Yoshiwara* (*Il quartiere delle geishe*) di M. Ophüls', *Corriere Padano*, 7 January 1938.

'*Sotto i ponti di New York* di A. Santell', *Corriere Padano*, 9 February 1938.

'*Angelo* di E. Lubitsch', *Corriere Padano*, 10 February 1938.

'*Candelabri dello zar* di G. Fitzmaurice; *Le tre spie* di V. Saville', *Corriere Padano*, 10 February 1938.

'*Charlie Chan alle Olimpiadi* di D. Zanuck; *Baci sotto zero* di N. Taurog; *La lucciola* di R. Z. Leonard', *Corriere Padano*, 16 February 1938.

'*La vergine di Salem* di F. Lloyd', *Corriere Padano*, 18 February 1938.

'*Scandolo di Grand Hotel* di D. Zanuck', *Corriere Padano*, 20 February 1938.

'*Un dramma sull'Oceano* di M. St Clair', *Corriere Padano*, 22 February 1938.

'*La Contessa Alessandra* di J. Feyder', *Corriere Padano*, 9 March 1938.

'*La fine della Signora Cheyney* di R. Boleslawsky', *Corriere Padano*, 10 March 1938.

'*Carnet de bal* di J. Duvivier', *Corriere Padano*, 12 March 1938.

'*Zanne e artigli* di F. Buck (documentario); *Prigioniero volontario* di D. Howard', *Corriere Padano*, 15 March 1938.

'*Il magnifico brutto* di G. Blystone', *Corriere Padano*, 16 March 1938.

'*Uragano* di J. Ford', *Corriere Padano*, 17 March 1938.

'*L'allegro cantante* di G. Righelli', *Corriere Padano*, 22 March 1938.

'*La gelosia non è di modo* di W. Lang (e di Zanuck)', *Corriere Padano*, 24 March 1938.

'*L'ultimo gangster* di E. Ludwig; *Voglio danzare con te* di M. Sandrich', *Corriere Padano*, 26 March 1938.

'*L'ultima partita* di F. A. Dwan', *Corriere Padano*, 31 March 1938.

'*Gli ultimi giorni di Pompei* di E. Schoedsack', *Corriere Padano*, 1 April 1938.

'*Un mondo che sorge* di F. Lloyd', *Corriere Padano*, 2 April 1938.

'*Il trionfo della primula rossa* di A. Korda', *Corriere Padano*, 7 April 1938.

'*Un colpo di fortuna* di M. Leisen', *Corriere Padano*, 12 April 1938.

'*Tovarich* di A. Litvak', *Corriere Padano*, 13 April 1938.

'*Millionaria su misura* di M. Curtiz', *Corriere Padano*, 20 April 1938.

'*Isola delle perle* di J. Hogan', *Corriere Padano*, 23 April 1938.

'*L'ultima nemica* di U. Barbaro', *Corriere Padano*, 3 May 1938.

'Gli inglesi a Malta' (review of a book by Luigi Preti), *Corriere Padano*, 6 May 1938.

'*I filibusteri* di C. B. DeMille', *Corriere Padano*, 7 May 1938.

'*La vita futura* di W. C. Menzies', *Corriere Padano*, 8 May 1938.

'Elzeviri a passo ridotto', *Corriere Padano*, 23 July 1938.

'Sul cinema nazionale', *Corriere Padano*, 23 July 1938.

'Taccuino', *Corriere Padano*, 14 September 1938.

'Una favola eroica sullo schermo: Luciano Serra italianissimo pilota', *Corriere Padano*, 26 October 1938.

'Conversazione (intervista a Silvana Jachino)', *Corriere Padano*, 19 November 1938.

'Per Nuova York', *Corriere Padano*, 10 December 1938.

'La rinascita del nostro cinema e la riorganizzazione industriale', *Corriere Padano*, 12 January 1939.

'Panoramica della produzione nazionale', *Corriere Padano*, 22 January 1939.

'*Los novios de la muerte* (poesia di un documentario)', *Corriere Padano*, 25 January 1939.

'Il problema dei soggetti . . .', *Corriere Padano*, 10 February 1939.

'Luci ed ombre dello schermo a Ferrara (a proposito di un progetto di anonimo per un film su Alfonso I D'Este e Lucrezia Borgia)', *Corriere Padano*, 22 February 1939.

'Interrogativi cinematografici', *Corriere Padano*, 23 February 1939.

'Corriere cinematografico', *Corriere Padano*, 13 April 1939.

'Vita selvaggia', *Corriere Padano*, 16 May 1939.

'L'albergo dei morti a Hollywood', *Cinema*, 25 June 1939.

'Una cronistoria del cinema' (review of Pasinetti's, *Storia del cinema*), *Cinema*, 10 July 1939.

'Panoramica', *Cinema*, 10 July 1939.

'Cronache del cinema', *Corriere Padano*, 14 July 1939.

'Umori del pubblico', *Cinema* no. 74, 25 July 1939.

'Coste e paghe', *Cinema*, 10 August 1939.

'Divismo balneare', *Cinema*, 10 August 1939.

'Povertà', *Cinema*, 25 September 1939.

'I custodi della civiltà', *Cinema*, 10 October 1939.

'Lo schermo. Del colore', *Corriere Padano*, 2 January 1940, p. 3.

'La scuola delle moglie', *Cinema*, 25 February 1940.

'Allarmi inutili', *Cinema*, 10 April 1940.

'La nuova colonia', *Cinema*, 25 April 1940.

'Un costumista', *Cinema*, 25 April 1940.

'Un tecnico del suono', *Cinema*, 25 April 1940.

'Il consiglio dei Dieci meno Uno' (interviews with Leo Longanesi, Piero Tellini, Cesare Zavattini), *Cinema*, 25 May 1940.

'L'ultima lezione di Nello Quilici', *Corriere Padano*, 8 August 1940.

'La settimana cinematografica di Venezia: *La peccatrice* di Palermi', *Corriere Padano*, 4 September 1940.

'La settimana cinematografica di Venezia: L'epopea dell'Alcazar in un film di Genina', *Corriere Padano*, 5 September 1940.

'La settimana cinematografica di Venezia: *L'ebreo Süss* e *Il cavaliere di Krujá*, *Corriere Padano*, 6 September 1940.

'La settimana cinematografico di Venezia: un delicato film di Camerini segna un successo della cinematografia italiana', *Corriere Padano*, 7 September 1940.

'Inaugurazione', *Cinema*, 10 September 1940.

'La sorpresa veneziana', *Cinema*, 10 October 1940.

'Vita impossibile del Signor Clark Costa', *Cinema*, 10 November 1940.

'Film di questi giorni: *Ombre rosse*', *Cinema*, 25 November 1940 (signed Vice).

'Il doppiaggio alla sbarra', *Film*, 21 December 1940.

'Due lustri di sonoro', *Cinema*, 25 December 1940 (with Gianni Puccini).

'Primo amore: film del trapasso', *Cinema*, 25 December 1940.

'Parole di un tecnico', *Cinema*, 25 December 1940.

'Plebiscito contro gli orrori del doppiato', *Bianco e Nero*, December 1940.

'Parla un operatore', *Cinema*, 25 February 1941.

'Chrysler apribile con strapuntini', *Cinema*, 25 March 1941.

'Distrazioni', *Cinema*, 10 April 1941.

'Conclusioni sul doppiato', *Cinema*, 25 April 1941.

'Lo spettacolo Roosevelt', *Cinema*, 10 August 1941.

'Per una storia della mostra', *Cinema*, 10–25 September 1941.

'Suggerimenti di Hegel', *Cinema*, 10 December 1942.

'L'Herbier sulle orme di Méliès', *Cinema*, 25 January 1943.

'Danza classica e cinema', *Cinema*, 25 April 1943.

'Battere le mani', *Cinema*, 1 May 1943.

'Gli intellettuali e il cinema', *Bianco e Nero*, May 1943.

'Commento a un'emigrazione', *Primato*, 15 May 1943.

'La questione individuale', *Lo Schermo*, August–September 1943.

'Prévert et Carné', *Lo Schermo*, August–September 1943.

'Il cimitero della celluloide', *Cinema*, 25 December 1943.

'Prima di Montmartre', *Cosmopolita*, 23 December 1944.

'Film di tutto il mondo a Roma', *Film d'oggi*, nos. 16, 17, 20, 6, 13 October, 3 November 1945.

'Marcel Carné, ovvero quasi un ritratto', *Fiera Letteraria*, 30 May 1946.

'Frigida America', *Film Rivista*, 31 August 1946.

'L'ultimo Disney', *Film Rivista*, 9 September 1946.

'Omaggio a Clair', *Film Rivista*, 13 September 1946.

'Omaggio a Renoir', *Film Rivista*, 19 September 1946.

'Il problema del colore', *Bianco e Nero*, 1948.

'Marcel Carné, parigino', *Bianco e Nero*, October 1948.

'Il colore non viene dall'America', *Sequenze* no. 1, 1949.

'La pazienza del cinema', *Cinema*, 30 January 1949.

(Ed.) 'Breviario del cinema', *Cinema*, (Nuova Serie) nos. 11, 16, 20, 24 March, June, August, October 1949.

'*La terra trema*', *Bianco e Nero*, July 1949.

'Che cosa pensano del pubblico', *Cinema* no. 73, 1 November 1951.

'Un passo avanti', *Cinema Nuovo*, 1 March 1953.

'Antonioni risponde a Chiarini', *Cinema Nuovo*, 15 May 1953.

'Annuale o biennale?', *Cinema Nuovo*, 15 August 1953.

'Suicidi in città', *Cinema Nuovo*, 15 March 1954.

'*I vinti*', *Cinema Nuovo*, 15 March 1954.

'Uno di nostri figli', *Cinema*, 25 July 1954 (with G. Bassani and S. Cecchi d'Amico).

'Domande e risposte', *Cinema Nuovo*, 25 January 1955.

'Domande e risposte', *Cinema Nuovo*, 25 April 1955.

'Lettere a Michele Lacalamita', *Bianco e Nero*, May 1958.

'Colloquio con Michelangelo Antonioni', *Bianco e Nero*, June 1958.

'Crisi e neorealismo', *Bianco e Nero*, September 1958.

'Crisi e neorealismo, risposta al questionario di, *Bianco e Nero*', *Bianco e Nero*, September 1958.

'Fare un film è per me vivere', *Cinema Nuovo*, March–April 1959 (also in English in *Filmviews*, Spring 1987).

'There Must be a Reason for Every Film', *Films and Filming*, April 1959.

'Une journée', *Positif* no. 30, July 1959.

'Questions à Antonioni', *Positif* no. 30, July 1959.

'Pourquoi j'ai fait L'Avventura', *Les Lettres Françaises*, 26 May 1960.

MANCEAUX, M. 'Entretien avec Michelangelo Antonioni', *L'Express*, 8 September 1960.

MAURIN, F. 'Entretien avec Antonioni', *L'Humanité-Dimanche*, 25 September 1960.

'Entretien avec Michelangelo Antonioni' (ed. André S. Labarthe), *Cahiers du Cinéma* no. 112, October 1960.

'Eroticism – the Disease of Our Age', *Films and Filming*, January 1961.

LABARTHE, A. S. 'Quatre questions à Antonioni', *France-Observateur* , 23 February 1961.

'La malattia dei sentimenti', *Bianco e Nero*, February–March 1961 (also in English in *Film Culture* no. 24, Spring 1962).

'Riflessioni sull'attore', *L'Europa Letteraria* no. 9–10, 1961.

'Nevrosi, disperazione e speranza', *Cinema Nuovo*, November–December 1962.

'Statement', *Motion* no. 5, March 1963.

'Il "fatto" e l'immagine', *Cinema Nuovo*, July–August 1963 (available in English as 'The Event and the Image', *Sight and Sound*, Winter 1963/64).

'La realtà e il cinema diretto', *Cinema Nuovo*, 167 January–February 1964; translated as 'Reality and cinema-verite' in S. Wake (ed.), *Blow-Up* (London: Lorimer, 1971).

'La nuit, l'eclipse, l'aurore' (interview with J.-L. Godard), *Cahiers du Cinéma* no. 160, 1964; in English in *Cahiers du Cinéma in English* no. 1, January 1966; in Italian in *Cineforum* nos. 36–37.

'Il deserto rosso', *Cahiers du Cinéma* no. 159, October 1964.

'Dichiarazioni di Michelangelo Antonioni su "Deserto Rosso"' in 'Deserto rosso' edited by F. Dorigo *Cineforum* no. 40, December 1964.

'Dix ans du cinéma français', *Cinema 65* no. 92, January 1965.

'Documenti. Un documentario sulla donna', *TVC* no. 1, 1966.

'Protagonista, non testimone l'Antonioni di Zabriskie Point', *Cinema Nuovo*, July–August 1968.

Antonioni's fictional writings

'Due angeli sotto la pioggia (impressioni di un soggiorno a Solda)', *Corriere Padano*, 6 August 1938.

'Strada a Ferrara', *Corriere Padano*, 8 October 1938.

'Ritratto', *Corriere Padano*, 18 December 1938.

'Antonioni à Hollywood: entretien', *Cinema 69* no. 137, June 1969.

'Licensiosità come ribellione', *Cinema Nuovo*, November–December 1969.

'La parola di Antonioni su Zabriskie Point', *Cineforum* nos. 92–93, May–August 1970.

'Antonioni parle', *Cinema 70* no. 147, June 1970.

'An interview with Michelangelo Antonioni' (with P. Billard) in S. Wake (ed.), *Blow-Up*, (London: Lorimer, 1971).

MANCINI, M. et al. 'Conversazione con Michelangelo Antonioni', *Filmcritica* no. 231, January–February 1973.

'La différence entre Pavese et moi, c'est que lui s'est suicidé et moi pas' (interview with Luisa Spagnoli), *Ecran* 18, 1973.

'Antonioni on the Seven-Minute Shot', *Film Comment*, July–August 1975.

'Antonioni after China: Art versus Science', *Film Quarterly*, vol. 28 no. 4, 1975 (interview with Gideon Bachmann).

'Da ragazzo suonavo il violino ma non amo la musica nei film', *Filmcritica*, nos. 305–306, May–June 1980.

'Antonioni parle de son nouveau film', *Image et Son* no. 351, June 1980.

'A Love of Today: An Interview with Michelangelo Antonioni', *Film Quarterly* vol. 36 no. 4, Summer 1983.

'Statement', *Le montagne incantate* (Biennale di Venezia, 1986).

ROUMETTE, S. 'Au bout de la nuit: entretien avec Michelangelo Antonioni', *Clarté* no. 34.

'Uomini di notte', *Corriere Padano*, 18 February 1939.

'Stanotte hanno sparato', *Cinema Nuovo*, 15 April 1953.

'Ho un storia vera che non posso girare', *Successo*, (Milan) February 1961.

'Appunti per un film da fare o da non fare', *Cinema Nuovo*, November–December 1977.

'Un uomo, una donna e una storia che poteva essere un film', *Cinema Nuovo*, March–April 1978.

'Quel bowling sul Tevere e inoltre Il deserto dei soldi', *Cinema Nuovo*, March–April 1976.

'Le idee non sono antipatiche né simpatiche', *Cinema Nuovo*, May–June 1976.

'Quattro uomini in mare', *Cinema Nuovo*, November–December 1976.

'Il "big bang" della nascita di un film', *Cinema Nuovo*, December 1981.

Acquilone: una favola del nostro tempo (Rimini: Maggioli, 1982).

'Una intensa emozione che la troupe interrompe', *Cinema Nuovo*, June 1982.

Quel bowling sul Tevere (Turin: Einaudi, 1983); published by Oxford University Press as, *That Bowling Alley on the Tiber*, in 1987.

Antonioni's screenplays, treatments (realised and not).

'Per un film sul fiume Po', *Cinema*, 25 April 1939.

'Terra verde (sunto per un film)', *Bianco e Nero*, October 1940.

Il grido, (ed. Elio Bartolini) (Bologna: Cappelli, 1957).

L'avventura, (ed. Tommaso Chiaretti) (Bologna: Cappelli, 1960).

L'eclisse, (ed. John Francis Lane) (Bologna: Cappelli, 1962).

'Makaroni (sceneggiatura)', *Cinema Nuovo*, May–June, July–August, September–October 1963 (with T. Guerra).

Il deserto rosso, (ed. Carlo Di Carlo) (Bologna: Cappelli, 1964).

Sei film, (*Le amiche, Il grido, L'avventura, La notte, L'eclisse, Il deserto rosso*) (Rome: Einaudi, 1964).

Blow-Up (Turin: Einaudi, 1967).

Writings on Antonioni

ABRUZZESE, A. 'Ideologia e poetica nel regista cinematografico' in *L'immagine filmica* (Rome: Bulzoni, 1974).

ADAIR, G. 'The Eagle has Three Heads: Il Mistero di Oberwald', *Sight and Sound*, vol. 50 no. 4, Autumn 1981.

AGEL, H. *Les Grands Cinéastes* (Paris: Editions Universitaires, 1959).

ALESSANDRINI, L. et al., 'Discutiamo su *Blow-Up*', *Rivista del Cinematografo* no. 1, 1968.

Zabriskie Point (introduction by Alberto Moravia) (Bologna: Cappelli, 1970).

Il primo Antonioni, (ed. Carlo Di Carlo) (Bologna: Cappelli, 1973) (includes, *Gente del Po, N.U., L'amorosa menzogna, Superstizione, Cronaca di un amore, I vinti, La signora senza camelie, Tentato suicidio*).

Chung Kuo: Cina, (ed. Lorenzo Cuccu) (Turin: Einaudi, 1974.

Professione: reporter, (ed. Carlo Di Carlo) (introduction by Stefano Reggiani) (Bologna: Cappelli, 1975).

The Passenger (with Mark Peploe and Peter Wollen) (New York: Grove Press, 1975).

Tecnicamente dolce (Turin: Einaudi, 1976).

Il mistero di Oberwald (ed. Gianni Massironi) ERI 1981.

Identificazione di una donna, (ed. Aldo Tassone) (Turin: Einaudi, 1983).

AMIEL, V. '*Identification d'une femme*', *Positif* no. 262, December 1982.

ANON. 'Vie del cinema nostro', *Cinema*, 10 July 1943.

ANON. 'Questo pubblico, queste masse', *Cinema*, 25 July–10 August 1943.

ANON. 'Editoriale', *Cinema*, 25 July–10 August 1943.

ANON. '*La signora senza camelie*', *Bianc e Nero*, no. 3 1953.

ANON. 'I vinti', Cinema Nuovo no. 31, 15 March 1954.

ANON. 'Blow-Up', Cinema 60 nos. 65–66, 1967.

ANON. 'Antonioni, un autore "moderno"', Cineforum 143, April 1975.

ANON. 'Mi ha affascinato giocare con il colore', Il Tempo 6 August 1980.

ANON. 'Note: Identificazione di un autore: Michelangelo Antonioni Ferrara, 1982–1983', Bianco e Nero no. 4, 1983.

APULEO, V. 'Attraverso l'emozione', Il Messaggero, 21 October 1983.

ARGAN, C. A. 'Statement', Le montagne incantate (Biennale di Venezia 1986).

ARGENTIERI, M. 'I vinti', Rinascita, 10 November 1962.

ARGENTIERI, M. 'Tre film al Festival di Venezia', Il Contemporaneo no. 77, October 1964.

ARGENTIERI, M. 'I "formalisti italiani"', Cinema 60 nos. 147, 148, 149 September–October, November–December 1982, January–February 1983.

ARISTARCO, G. 'Cronaca di un amore', Cinema, 15 November 1950.

ARISTARCO, G. 'La signora senza camelie', Cinema Nuovo, 15 March 1953.

ARISTARCO, G. 'L'amore in città, Cinema Nuovo, 15 January 1954.

ARISTARCO, G. 'Il lungo coltello', Cinema Nuovo, 25 September 1955.

ARISTARCO, G. 'Il grido', Cinema Nuovo, 15 October 1957.

ꞭTARCO, G. 'Cronache di una crisi e ᵔ strutturali dell'anima', Cinema ʼanuary–February 1961.

Ɬ. 'L'universo senza qualità', ᵔ May–June 1962.

cinema italiano dopo ᵔrni del CUC no. 6, 1964.

Ionna nel deserto di ᵔ Nuovo, January–Fe-

ARISTARCO, G. 'Evoluzione di Antonioni in Zabriskie Point', Cinema Nuovo, May–June 1970.

ASOR, ROSA A. Scrittori e popolo (Rome: Samonà e Savelli, 1969).

ASTRUC, A. 'Il grido', L'Express, 11 December 1958.

ATTOLINI, V. 'Poetica e stile in Michelangelo Antonioni', Giovane Critica no. 7, February–March 1965.

AUDE, F. 'L'Adieu aux femmes', Positif 263, January 1983.

AUDE, F. AND THIRARD, P.-L. 'Entretien avec Michelangelo Antonioni', Positif 263, January 83.

BALDELLI, P. 'Le due strade di Antonioni', Filmselezione 7, 1961.

BALDELLI, P. 'Antonioni dalla California: L'Europa è un museo', Il Dramma, April 1970.

Baldelli, P, Cinema dell'ambiguità (Rome: Samonà e Savelli, 1971).

BARRAL, J. 'Notes sur L'avventura', Positif no. 35, July–August 1960.

BARTHES, R. 'Caro Antonioni . . .', Bologna Incontri no. 2, February 1980.

BARTOLINI, E. 'Omaggio a Antonioni', Europa Letteraria nos. 9–10, 1961.

BASSOTTO, C. 'Ritratto di Michelangelo Antonioni', Cineforum no. 6, August 1961.

BAZIN, A., MAYOUX, M., RICHER, J.-J. 'Petit dictionnaire pour Venise', Cahiers du Cinéma no. 27, October 1953.

BAZIN, A. 'I vinti', Cinema Nuovo, 15 September 1953.

BAZIN, A. 'Le neo-réalisme se retourne', Cahiers du Cinéma no. 69, March 1957.

BELMANS, J. 'Michelangelo Antonioni ou l'état de crise', Le Thryse, Brussels, 1965.

BELMANS, J. 'La fonction du décor dans l'œuvre de Michelangelo Antonioni', Le Progrès no. 16, Brussels, 1968.

BENAYOUN, R. 'La Donna Senza Camelie', Positif no. 30, July 1959.

BENAYOUN, R. 'Trois tempéraments à leur parfaite extrémité', *Positif* no. 117, June 1970.

BENAYOUN, R. 'Une dialectique du détachement: *Identification d'une femme*', *Positif* 263, January 1983.

BERGALA, A. 'L'exercice et la répétition', *Cahiers du Cinéma* no. 342, December 1982.

BERNARDINI, A. *Michelangelo Antonioni da Gente del Po a Blow-Up* (Milan: I Sette, 1967).

BEYLIE, C.'Haute gamme', *Cahiers du Cinéma* no. 91, January 1959.

BEZZOLA, G. 'Renoir, Visconti, Antonioni', *Cinema Nuovo* no. 18, 1 September 1953.

BIAGI, E. 'Dicono di Lei Antonioni', *La Stampa*, 25 March 1973.

BIANCHI, P. 'Una porta spalancata sul deserto amoroso', *Il Giorno*, 5 March 1975.

BIARESE, C. AND TASSONE, A. *I film di Michelangelo Antonioni* (Rome: Gremese Editore, 1985).

BILLARD, P. 'Michelangelo Antonioni: un cinéaste du "mal de vivre"', *France-Observateur* no. 4, December 1958.

BIRAGHI, G. '*Professione: reporter*', *Il Messaggero*, 2 March 1975.

BOATTO, A. 'Le strutture narrative in Antonioni' in C. Di Carlo, *Michelangelo Antonioni* (Rome: Edizioni *Bianco e Nero*, 1964).

BOLLERO, M. 'Il documentario: Michelangelo Antonioni', *Sequenze* no. 4, Parma, December 1949.

BOLZONI, F. 'Un ritratto di Antonioni', *Rivista del Cinema Italiano* no. 10, October 1954.

BOLZONI, F. 'Un regista: Michelangelo Antonioni', *Ferrania* vol. 11 no. 1, January 1957.

BONITZER, P. 'Désir désert', *Cahiers du Cinéma* nos. 262–263, January 1976.

BONITZER, P. 'Il concetto di scomparsa', in *Michelangelo Antonioni: Identificazione di un autore* (Parma 1985).

BONITZER, P. 'Les images, le cinéma, l'audiovisuel', *Cahiers du Cinéma* no. 404, February 1988.

BORDE, R. 'Un cinéma de la vérité subjective', *Les Temps Modernes*, December 1960–January 1961.

BORELLI, A. 'Il cinema italiano e la crisi della società borghese', *Cinemasud* 27, 1962.

BRAMBILLA, C. 'Una fuga impossibile', *La notte*, 5 March 1975.

BRATINA, D. '*Zabriskie Point/Easy Rider*', *Cineforum* nos. 92–93, May–August 1970.

BRUNETTA, G.-P. *Forma e parola nel cinema* (Padua: Liviana, 1970).

BRUNO, E. '*Cronaca di un amore*', *Filmcritica* no. 2, January 1951.

BRUNO, E. '*Il grido*', *Filmcritica* no. 74, January 1958.

BRUNO, E. '*Il deserto rosso*', *Filmcritica* no. 146, June 1964.

BRUNO, E. 'La irrealtà fisica di Michelangelo Antonioni' in *Tendenze del cinema contemporaneo* (Rome: Samonà e Savelli, 1965).

BRUNO, E. 'L'immagine e l'avvenimento', *Filmcritica* no. 206, April 1970.

BRUNO, E. 'Senso (filmico) dell'intrascrivibile', *Filmcritica* no. 231, January–February 1973.

BRUNO, E. 'La Cina di Antonioni', *Filmcritica* no. 231, January–February 1973.

BUFFA, M. 'Lo sguardo/ripresa di *Professione Reporter*', *Filmcritica* no. 231, January–February 1973.

Burch, N. *Theory of Film Practice* (New York: Praeger 1973).

BUTOR, M. 'Rencontre avec Antonioni', *Les Lettres Françaises*, 14 June 1961.

CALDERONI, G. 'Que pensez-vous de la censure?', *Cinéma*, 15 March 1952.

CALDIRON, V. 'Il gruppo Cinema 1941–43 nella cultura d'avanguardia', *Cinema Nuovo*, 1 May 1957.

CALVINO, I. '*Le amiche*', *Notiziario Einaudi*, November 1955.

CALVINO, I. '*L'eclisse*', *Il Giorno*, 29 April 1962.

CALVINO, I., FORTINI, F., FERRATA, G., SOAVI, G., TARIZZO, D. 'Quattro domande sul cinema italiano', *Cinema Nuovo*, January–February 1961.

CAMERON, I. 'Michelangelo Antonioni', *Film Quarterly* no. 1, 1962.

CAMERON, I. AND WOOD, R. *Antonioni* (London: Studio Vista, 1970).

CANBY, V. 'Antonioni's Haunting Vision', in M. Antonioni, M. Peploe, P. Wollen, *The Passenger* (New York: Grove Press, 1975).

CANNAVO, G. 'Antonioni sulla via di Camus', *Cinema Nuovo*, July–August 1961.

CANNISTRARO, P. V. *La fabbrica del consenso: fascismo e mass media* (Bari: Laterza, 1975).

CAPELLE, A. 'Antonioni parle . . .', *Arts*, 17 August 1966.

CARPI, F. 'Michelangelo Antonioni', *Cinema Nuovo*, 15 March 1957.

CARPI, F. *Cinema italiano del dopoguerra* (Milan: Schwarz, 1958).

CARPI, F. *Michelangelo Antonioni* (Guanda, 1958).

CARRÈRE, E. 'De retour en Italie: *Identification d'une femme*', *Positif* no. 263, January 1983.

CASETTI, F., FARASSINO, A., GRASSO, A., SANGUINETTI, T. (Il gruppo Cinegramma) 'Neorealismo e cinema italiano degli anni '30', in Lino Micciché (ed.), *Il neorealismo cinematografico italiano* (Venice: Marsilio, 1975).

CASIRAGHI, U. 'La lunga notte dei sentimenti nell'*Eclisse* di Antonioni', *L'Unità*, 13 April 1962.

CASIRAGHI, U. 'Il nuovo film di Antonioni sugli schermi italiani: un reporter esplora sé stesso', *L'Unità*, 5 March 1975.

CASTELLANI, L. '*Il deserto rosso*', *Rivista del Cinematografo* nos. 9–10, 1964.

CASTELLO, G. C. 'Troppi "Leoni" al Lido', *Cinema* no. 116, 31 August 1953

CASTELLO, G. C. '*L'amore in città*', *Cinema* no. 123, 15 December 1953.

CASTELLO, G. C. '*Le amiche*', *Film*, October 1955.

CASTELLO, G. C. 'La seconda settimana della mostra', *Film* no. 3, October 1955.

CASTELLO, G. C. 'Coerenza di Antonioni', *Il Punto*, 8 October 1960.

CATAVELLI, G. '*Blow-Up*', 15 November 1967.

CATAVELLI, G. 'Professione: reporter', *Libertà*, 3 April 1975.

CAVALLARO, G. 'Michelangelo Antonioni, simbolo di una generazione', *Bianco e Nero*, September 1957.

CAVALLARO, G. 'Colloquio con Michelangelo Antonioni', *Bianco e Nero*, June 1958.

CAVALLARO, G. 'Antonioni', in *Venti anni di cinema italiano* (Rome: Sindacato Nazionale Giornalisti Cinematografici Italiani, 1965).

CECCHI, E. 'American Literature and the Cinema', *Filmviews* no. 135, Autumn 1988.

CERVONE, PAOLO 'Antonioni scopre l'elettronica', *Corriere della Sera*, 30 June 1981.

CHATMAN, S. *Antonioni or, The Surface of the World* (Berkeley and Los Angeles: University of California, 1985).

CHIARETTI, T. 'Cinema romanzesco e della realtà', *Cinema 60* no. 5, November 1960.

CHIARETTI, T. 'La monade orgogliosa', *La Fiera del Cinema* no. 3, March 1962.

CHIARETTI, T. 'Infelicità e sentimento in Antonioni', *Cinema 60* no. 45, September 1964.

CHIARETTI, T. 'Affettuosamente incolore', *Cinema 60* no. 45, September 1964.

CHIARETTI, T. 'Problemi estetici in Antonioni', *Centro-film* nos. 36–37, 1965.

CHIARINI, L. '*Signora senza camelie*', *Cinema Nuovo*, 1 April 1953.

CHIARINI, L. 'Ancora sulla *Signora senza camelie*', *Cinema Nuovo*, 1 June 1963.

CHINOL, E. 'Film poesia e film letteratura', *Cinema Nuovo*, 15 July 1953.

CINEMA NUOVO 'Protagonista, non testimone l'Antonioni di Zabriskie Point', *Cinema Nuovo*, July–August 1968.

'Cinémonde Fait le procès de Michelangelo Antonioni', *Cinémonde*, 31 January 1961.

CLAY, J. 'La blessure secrète de Michelangelo Antonioni', *Realités* no. 193, February 1962.

CLOUZOT, C. '*Blow-Up*', *Cinema 67* no. 116, May 1967.

CLUNY, C.M. 'Michelangelo Antonioni', *Cinéastes I* (Brussels: Casterman, 1971).

COLLET, J. 'Antonioni ou le désert de l'amour', *Radio Cinema* no. 559, 2 October 1960.

COLOMBO, F. 'La metamorfosi di Antonioni', *La Stampa*, 11 July 1974; in English as 'Visual structure in a film by Antonioni', *Quarterly Review of Film Studies* vol. 2 no. 4, November 1977.

COLOMBO, L. G. 'Coerenza estetica e morale nell'opera di Antonioni', *Il Cittàdino*, 8 February 1959.

CONTENTI, F. 'Le spirali del senso', *Filmcritica* 331, January 1983.

CONTINI, E. 'Il documentario', in *Il neorealismo italiano* (Venice: Quaderno a cura della Direzione della Mostra Internazionale d'arte cinematografica, 1951).

COSSATO, V. 'Antonioni per poco battuto la Cina', *Il Giorno*, 17 November 1974.

COSULICH, C. 'Una lunga attesa di morte nella fuga di un uomo in crisi', *Cinema*, 2 March 1975.

COWIE, P. *Antonioni, Bergman, Resnais* (London: Tantivy Press, 1963).

CUCCU, L. *La Visione come problema* (Rome: Bulzoni, 1973).

CUCCU, L. 'Identificazione di una donna: prima ipotesi per la definizione dello stile', *Bianco e Nero*, January–March 1983.

CUEL, F. 'Il postino suona sempre due volte', *Cinématographe* no. 70, September 1981.

CURTIS, H-L. 'Antonioni au naturel', *Combat*, 20 April 1961.

DANEY, S. AND TOUBIANA, S. 'La méthode de Michelangelo Antonioni', *Cahiers du Cinéma* no. 342, December 1982.

DECAUX, E. 'Le mystère d'Oberwald', *Cinématographe*, October 1980.

DEL FRA, L. 'Con una pistola in mano sono subito simpatici' *XXX* no. 30, 1 March 1954.

DELLA VOLPE, G. 'Antonioni e l'ideologia borghese' in C. Di Carlo (ed.), *Michelangelo Antonioni* (Rome: Edizioni Bianco e Nero, 1974).

DEMEURE, J. 'Suicide manqué', *Positif* no. 30, July 1959.

DE SANTI, G. '*Identificazione di una donna*', *Cineforum* no. 12, December 1982.

DE SANTIS, G. 'Per un paesaggio italiano', *Cinema*, 25 April 1941.

DE SANTIS, G. AND M. ALICATA 'Verità e poesia: Verga e il cinema italiano', *Cinema*, 10 October 1941.

DE SANTIS, G. AND M. ALICATA 'Ancora di Verga e del cinema italiano', *Cinema*, 25 November 1941.

DE SANTIS, G. 'Il linguaggio dei rapporti', *Cinema*, 25 December 1941.

DI CARLO, C. (ed.) *Michelangelo Antonioni* (Rome: Edizioni Bianco e Nero, 1964).

DI CARLO, C. 'Ritorna in TV la Cina vista da Michelangelo Antonioni', *L'Unità*, 23 August 1979.

DI CARLO, C. 'Antonioni parle de son nouveau film', *Image et Son* no. 351, June 1980.

DI CARLO, C. 'Nei colori di Antonioni un futuro già cominciato', *L'Unità*, 3 September 1980.

DI CARLO, C. (ed.) *Michelangelo Antonioni: identificazione di un autore* (Rome: Pratiche, 1983–85).

DI GIAMMATTEO, F. '*Cronaca di un amore*', *Bianco e Nero*, April 1951.

DI GIAMMATTEO, F. 'Quattro film italiani', *Rivista del Cinema Italiano*, vol. 2 nos. 4–5, April-May 1953.

DI GIAMMATTEO, F. 'Tra dubbi e penose incertezze i migliori verso il realismo', *Ras-*

segna del Film vol. 2 no. 16, July–August 1953.

DI GIAMMATTEO, F. 'Michelangelo Antonioni', *Comunità*, Milan, February 1956.

DI GIAMMATTEO, F. AND TINAZZI, G. *Michelangelo Antonioni* (Padua: CUC, 1961).

DI GIAMMATTEO, F. 'Michelangelo Antonioni', in C. Di Carlo (ed.), *Michelangelo Antonioni* (1964).

DONIOL-VALCROZE, I. 'Une robe de tulle bleu ciel', *Cahiers du Cinéma* no. 75, October 1957.

DORIGO, F. (ed.) 'Il deserto rosso', *Cineforum*, December 1964.

DORT, B. 'Incertezze antonioniane', in C. Di Carlo (ed.), *Michelangelo Antonioni* (1964).

ECO, U. '*De interpretatione*, or the difficulty of being Marco Polo', *Film Quarterly*, vol. 30 no. 4, Summer 1977.

ECO, U. 'Antonioni "impegnato"', in C. Di Carlo (ed.), *Michelangelo Antonioni* (1964).

EPSTEIN, R. 'Antonioni Speaks . . . and Listens', *Film Comment*, July–August 1975.

FERNANDEZ, D. 'Antonioni, poète du matriarcat', *NRF*, 1 November 1960.

FERRARA, G. *Il nuovo cinema italiano* (Florence: Le Monnier, 1957).

FERRERO, A. 'La presenza d'Antonioni nel cinema italiano', *Cinestudio* no. 5, November 1962.

FERRERO, A. 'Le amiche', *Cinestudio* no. 5, November 1962.

FERRERO, A. 'Il deserto di Antonioni e la collera di Pasolini', *Cinema Nuovo*, September–October 1964.

FERRUA, P. 'Blow-Up from Cortazar to Antonioni', *Film and Literature Quarterly* vol. IV no. 1, Winter 1976.

FINK, G. 'Antonioni e il giallo alla rovescia', *Cinema Nuovo*, March–April 1963.

FINK, G. 'Una politica degli autori negli anni cinquanta', in G. Tinazzi (ed.), *Il cine-ma italiano degli anni 50* (Venice: Marsilio, 1979).

FLAIANO, E. '*Cronaca di un amore*', *Il Mondo*, 23 December 1950.

FOFI, G. *Capire con il cinema* (Milan: Feltrinelli, 1977).

FORTINI, F. 'Il realismo italiano nel cinema e nella narrativa', *Cinema Nuovo*, 15 June 1953.

FREDDI, L. *Il cinema* (Rome: L'Arnia, 1949).

GARDIN, G.B. 'Antonioni e Bergman alle prese col colore', *Cinema 60* no. 45, 1964.

GERMANI, S.G. 'Identificazione di una donna', *Filmcritica* nos. 339–340, November–December 1983.

GIACCI, V. 'Un film di fantasmi: *Il mistero di Oberwald*', *Filmcritica* nos. 307–309, September–November 1980.

GILLIAT, P. 'About Reprieve' in M. Antonioni, M. Peploe, P. Wollen, *The Passenger* (New York: Grove Press, 1975).

GILMAN, R. 'About nothing – with precision', *Theatre Arts* vol. 46 no. 7, July 1962.

GILSON, R. 'Michelangelo Antonioni de *Gente del Po* à *Il grido*', *Les Temps Modernes* no. 158, April 1959.

GLISERMAN, M. 'The Passenger: An Individual in History', *Jump Cut* no. 8, August–September 1975.

GOW, G. 'Michelangelo Antonioni's Film *Zabriskie Point*', *Films and Filming* no. 21, 1975.

GOZLAN, G. '*Le Cri* ou la faillite de nos sentiments', *Positif* no. 35, July–August 1960.

GOZLAN, G. '*La signora senza camelie*', *Positif* no. 38, March 1961.

GRANDE, M. 'La condizione estetica tra lettura e semiosi (a proposito di *Professione: reporter*)', *Filmcritica* no. 231, January–February 1973.

GRAZIANI, S. 'Il fotografo Thomas e il mezzo psicologia', *Cinema Nuovo* no. 196, November–December 1968.

GRAZZINI, G. 'Antonioni nella "spirale"', *Corriere della Sera*, 12 December 1971.

GRAZZINI, G. 'Antonioni: saper leggere dentro le cose', *Corriere della Sera*, 5 March 1975.

GRAZZINI, G. *Gli anni sessanta in cento film* (Bari: Laterza, 1977).

GRIFFITHS, K. 'Antonioni's Technological Mysteries', *Framework* nos. 15–17, Summer 1981.

GROSOLI, F. 'Cinema / storia: memoria del passato e lettura del contemporaneo', *Cinema e Film* nos. 16–17, July–December 1978.

GUGLIELMINO, G. M. 'Violento attacco cinese alla "Cina" di Antonioni', *Gazetta del Popolo*, 31 January 1974.

GUGLIELMINO, G. M. '*Professione: reporter* di Michelangelo Antonioni', *Gazzetta del Popolo*, 1 March 1975.

HUSS, R. (ed.) *Focus on Blow-Up* (Englewood Cliffs New Jersey: Prentice-Hall, 1971).

KAPLAN, N. 'Quelques pas dans l'Aventure', *Positif* no. 35, July–August 1960.

KAUFFMAN, S. '*Zabriskie Point*', *The New Republic* no. 162, 14 March 1970.

KEZICH, T. '*I vinti*', *Sipario* no. 95, March 1954.

KEZICH, T. '*Professione: reporter*', *Panorama*, 6 March 1975.

KEZICH, T. 'Statement', *Le montagne incantate* (Biennale di Venezia 1986).

KRAL, P. 'Traversée du désert: de quelques constantes antonioniennes', *Positif* no. 263, January 1983.

KYROU, A. '*I vinti*', *Positif* no. 30, July 1959.

LABARTHE, A. S. '*Le amiche*', *Cahiers du Cinéma* no. 110, August 1960.

LABARTHE, A. S. 'Antonioni hier et demain', *Cahiers du Cinéma* no. 110, August 1960.

LABARTHE, A. S. 'Le facteur rhésus et le nouveau cinema', *Cahiers du Cinéma* no. 113, November 1960.

LAURA, E.G. 'Cannes '60: crisi dei valori umani', *Bianco e Nero*, May–June 1960.

LANE, J.F. 'Antonioni and the Two-Headed Monster', *Sight and Sound* vol. 49 no. 1, Winter 1979–1980.

LEFEVRE, R. '*Blow-Up*', *Image et Son*, November 1967.

LEPROHON, P. *Michelangelo Antonioni*, Cinéma d'aujourd'hui (Paris: Seghers, 1962).

LYONS, R. *Michelangelo Antonioni's Neo-realism: A World View* (New York: Arno Press, 1974).

MANCINI, M. 'Il corpo e la favola', *Filmcritica* no. 252, March 1975.

MANCINI, M. AND PERRELLA, G. *Michelang elo Antonioni: Architetture della visione* (Rome: Coneditor Consorzio Coop, 1986).

MANCIOTTI, M. '*Identificazione di una donna*', *Il Secolo XIX*, 12 November 1982.

MANGINI, C. 'Diventano amiche le donne sole di Pavese', *Cinema Nuovo*, 10 June 1955.

MARCABRU, P. 'Antonioni: la poésie et le désenchantement', *ARTS*, 14 June 1961.

MARTIN, M. '*Zabriskie Point*: détruire dit-il', *Cinema 70* no. 147, June 1970.

MARTINI, S. '*La signora senza camelie* non offende il cinema italiano', *Cinema Nuovo*, 1 March 1953.

MAZZOCHI, G. 'Le cinque strade di Antonioni', *Il Punto*, 11 March 1961.

MICCICHE, L. '*Le amiche*', *Schermi* no. 9, 1958.

MICCICHE, L. 'Dove corri America?', *Avanti!*, 29 March 1970.

MICCICHE, L. '*Professione: reporter* di Michelangelo Antonioni', *Cinema 60* no. 101, January–February 1975.

MICCICHE, L. 'Inutile la fuga dalla propria prigione', *Avanti!*, 2 March 1975.

MICCICHE, L. 'La solitudine esistenziale di Antonioni', *Avanti!*, 2 November 1982.

MICHA, R. "L'eau dans l'œuvre d'Antonioni", *Critique*, April 1965.

MICHELI, S. 'Il personaggio femminile nei film di Antonioni', *Bianco e Nero* no. 1, 1967.

MORANDINI, M. 'Film da discutere: *L'avventura*', *Il Nuovo Spettatore Cinematografico* no. 15, 1960.

MORANDINI, M. '*L'avventura*', *Schermi* nos. 23–24, 1960.

MORAVIA, A. '*Cronaca di un amore*', *L'Europeo* no. 297, November 1950.

MORAVIA, A. '8 ¾: Moravia interroga Antonioni sul suo ultimo film *Blow-Up*', *L'Espresso*, 22 January 1967.

MORAVIA, A. 'Una bella bara a due piazze', *L'Espresso*, 6 March 1975.

MOSTRA INTERNAZIONALE DEL NUOVO CINEMA '*Luciano serra, pilota*', Nuovi materiali sul cinema italiano 1929–1943 vol. II, quaderno informativo 72 (Ancona 1976).

MUSATTI, C. 'Tempo e regressione istintuale nell'America di Antonioni', *Cinema Nuovo*, September–October 1970.

MUSATTI, C. 'L'ultimo Antonioni dinanzi a uno psicologo', *Cinema Nuovo*, September–October 1972.

MUSSOLINI, V. 'L'emancipazione del cinema italiano', *Cinema*, 25 September 1936.

MUSSOLINI, V. 'Un momento critico', *Cinema*, 25 November 1938.

MUSSOLINI, V. 'Alcune cifre', *Cinema*, 25 December 1938.

MUSSOLINI, V. 'Importazione ed esportazione cinematografica', *Cinema*, 25 November 1939.

MUSSOLINI, V. 'Constatazioni', *Cinema*, 10 May 1941.

NOWELL-SMITH, G. 'Shape Around a Black Point', *Sight and Sound*, Winter 1963/64.

ONGARO, A. 'Antonioni: *L'Europeo* intervista', *L'Europeo*, 5 March 1975.

PANDOLFI, V. 'Il palcoscenico di Antonioni', *Cinema Nuovo*, 1 November 1957.

PANICELLI, I. 'Statement', in *Le montagne incantate* (Biennale di Venezia 1986).

PASOLINI, P. P. 'Il cinema di poesia', *Empirismo eretico* (Milan: Garzanti, 1972; recently translated into English as *Heretical Empiricism*, University of Indiana Press, 1988).

PECORI, F. 'Borato e gesso', *Filmcritica* no. 206, April 1970.

PERRY, T. 'Men and Landscapes: Antonioni's *The Passenger*', *Film Comment*, July–August 1975.

PESTELLI, L. 'Antonioni in un deserto rosa', *La Stampa*, 1 March 1975.

PIETRANGELI, A. 'Analisi spettrale del film realistico', *Cinema*, 25 July 1942.

PIETRANGELI, A. 'Verso un cinema italiano', *Bianco e Nero*, August 1942.

PIETRANGELI, A. AND MESTOLO ' A proposito di Ossessione', *Cinema*, 10 July 1943.

PIRELLA, A. 'Antonioni o la crisi della semanticità visiva' in C. Di Carlo, *Michelangelo Antonioni* (1964).

PLEBE, A. AND BRUNO, E. 'Per un cinema italiano di tendenza', *Filmcritica* nos. 156–157, April-May 1965.

POLACCO, G. '*Professione: reporter*', *Momento-Sera*, 3–4 March 1975.

PONZI, M. 'Comportamenti e imprevisti: *Blow-Up*', *Cinema e Film* vol. 1 no. 4, Autumn 1967.

PORTOGHESI, P. 'Statement', in *Le montagne incantate* (Biennale di Venezia, 1986).

RAI *Il mistero di Oberwald*, n.d.

RANIERI, T. *Michelangelo Antonioni* (Università degli studi di Trieste, 1957–1958).

RANVAUD, D. '*Il mistero di Oberwald*', *Monthly Film Bulletin*, September 1981.

REGGIANI, S. 'Se Antonioni non è più lui', *La Stampa*, 29 June 1973.

REGGIANI, S. '"Come ho inventato il film"', *La Stampa*, 28 February 1975.

RENMIN RIBAO 'A Vicious Motive, Despicable Tricks – A Criticism of M. Antonioni's

Anti-China Film "China"' reprinted in *Chinese Literature* no. 3, 1974.

RENZI, R. 'Stile e coscienza morale di Michelangelo Antonioni', *Emilia*, April 1954.

RENZI, R. 'I quattro della crisi', *Cinema Nuovo*, 1 December 1957.

RENZI, R. 'Cronache dell'angoscia in Michelangelo Antonioni', *Cinema Nuovo*, May–June 1959.

RENZI, R. 'Ingrandimento il papa Satan di Antonioni', *Cinema Nuovo*, January–February 1968; with a reply from Antonioni in July–August 1968; and a reply to that from Renzi in November–December 1968.

RENZI, R. 'Jancsó tende la mano a Michelangelo Antonioni', *Cinema Nuovo*, January–February 1970.

RENZI, R. 'Antonioni nelle vesti del drago bianco', *Cinema Nuovo*, May–June 1974.

RICCIOLI, G. 'Le strizzatine d'occhio di Antonioni', *Cinema 60* no. 7, January 1961.

RICCIOLI, G. 'Infelicita e sentimento in Antonioni', *Cinema 60* no. 45, 1964.

ROBUTTI, E. '*Il grido*', *La Squilla* (Bologna), 17 October 1957.

RODA E. '37 domande a Michelangelo Antonioni', *Il Tempo*, 4 July 1957.

RONDI, G. L. '*Professione: reporter*', *Il Tempo*, 2 March 1975.

RONDI, G. L. 'La professione del reporter in fuga', *Il Settimanale*, 15 March 1975.

RONDI, G. L. '*Il mistero di Oberwald*', *Il Tempo*, 9 August 1981.

RONDOLINI, G. 'Antonioni pittore di montagne incantate', *La Stampa*, 14 September 1983.

RONDOLINI, G. 'Statement', in *Le montagne incantate* (Biennale di Venezia 1986).

ROUD, R. '*The Passenger*', *Sight and Sound*, Summer 1975.

SADOUL, G. 'Le poids de la solitude', *Les Lettres Françaises*, 10 December 1958.

SADOUL, G. 'Michelangelo Antonioni comme je l'ai vu', *Les Lettres Françaises*, 26 May 1960.

SADOUL, G. 'Puro come "La notte"', *Filmcritica* no. 105, January 1961; original in *Les Lettres Françaises*, 1 March 1961.

SADOUL, G. 'Que tombent ces vagues de brique', *Les Lettres Françaises*, 8 June 1967.

SAINDERICHIN 'Signe particulière: néant', *Cahiers du Cinéma*, no. 342, December 1982.

SALINARI, C. et al., 'Le idee e il linguaggio di Antonioni', *Il Contemporaneo* no. 49, June 1962.

SALTINI, V. 'Il cinema della soggettività', *Bianco e Nero*, November–December 1964.

SAMUELS, C. T. 'An Interview with Antonioni', *Vogue* (USA), 15 March 1970.

SAMUELS, C. T. 'An Interview with Antonioni', *Film Heritage* vol. 5 no. 3, Spring 1970.

SAMUELS, C. T. 'Puppets: from Z to *Zabriskie Point*', *The American Scholar* no. 18, Autumn 1970.

SANTUARI, A. 'Identificazione incerta tra cinema e realtà', *Paese Sera*, 9 March 1981.

SANTUARI, A. 'Antonioni col colore spiega "Il mistero"', *Paese Sera*, 30 August 1981.

SEGUIN, L. 'Le Cri', *Positif* no. 30, July 1959.

SIBILLA, G. 'Michelangelo Antonioni', *Bianco e Nero*, January 1954.

SICILIANO, E. 'Che leggono i registi: Il rifiuto d'Antonioni', *La Stampa*, 5 August 1972.

SICLIER, J. 'Il ritorno del viaggiatore' in M. Antonioni, *Identificazione di una donna*, (Turin: Einaudi, 1983).

SIMON, J. AND GELMIS, J., LAST, M., STAR, H., LEES, A. 'Antonioni: What's the Point?', *Film Heritage* vol. 5 no. 3, Spring 1970.

SINGER, E. 'Parigi scopre le facce di Antonioni', *La Stampa*, 26 March 1985.

SKORECKI, L. '*La signora senza camelie*', *Cahiers du Cinéma* no. 297, February 1979.

SLOVER, G. 'Blow-Up: medium, messaggio, miti e finzione', Strumenti Critici no. 5, 1968.

SPINAZZOLA, V. 'Michelangelo Antonioni regista', Film 1961 (Milan: Feltrinelli, 1961).

STANTON, E. 'Antonioni's The Passenger. A Parabola of Light', Film and Literature Quarterly vol. 5 no. 1, Winter 1977.

STRICK, P. Antonioni (London: Motion Publications, 1963).

TAILLEUR, R. 'Chronique d'un amour', Positif no. 30, July 1959.

TAILLEUR, R. AND THIRARD, P.-L. Antonioni (Paris: Editions Universitaires, 1963).

TARNOWSKI, J.-F. 'Identification d'une œuvre: Antonioni et la modernité cinematographique', Positif no. 263, January 1983.

TASSONE, A. 'Michelangelo Antonioni' in A. Tassone, Parla il cinema italiano, vol. 1 (Milan: Il Formichiere, 1979)

TASSONE, A. 'Antonioni critico cinematografico (1935–1949)', Bianco e Nero, 1985.

TEMPESTI, F. 'Il linguaggio dell'Avventura', Cinema Nuovo, November–December 1960.

THIRARD, P.-L. 'Antonioni ou les révisions nécessaires', Les Lettres Nouvelles, December 1960.

THIRARD, P.-L. 'Femmes entre elles', Positif no. 30, July 1959.

THIRARD, P.-L. 'Michelangelo Antonioni', Premier Plan no. 15, 1960.

TILLIETTE, X. 'Cadrages sur Antonioni', Etudes, July–August 1961.

TINAZZI, G. 'Antonioni e il romanzo della crisi', Cenobio no. 2, 1961.

TINAZZI, G. 'La via della regressione naturale', Giovane Critica no. 7, February–March 1965.

TINAZZI, G. Antonioni (Il castoro cinema, 1974).

TINAZZI, G. 'La dilatazione del dubbio', Cinema e Cinema no. 4, 1975.

TISO, C. 'Oggettività filmica e visione onirico-fantascientifica', Filmcritica no. 206, April 1970.

TISO, C. 'Prassi e procedimenti narrativi del film: il ribaltamento della favola come svolgimento della fiction (2): Professione: reporter e il ribaltamento del "doppio"', Filmcritica no. 231, January–February 1973.

TOMASINO, R. 'Antonioni: il meta-segno del cinema "astratto"', Filmcritica no. 231, January–February 1973.

TORNABUONI, L. 'L'intervista della domenica: Michelangelo Antonioni: io e il cinema, io e le donne', Corriere della Sera, 12 February 1978.

TORNABUONI, L. 'Antonioni sul mare del futuro', La Stampa, 19 December 1982.

TOTI, G. 'L'eclisse intellettuale e il cinema alienato', Cinema 60 nos. 21–22, 1962.

TREBBI, F. Il testo e lo sguardo (Bologna, 1976).

TUMIATI, G. 'Antonioni uno e due', L'illustrazione italiana , September 1960.

TURRONI, G. 'James Joyce e il III° episodio di I vinti', Filmcritica nos. 34–35, April–May 1954.

UNGARI, E. 'Michelangelo sterminatore', Cinema e Film, vol. IV nos. 11–12, Summer–Autumn 1970.

VACCARI, L. 'Professione contro', Il Messaggero, 31 August 1983.

VALLI, B.M. 'Ventisette domande a uno sceneggiatore: Tonino Guerra' in B.M. Valli (ed.), L'ultimo cinema 1980 (Studiforma, 1982).

VALOBRA, F. 'Fitzgerald e il cinema italiano contemporaneo', Centrofilm nos. 22–23, 1961.

VESCOVO, M. 'L'informale in Antonioni come fonte di realismo', Cinema Nuovo, January–February 1971.

VIAZZI, G. 'Il grido', Il Contemporaneo, 14 December 1957.

VIAZZI, G. ET THIRARD, P-L. 'Un écrivain nommé Antonioni', *Positif* no. 30, July 1959.

VISCONTI, L. 'Cadaveri', *Cinema*, 10 June 1941.

VISCONTI, L. 'Il cinema antropomorfico', *Cinema*, 25 September–25 October 1943.

VOGLIONO, B. 'Michelangelo Antonioni', *Centrofilm* no. 3, Centro universitario cinematografico Torino 1959.

WALSH, M. 'Antonioni's Narrative Design: *The Passenger*', *Jump Cut* no. 8, August–September 1975.

ZAND, N. AND MARCORELLES, L. 'Antonioni et le monde des sentiments', *France-Observateur*, 15 September 1960.

ZANELLI, D. (ed.) 'Quel mio grande e ingenuo amore per il cinema' (intervista con V. Mussolini), *Cinema Nuovo*, August–October 1983.

Jeanne Moreau as Lidia in LA NOTTE *(1960)*

Filmography

What follows is not a proper filmography but rather a list of films Antonioni made and was involved in and their most basic credits; there are a number of complete filmographies that may be consulted. The most comprehensive in English are in Seymour Chatman, *Antonioni, or The Surface of the World* (Berkeley and Los Angeles: University of California, 1985) and in Ted Perry and René Prieto, *Michelangel Antonioni: A guide to references and resources* (Boston: G. K. Hall, 1986); and there is one in Italian in Carlo Di Carlo (ed.) *Identificazione di un autore* (Rome: Pratiche, 1983–85).

Antonioni worked as an assistant director on *I due foscari* (1942) by Enrico Fulchignoni and on *Les Visiteurs du soir* (1942) made by Marcel Carné; he was second-unit director on Alberto Lattuada's *La tempesta* (1958).

In collaboration with others he worked on the scripts of *I due foscari*, Roberto Rossellini's *Un pilota ritorna* (1942), Giuseppe De Santis' *Caccia tragica* (1947) and Federico Fellini's *Lo sceicco bianco*. In 1955, he produced *Uomini in più*, a documentary on overpopulation and emigration from Italy, directed by Niccolò Ferrari.

Between 1943–1950, Antonioni made a number of short documentaries; his feature film career began with *Cronaca di un amore* (1950).

Shorts
GENTE DEL PO (1943–1947). Surviving footage 9 mins.

N.U. – NETTEZZA URBANA (1948). 9 mins.

L'AMOROSA MENZOGNA (1948–1949). 10 mins.

SUPERSTIZIONE – NON CI CREDO! (1949). 9 mins.

SETTE CANNE, UN VESTITO (1949). 10 mins.

LA FUNIVIA DEL FALORIA (1950). 10 mins.

LA VILLA DEI MOSTRI (1950). 10 mins.

LE CITTÀ DEI MONDIALI: ROMA (1990). 8 mins.

Features
CRONACA DI UN AMORE (1950). *sc* – Antonioni, with Daniele D'Anza, Silvio Giovanietti, Francesco Maselli, Piero Tellini. *ph* – Enzo Serafin. *m* – Giovanni Fusco. *l.p.* – Lucia Bosè (*Paola*), Massimo Girotti (*Guido*), Ferdinando Sarmi (*Enrico Fontana*). 96 mins.

I VINTI (1952). *sc* – Antonioni, with Suso Cecci D'Amico, Giorgio Bassani, Diego Fabbri, Turi Vasile. *ph* – Enzo Serafin. *m* – Giovanni Fusco. *ed* – Eraldo Da Roma. *l.p.* – (French episode) Jean-Pierre Mocky (*Pierre*), Etchika Choureau (*Simone*); (Italian episode) Franco Interlenghi (*Claudio*), Anna-Maria Ferrero (*Marina*); (British episode) Peter Reynolds (*Aubrey*), Fay Compton (*Mrs Pinkerton*), Patrick Barr (*Kent Watton*). 110 mins.

LA SIGNORA SENZA CAMELIE (1953). *sc* – Antonioni, with Suso Cecci D'Amico, Francesco Maselli, P. M. Pasinetti. *ph* – Enzo Serafin. *m* – Giovanni Fusco. *l.p.* – Lucia Bosè (*Clara Manni*), Andrea Cecchi (*Gianni Franchi*), Ivan Desny (*Nardo*), Gino Cervi (*Ercole*), Alain Cuny (*Lodi*). 105 mins.

TENTATO SUICIDIO (episode of *L'Amore in Città*) (1953). From an idea by Cesare Zavattini. *ph* – Gianni Di Venanzo. *ed* – Eraldo Da Roma. *m* – Mario Nascimbene. Non-professional actors. 20 mins.

LE AMICHE (1955). *sc* – Antonioni, with Suso Cecci D'Amico, Alba De Cespedes, from the novel *Tra donne sole* by Cesare Pavese. *ph* – Gianni Di Venanzo. *ed* – Eraldo Da Roma. *m* – Giovanni Fusco. *l.p.* – Eleonora Rossi Drago (*Clelia*), Valentina Cortese (*Nene*), Yvonne Furneaux (*Momina*), Madeleine Fischer (*Rosetta*), Franco Fabrizi (*Cesare*), Ettore Manni (*Carlo*), Gabriele Ferzetti (*Lorenzo*). 104 mins.

IL GRIDO (1957). *sc* – Antonioni, with Elio Bartolini, Ennio De Concini. *ph* – Gianni Di Venanzo. *ed* – Eraldo Da Roma. *m* – Giovanni Fusco. *l.p.* – Steve Cochran (*Aldo*), Alida Valli (*Irma*), Betsy Blair (*Elvia*), Dorian Gray (*Virginia*), Lyn Shaw (*Andreina*), Mirna Girardi (*Rosina*). 102 mins.

L'AVVENTURA (1959). *sc* – Antonioni, with Elio Bartolini, Tonino Guerra. *ph* – Aldo Scavarda. *ed* – Eraldo Da Roma. *m* – Giovanni Fusco. *l.p.* – Monica Vitti (*Claudia*), Lea Massari (*Anna*), Gabriele Ferzetti (*Sandro*). 145 mins.

LA NOTTE (1960). *sc* – Antonioni, with Ennio Flaiano, Tonino Guerra. *ph* – Gianni Di Venanzo. *ed* – Eraldo Da Roma. *m* – Giorgio Gaslini. *l.p.* – Marcello Mastroianni (*Giovanni Pontano*), Jeanne Moreau (*Lidia Pontano*), Monica Vitti (*Valentina*). 122 mins.

L'ECLISSE (1962). *sc* – Antonioni and Tonino Guerra, with Elio Bartolini, Ottiero Ottieri. *ph* – Gianni Di Venanzo. *ed* – Eraldo Da Roma. *m* – Giovanni Fusco. *l.p.* – Monica Vitti (*Vittoria*), Alain Delon (*Piero*), Francisco Rabal (*Riccardo*). 125 mins.

IL DESERTO ROSSO (Red Desert) (1964). *sc* – Antonioni and Tonino Guerra. *ph* – Carlo Di Palma. *ed* – Eraldo Da Roma. *m* – Giovanni Fusco. *l.p.* – Monica Vitti (*Giuliana*), Richard Harris (*Corrado*), Carlo Chionetti [Carlo De Pra] (*Ugo*). 120 mins (UK and US, 116 mins).

PREFAZIONE (episode of *I tre volti*) (1965). *sc* – Antonioni. *ph* – Carlo Di Palma. *l.p.* – Soraya, Ivano Davoli. 25 mins.

BLOW-UP (1966). *sc* – Antonioni and Tonino Guerra, from a story by Julio Cortázar. *ph* – Carlo Di Palma. *ed* – Frank Clarke. *m* – performed by The Yardbirds and The Lovin' Spoonful. *l.p.* – David Hemmings (*Thomas*), Vanessa Redgrave (*Jane*), Sarah Miles (*Patricia*). 111 mins.

ZABRISKIE POINT (1969). *sc* – Antonioni and Tonino Guerra, with Fred Gardner, Sam Shepard, Clare Peploe. *ph* – Alfio Contini. *editing assistant* – Franco Arcalli. *m* – Pink Floyd, The Rolling Stones and others. *l.p.* – Mark Frechette (*Mark*), Daria Halprin (*Daria*), Rod Taylor (*Lee Allen*). 110 mins.

CHUNG KUO CINA (1972). *ph* – Luciano Tovoli. *ed* – Franco Arcalli. *Musical Consultant* – Luciano Berio. Original running time (for Italian television), 220 mins; subsequent film and TV versions between 130 and 104 mins.

THE PASSENGER (Professione: reporter) (1975). *sc* – Mark Peploe, Peter Wollen, Michelangelo Antonioni. *ph* – Luciano Tovoli. *ed* – Franco Arcalli, Michelangelo Antonioni. *l.p.* – Jack Nicholson (*David Locke*), Maria Schneider (*The Girl*). European version, 127 mins; English-language version, 122 mins.

IL MISTERO DI OBERWALD (1980). *sc* – Antonioni and Tonino Guerra, from the play *L'Aigle à deux têtes* by Jean Cocteau. *ph* – Luciano Tovoli. *ed* – Michelangelo Antonioni, Francesco Grandoni. *Musical Consultant* – Guido Turchi. *l.p.* – Monica Vitti (*The Queen*), Franco Branciaroli (*Sebastian*), Paolo Bonacelli (*Count Foehn*), Elisabetta Pozzi (*Edith de Berg*). 129 mins.

IDENTIFICAZIONE DI UNA DONNA (1982). *sc* – Antonioni and Gérard Brach, with Tonino Guerra. *ph* – Carlo Di Palma. *ed* – Michelangelo Antonioni. *m* – John Foxx. *l.p.* – Tomas Milian (*Niccolò Farra*), Christine Boisson (*Ida*), Daniela Silverio (*Mavi*). 128 mins.

Monica Vitti
in L'ECLISSE

Index